THE REAL McRAE

Colin McRae was born in Lanarkshire, Scotland, in 1968. He won the British Rally Championship for the first time in 1991 and became the youngest ever World Rally Champion in 1995, at the age of 27.

Derick Allsop has joined forces with his friend Colin McRae to document this incredible sporting story. Derick is the country's foremost motorsport journalist and has written books with many iconic figures in the past, including Michael Schumacher and George Best. Previous titles also include *Formula One Uncovered* (Headline, 1998) and *Kicking in the Wind* (Headline, 1997).

7 9 10 8 6

This edition published 2002
First published in 2001 by Ebury Press,
an imprint of Ebury Publishing
A Random House Group Company

The Random House Group Limited Reg. No. 954009

www.randomhouse.co.uk

A CIP catalogue record for this book
is available from the British Library

The Random House Group Limited supports The Forest Stewardship
Council (FSC), the leading international forest certification organisation.
All our titles that are printed on Greenpeace approved FSC certified paper
carry the FSC logo. Our paper procurement policy can be found at:
www.rbooks.co.uk/environment

Mixed Sources
Product group from well-managed
forests and other controlled sources
www.fsc.org Cert no. TT-COC-2139
© 1996 Forest Stewardship Council
FSC

Printed in the UK by CPI Cox & Wyman, Reading, RG1 8EX

ISBN 9780091883966

To buy books by your favourite authors and register for offers visit
www.rbooks.co.uk

THE REAL
MᶜRAE

THE AUTOBIOGRAPHY OF THE PEOPLE'S CHAMPION

Colin McRae
and Derick Allsop

EBURY PRESS

Acknowledgements

Just as the driver and co-driver require the backing and forbearance of a whole team and more to put them on the road, so the author and co-author are indebted to many for helping them into print. We would like to thank, in particular, Martin Whitaker and Ford, Malcolm Wilson and M-Sport, Nicky Grist, Bernie Shrosbree, Jimmy and Margaret McRae, Alison McRae, Alister and Stuart McRae, Mark Wilford, Georgina Baskerville and David Windsor at Avenue Communications, David Richards and Subaru, Lanark Tourist Information Centre, Matt Neal, Colin Morrison, Ian Hughes, Graham and Tracey Ogden, Neil and Bob Fountain.

A special word of thanks to Tommi Makinen, for kindly contributing the foreword, and to Steve Fellows and Subaru. We wish also to express our appreciation of the unflinching support from Jean-Eric Freudiger, Sue, Kate and Natalie Allsop, and the encouragement and enthusiasm of Hannah MacDonald and all at Ebury Press.

Contents

Acknowledgements   **iv**
Foreword   **vii**
Introduction   **ix**

1. A Town Fit for Heroes   **1**

2. Keeping it the Family   **21**

3. Into the Blue   **40**

4. The Final Ascent   **60**

5. Partners   **83**

6. Changing Times   **102**

7. Focus of Attention   **124**

8. My Greatest Escape   **145**

9. Friends and Rivals   **178**

10. Team Game   **195**

11. Centre Stage   **215**

12. Home Ground   **239**

13. Renewed Challenge   **259**

14. Starting All Over Again   **291**

Foreword

To my mind there is no more exciting sight in sport than a World Rally Championship car driven to the limit and no-one I have competed against does that better than Colin McRae. He drives not only with phenomenal skill, speed and courage, but also with a style that all rally fans love to see. When Colin is on a stage, people want to watch. That says it all. No wonder he has such a huge following in Britain and indeed all over the world.

I have had occasion to rue Colin's pace and commitment because when he has the bit between his teeth there is no harder man to beat. Yet at the same time I have admired his performances just like any other lover of rallying. He has a rare talent and that is invaluable to our sport.

Above all, I am proud to be able to call Colin a friend. During a rally we are the fiercest of opponents but I like to think we have a mutual respect. And when the work is done I enjoy having a drink and a chat with Colin. Mind you, we are still very competitive away from the rally stages. We both like motorbikes and we've had some terrific fun riding in Finland. I suppose I had an unfair advantage, being at home, and he's threatening to get his own back in Britain!

I look forward to many more great fights and good times with Colin.

Tommi Makinen
World Rally Champion, 1996–99

Introduction

Three wins in a row; from nowhere to the top of the World Rally Championship. It was the stuff of dreams, the kind of run you dare not hope for at this level of the sport. A hat-trick of victories – in Argentina, Cyprus and Greece – had re-launched my 2001 title challenge and banished the frustrations of the previous rallies, when a succession of mishaps, technical glitches and mechanical failures threatened to leave my Ford team-mate, Nicky Grist, and I stranded.

And yet more than that, those wins vindicated my decision to carry on competing after the most horrific accident of my career. As I was trapped, upside down, in the wreckage of my Focus, in a Corsican ravine on that fateful autumn day of 2000, I thought not only that my career could be over, but that I might not survive the ordeal. I drifted in and out of consciousness, helpless and disorientated, my cheekbone smashed.

My memories of the crash and its aftermath are vague and confused. I remember clipping a rock on the inside of the road and going off the road on the outside. I recall the taste of blood and the terror as I smelt petrol, and still no-one was getting me out of there. Nothing seemed to be happening. And I remember thinking I didn't need this anymore. I'd won the World Championship in 1995. I'd got 20 rally victories to my name and I'd made enough money to keep my family in comfort for the rest of our lives. If I managed to escape this one I could enjoy life without any more risks or pressures.

It was, though, a big if. I honestly feared I was going to die and everything I've been told since then confirms that I really was in a perilous position. That accident could have killed me. The rescue crews were apparently at a loss as to how to release me and it was mainly due to the initiative and efforts of Nicky and Bernie Shrosbree, our trainer, that I was freed in time.

But once I knew I was safe and on the mend, all those thoughts of quitting disappeared. I was still in with a chance of the Championship and I was determined to be in the car for the next rally. I'm sure that was the best thing I could have done. I picked up a point in that San Remo Rally, the best point I've ever scored. The Championship eluded me but I was back in business, and looking forward to chasing more victories in 2001. I felt sure I could still beat the best, still win rallies and still fulfil my ambition of taking a second world title.

I would be lying if I said I was able to put Corsica completely out of my head. I probably think about the dangers more now than I did before that accident. But what concerned me most of all was not knowing exactly what happened. When I have an accident I want to know why. There was so much of that accident that I couldn't – and still can't – remember.

Danger comes with the territory in rallying. You have to accept it and all of us involved do so. But although the danger might be at the back of your mind, you can't afford to dwell on it because then it would affect your performance and if that happens you might as well pack it in.

I think my results in 2001 prove that I haven't allowed Corsica to affect my driving. A lot of people criticised me in the past for having too many accidents. They even called me McCrash for a while. But I have no regrets about the way I drive. It's brought me success, the big contract and an appreciative following. Being Mr Consistent is simply not my style. I prefer the fast and exciting way, and so do the fans. The crowds respond to the guy who is willing to go for it and drive on the edge. It's what people want to see and what manufacturers want because it's the kind of driving that gets you noticed and therefore their car noticed. The thrill for me is driving fast and driving to win. Ever since I was a young driver, starting out in rallying, I have had belief in my ability to do that. I realised I had natural car control, an instinctive feel for it. When you take up any sport it's for the pure enjoyment and I was no different. I loved the speed and the buzz it gave me. And I was captivated by the challenge of driving a car on the limit. It was the biggest kick anyone could have had. When things are going well I still love it, I still get that buzz. But I have to admit that the enjoyment isn't quite what it was when I was a youngster. The World Rally Championship has become serious business and the big kick for me now is the result. When you're not getting the results, and especially when the reasons are beyond your control, it can be difficult to maintain your enthusiasm and motivation.

I have had my share of those difficult periods through my career, but thankfully the highs have eclipsed the lows. The success we had in 2001 made all the earlier setbacks and dismay worthwhile. I was winning rallies and winning well. And I was competing for the World Championship again. There's nothing quite like climbing to the top of that Championship table and seeing the No. 1 plate on the side of your car. That's why we're here. That's why we expose ourselves to the dangers and our families to the anxieties. And that's why I still want more of it.

A Town Fit for Heroes

When it comes to heroes, Sir William Wallace was always going to be a hard act to follow. He was a champion of the very highest order in Scotland who led the early resistance forces against English rule. He is exalted in Lanark despite the fact that he burned down the town in May 1297. Wallace and his 30-strong band of patriots killed Lanark's English sheriff.

The momentum of his patriotic war garnered popular support and his army terrorised the English, north and south of the border. The enemy was driven from his beloved land and Wallace was proclaimed Guardian of the kingdom. However, his position was undermined by jealous Scottish nobles and he continued his struggle as a guerrilla leader until he was captured on August 5, 1305. He was taken to London, tried for treason and executed.

The venerated Wallace still watches over the people of Lanark, the historic market town on the Clyde, less than 30 miles up-stream from Glasgow.

His statue dominates the town steeple of St Nicholas' Church, which draws the eye down the broad thoroughfare that is High Street.

Today all the familiar town centre retail names, north and south of the border, ply their trade here. Woolworths, Boots, WH Smith, Thomas Cook, Victoria Wine. You'll also find the obligatory Indian restaurant, the Taj Mahal and the one obvious sign of nationalistic spirite identifies the Chinese restaurant, the McChan!

Every summer a tradition dating back to the 12th century, when Lanark was established as a Royal Burgh, brings the townsfolk down the hill towards Wallace's corbelled niche and the focal point of the Lanimer celebrations. The procession and accompanying festivities – official or otherwise – are woven into the fabric of this community.

Another more recently established ritual in these parts honours heroic doing of a very different kind. No member of the McRae family would claim to be the latter day Braveheart but their achievements in rallying are honoured and celebrated annually by the 8,000 strong population. The McRae Stages is a round of the Scottish Rally Championship held here and supported by the eponymous driving clan with due relish.

Jimmy McRae set the wheels of this fabled dynasty in motion, switching from bikes to cars with such assurance he won the British Rally Championship five times. He and his wife, Margaret, had three sons and two of them were drawn to competition on wheels. Youngest son

Stuart opted for a career in catering while middle son Alister followed in the tracks and slides of his father and big brother Colin to become a regular competitor in the World Rally Championship. Alister's ultimate objective is to emulate Colin's greatest feat and become world champion.

Colin McRae was Britain's first winner of the World Rally Championship and the youngest from any nation to claim the title when he was crowned in 1995, at the age of 27, accomplishment enough to command hero status. And yet there was more to this son of Lanark and his driving than could be measured by sporting landmarks. Unassuming to the point of diffidence out of the car, he was a fearless extrovert at the wheel, captivating an ever-growing fan club with his high speed audacity. His reluctance to compromise a natural flamboyance and determination to be first has brought him into conflict at times with his own bosses and the sport's authorities. It has also exposed him to some spectacular and terrifying crashes.

But it has always served to confirm his unrivalled stature with those who venture deep into the forests, regardless of the hour or the elements, to witness at close quarters the unbridled commitment of a master on the edge.

Britons are united under the McRae banner. Sir William Wallace could scarcely have entered such a claim on his CV.

It all began in Lanark Hospital on August 5 (spooky coincidence, or what?) 1968, when a 21ins, 7lb 14oz boy was born to Margaret and Jim McRae. They take up the story:

Margaret McRae: *'We called him Colin and gave him a second name of Steele, Jim's mother's maiden name. He was a bit of a Billy Bunter as a boy. He liked his food and had really chubby chops. Not like now, he's far too thin. He was the most mischievous of the three boys. Alister arrived in 1970, Stuart in 1972.*

'Colin was always keen to explore the big outside world. We lived in Blackwood, just a few miles from Lanark, when he was young. We had to tie up the gates because he was prone to go wandering off. Jim's mother lived just four houses from us and he liked to go and see gran McRae. One day, when he was about three, he was out in the garden playing with his bike when I suddenly realised I hadn't heard him for a while. I went outside and there was the bike parked at the gates, but no Colin. He'd obviously used it as an escape route. He'd climbed up on the bike, over the gate and was off. I checked at his gran's house but he wasn't there. He had apparently gone to see his cousin. But he wasn't there so Colin crossed the main road, found his way to the park and I eventually found him playing on the swings.

'He did the same thing when I was visiting a friend in another village not far away. My mother lived in the same village. He was in the back yard, playing with the other kids. They all came in for milk and biscuits, but not Colin, and nobody knew where he was. He'd wandered off again, crossing a couple of roads, to go to his gran's. But my mum wasn't in because she worked and we found him standing in her front garden with a huge pair of binoculars round his neck and his

hat and wee coat on, saying, "Gran's not here". He was a horror, he really was.

'Alister was fairly quiet compared with Colin. They were quite happy playing together and were very close, although Colin tended to want to go somewhere else and find something else to do. Stuart's always been different from the other two. He wasn't mechanically minded like Colin and Alister. Colin was always into Lego and Meccano, things like that, and he always had this thing about cars, even from a very early age.

'When he was no more than a year old he absolutely loved to stand on the driving seat of my car while it was parked outside the door. He'd play with the wheel and the gear lever, though of course I knew he couldn't actually move anything and was quite safe. I didn't think at the time that I might have set something going. I was just delighted it got him out of my hair!

'My mum and dad often used to take Colin for a run in the car and in those days you could sit your child on your knee in the front. Without our ever telling him, he seemed to know the different makes of cars. He'd say, "oh, here's a Ford Anglia, granddad", and "here's an Escort". From a young age he knew them all. How he did I don't know. When mum and dad came to the house he had to go out and sit on granddad's knee to drive the last few yards with him. That was from about two. Jim went to Stirling to pick up a couple of aunts of mine to visit one day and of course Colin's in the front window asking, "When's daddy coming home?" So when they arrived he ran out and got onto Jim's knee and steered the car right into the* *garage. My aunt talked about it for years this tiny wee tot who parked the car.'*

Jim: *'When we got married we renovated an old cottage which was about 100 yards down the road from my father's house. That was in Blackwood. My father was the local blacksmith. It was his father's business and his father's before that. My father had a place under his house which he used as a workshop and when he went into semi-retirement he'd do gates for people and sharpen lawn-mowers, things like that. He called it the "dook", a good old Lanarkshire word for an underground workshop.*

'Colin could walk to his grandpa's, so we'd watch him go up the road. He'd spend hours there, working away with him. He was good company for my father. Then he'd come back home, up to his eyes in grease. I think he got his fascination for mechanical things, engineering and so on, from that and the garage I had at the house. I was scrambling at the time and had bikes around, so I suppose you could say he was born into it.

'When I left school I wanted to be a mechanic but never really got a proper opportunity. I joined a heating, plumbing and electrical company in Blackwood, then went to a company in Glasgow as a junior quantity surveyor. I ended up as chief surveyor for them but I always had the notion to have my own business. Then one day, a surveyor who worked for me came in to say he'd been speaking to an old guy in Lanark who wanted to sell his plumbing and heating business. My father gave me a hand and I bought the business, Allan

Wallace Ltd. I don't know if there was any connection with William Wallace!

'This was in 1973. Colin was five and had already developed an interest in cars. When he was a pain in the backside in the house, Margaret would put him in a car seat in the car and he would be as happy as Larry, steering the wheel of the car. It was always cars and bikes for Colin, just like me. He wasn't interested in football or other sports.

'There was a panic one day when Colin was about two. I was working in Glasgow and got a phone call saying it looked as though Colin would have to be taken to hospital. He had been mucking about with a three-wheeler bike. He had it upside down and was oiling the chain or something and got his small finger caught in the wheel of the chain. Margaret couldn't move it and he was screaming. She ran up the back to a retired farmer for help but he couldn't get it out. He went back for his clippers and cut the chain to get Colin's finger out. That's the kind of thing he got up to. He was always inquisitive.

'When he was maybe three years old my mother caught him mothering a stray boxer dog they had taken in. This boxer wouldn't do what it was told, it just lay about. It wasn't a very interesting dog and one day Colin was poking it in its ear with a welding wire. My mother had a fit, grabbed it off Colin and asked him what he was doing. He said he was trying to see if it would come out of the other ear.

'When I bought the business in Lanark I sold my scrambles bike because I couldn't afford to injure *myself, but a year later I had the inclination to start again. Then I came off and landed on the marking ropes, which burnt through where it hurt. I thought, "bugger this". I was turned 30 then and Margaret had always hated bikes. I went to see a stage of the RAC Rally and thought it looked fun. I went to a local car club, did my first rally in a 1200 Mark I Cortina and that's how it all came about. I got the rallying bug.*

'In the early days rallying was a family outing. Margaret would come on the events with the boys and bring the sandwiches, coffee and stuff. Colin got interested then. He certainly wasn't interested in lessons at school, all his reports said, "Could do better – if he concentrated". He was more interested in bikes and cars.

'Although I hadn't been scrambling for years I kept a trials bike which came in a box. I was that busy I never had time to build it and Colin was always at me, "When are we building this bike?" He got my father down one day and they opened the box and built it up. The first bike Colin had was a 75cc Honda schoolboy scrambles bike. Margaret hated it. It was worse having her son do it than her husband. But he was good and he won the Scottish Schoolboys Championship the first year with that bike.'

Margaret: *'I was relieved when Jim moved from bikes to cars but then I had the scenario all over again. It was a nightmare. I was never happy when the boys were on bikes. Alister was very much into bikes too. More so, actually, than Colin. He would have carried on longer but he damaged* *his knees and the orthopaedic surgeon said, "Pack this in, boy, or you're going to be really crippled when you're older". Otherwise he would have carried on. He absolutely loved it.*

'I lost count of how many times they hurt themselves. I didn't very often go and watch them because I found it too difficult to watch. Cars were the lesser of two evils. With cars you feel they have more protection than they have on a bike. I always thought it was a safer sport.'

Jim: *'From the age of about 14 Colin worked a couple of nights a week and on a Saturday with a guy who had a garage, Archie's Autos. When he left school he tried to get work as a mechanic at a couple of garages but there was nothing doing. He started working for me on the heating side but even then his mind was obviously on rallying.*

'I don't know when he first drove a car but I've heard all sorts of stories! I heard about the plumbing vans being used by him and one of his friends, Robbie Head, who was also into trials bikes and later got into rallying. If a van failed an MOT or we were changing a van it would disappear and they would knock hell out of it somewhere.

'What surprised me very much with Colin was that he wanted to get into cars as soon as he could and he found out he could have a competition licence for autotests when he was 16. I told him he would have to sell his scrambles bike to buy the Mini that he wanted to go autotesting with and he did. For anyone who likes the thrill of speed, autotesting is tame. It's in and out of cones in a car park, but I think it was just the fact he could

drive a car before he had a road licence.

'He just observed and picked up all he needed to drive. I once went and sat with him in practice in a Sunbeam and gave him some basic tips, as you would anybody. Then I co-drove for him in the first Nova he had and vowed I would never do it again! Colin's a total natural. You know if you sit beside someone that if they've got their ears tuned to the throttle and clutch it's so much smoother, and he was like that. I always remember that rally I did with him, the Galloway Hills. For the first two or three stages I was telling him, "Back off, steady, steady". Into the afternoon we were on a stage I knew and I said to him, "Flat out, it's okay, over the crest, go, go". At the end he turned to me and said, "That's the first time you've told me to go quicker".

'There was always an element of worry, but no more than any mum and dad would have if their kids were going to Edinburgh or Glasgow night-clubbing at weekends. You will always want to know they are in the right environment and that they are as safe as they can be. The good thing about rallying now is that the cars are so strong and drivers are able to walk away from major accidents. Well, mostly, anyway.

'I think the McRae name helped Colin initially. It perhaps opened doors to people I knew and then, when things weren't going so well, I was able to put a word in the right place. Ultimately Colin had to prove himself and he did so. I'm sure Alister could be just as good as Colin but unfortunately for him the McRae name has probably been more of a hindrance than a help. Following me and *then Colin has made it particularly hard for him. I'm sure that had his name been Alister Something Else then he would have found it easier to get a competitive car.*

'It would have been even more difficult for Stuart, but after showing an initial interest he never really got into rallying. He once asked if he could have a run in a rally car so the other lads told him to go down to the workshop and they'd dig out the Nova for him. Colin offered to co-drive for him on his first rally.

'Stuart was full of enthusiasm, they got the car out and started cleaning it up. There was a lot of work to be done on the car and he must have been on it for three hours that first night. The next night he managed an hour and the following night he didn't turn up. Alister and Colin told him that if he was really interested and wanted to drive the car he had to work on it as well. He couldn't just turn up when it was ready. The work went no further. They pushed the car back into the corner and Stuart never did a rally.

'Stuart was always more interested in the hotel and catering trade, even before leaving school. He had a part-time job working in a restaurant. Alister worked with me on the plumbing and heating side, Colin as a mechanic. Just like me, they caught the rallying bug.'

*   *   *

You can never quite pinpoint events when you were very young but some of my earliest memories are of times spent with my grandfathers.

I called my father's father grandpa and used to be with him whenever I could, down in his workshop under the house. I'd be with him in the dook 12 hours a day if I could, getting under his feet but having a great time.

My mum's dad was granddad and whenever I could I would be in the car with him, sitting on his knee, steering his car at every opportunity. I can remember that very clearly. I can also remember identifying cars while I was riding with my grand-parents. We used to have a competition to see who could identify a car first. I think a lot of young kids are fascinated with cars and I was in a position to be a lot closer to them.

I was always more interested in cars and bikes than any other kind of sport. I played football at school because that was what they played, but I wasn't really bothered about it. I also played rugby now and then but I was never really into it. I did a bit of water skiing later, but as a young kid I just liked getting into mischief with friends. We'd maybe go down to the river, using fishing as an excuse, but really we were mucking about. We got into trouble now and then with farmers. We used to nick apples and get up to all the things normal kids do. It was the buzz, the chase. We didn't get caught very often. Usually we'd get away with it.

I went to Robert Owen Junior School in Lanark and then to Lanark Grammar School. I was never too bothered about school. I sat five O levels and passed three. I wasn't academic at all. I was better on the crafts side. The only A grade I got was in metalwork. I spent most of the time gazing out of the window, wanting to get out there and enjoy myself. It was always outdoor activities that interested me.

I had my share of horror teachers, especially at secondary school. I think everybody in the class got belted at least once. I was certainly glad to get away from some of them. They were local people and I still see them walking up and down the street. I definitely don't stop and speak to them. I just drive past and keep my head down. School was never my favourite place.

However my favourite indoor place was grandpa's dook. We used to build bogeys, carts made from bits of wood and old wheels which we used to race down the steepest hill we could find. Alister was a wee bit younger and at that age a couple of years seems a big difference, so I'd prefer to play with boys of my own age around the town. There would usually be four or five of us. There are a few hills in Lanark and the only way is down!

I was desperate for a motorcycle for as long as I can remember but my mother was never that enthusiastic. A friend of mine at primary school, Robin Anderson, moved into a big house on the south side of Lanark and he and his brother had motorbikes. I was up there one day and we were playing around with them. I thought those bikes were great. When I came back at night I was really down in the dumps because the fun was over.

My father could see that, so a couple of weeks later he got me a bike. I was nine years old. It was brilliant, all I'd ever wanted. It was a Honda XR 75 which I just rode locally in the fields round about. My cousins had a farm that we used to go up to and we had permission to ride there. I fell off a few times but I had no really bad scrapes and it never put me off. The biggest problem was finding new places where we were allowed to ride our bikes.

One day we were at our house and my parents were away. A couple of friends and I were messing around with my father's trials bike. He obviously didn't know about it – not until later, anyway! We started riding around on the public road and one of my friends hit a wall and tore all his knuckles. The next thing we knew the police turned up. They wanted to know where my parents were and I told them they weren't in. I was thinking, 'They don't know about this and they're not going to find out.' But of course we all had to give our names to the police and we realised they would find out when they came back. We put the bike in the garage and sat there panicking for hours, waiting for them to come home.

Eventually the father of one of the other lads came to the door with a policeman. We thought, 'That's it, we're done for now. We'll not be allowed to ride the bikes again.' But in fact when my dad got back it wasn't as bad as I'd feared and it all blew over. He gave me the normal rollicking and told me not to do it again, but it was worse getting that from the policeman. A couple of weeks later we were back out on the bikes again.

But I didn't just want to play around with bikes. I felt right from the start that I was quite good on a bike and knew what I was doing, so I wanted to compete. I had a friend, Dave Manser from

Cumbria, who was competing at the time. He was a bit older than me and I used to go to meetings with him and his father. My father was right into rallying at that time and also had the plumbing business so he was struggling to find time to take me. I loved it because competing was what it was all about, trying to beat the person in front of me.

I was 11 when I went to my first meeting. It was in the Wrexham area. It was a long way to go but these friends were going there and I just had to hitch up with them. It went reasonably well, although the bike I had wasn't great. The other bikes were slightly more advanced but I finished at the front end of the field so it wasn't bad.

I moved on to a better bike after that and made a pretty rapid rise. When I was 13 I won the Scottish Junior Scrambles Championship. I just wish I could have competed more often in England because the competition was a bit limited in Scotland. Another problem was the fact that my father was away so much and it was a little awkward relying on other people to take me all the time. It was quite difficult to get people to go down south. My mum certainly didn't fancy it. She came to a couple of meetings but sat in the car rather than watch the race. She hated it.

During that period I never got really hurt. I was winded a few times and had my share of bumps and bruises, but no broken bones. I was probably the only lad who didn't break a bone. A lot of the others running at the front got injuries. The year I won the Scottish Championship a guy called Ian Hill, who was very quick, broke his arm two thirds of the way through the season, which meant he missed a couple of rounds. I got far enough in front of him that he couldn't catch me.

Competing in cars didn't really figure in my thoughts at that stage. It was all bikes – motocross and road racing, as well. I would have liked to have had a go at road racing but there was definitely no support from my mother on that idea! She was hoping my interests would take me on an entirely different route. Dad was quite comfortable with it. He'd done it all himself and understood my enthusiasm for bikes. Fathers and sons accept there's a wee bit of danger but don't worry too much.

Alister was starting to race at about this time as well, so you can imagine mum then! He was very good but had to stop because of his knees. He had two operations and the surgeon told him he wouldn't be able to walk properly if he continued. He was not far off getting a works ride for the British Championship. He had quite a few offs and injuries. I was the more controlled one then. That situation rather reversed itself later!

I simply didn't like hurting myself. When I am in a car I feel quite secure. On a bike I was pretty sensible and I still am. I'm certainly not a coward but I just couldn't see the attraction of pain. It was happening all about me. Riding was fun for me, even though I wanted to win. Alister was getting to the stage where he had to produce results if he wanted to get sponsorship deals on bikes and that's what makes the difference. You can ride at 90 per cent all day and be well within your limits, but it's when you start to push, looking for the little extra that wins races, that it becomes a bit dangerous.

You can never be sure how you might have done in other areas but I did fancy road racing: circuits, Grand Prix 500, that sort of thing. I'd always wanted to have a go at the TT as well – until I went to the Isle of Man to see it for the first time. Now I don't regret not having done it. As soon as I saw the top guys coming round the first time it changed my mind completely. I thought, 'I'll give that one a miss, thank you.' It's frightening. That's the only way you can describe it.

Dad took up rallying as a way of getting away from the business at weekends and was doing well when I was racing bikes. He'd gone through the stage of working on his own cars and was now driving works-prepared cars. A lot of people work on their cars for years but he did that for only two or three years. And he didn't start until he was 30. Nowadays you wouldn't think about starting at that age because it couldn't happen.

Just going out with dad, testing and sitting in the car with him, must have influenced me. I was into speed and this was another way in. When he was driving with Opel his main mechanics, Alex Strathdee and Ian Anderson, would let me go in the van with them, clean the windscreen, get the jacks out and do that sort of stuff. That gets you into it. You get into the environment, you see it all, you understand it all at a very early age.

But I was still into the bikes. When I was 12 I moved up in the motocross classes, with a new bike, racing against boys who were a year older than me. Dad was quite keen for me to stay on bikes but mum was putting a lot of pressure on him, so he pointed me in the direction of trials bikes, which were a lot slower and not quite as dangerous. I wanted to continue in motocross but I got a nice new trials bike and I enjoyed it. It was a good level and I got my satisfaction from improving. I did that when I was 14 and 15 and won the Scottish Intermediate title. I went back to motocross when I was 16 because I missed that extra speed.

By then I was already messing about with cars. I learned how to drive just by watching mum and dad and my grandparents. It looked fairly straightforward. I started driving cars up and down the drive at home as soon as I could reach the pedals. I'd jump into whatever car was parked there with the keys in the ignition and find an excuse to move it. I was about 12 then. By the age of 14 I was looking for a bit more fun.

Another friend of mine, Sandy Mitchell, from Rigside, which is about five miles out of Lanark, was tinkering with cars and at school one day he asked me if I fancied going over at the weekend. He had an old Mini that he'd got from the scrap yard and was sorting it out. Once it was ready he was going to race it around the old mines in front of his house. So I went over there and it was great fun blasting about the mines. I could handle the car okay but it was a big wide open area so that didn't matter too much, anyway.

I realised there was some real fun to be had here so next we got hold of an old Bedford van, which was one of the plumbing and heating vans at my dad's company that had failed its MOT. I managed to persuade my old man to let me have it. I sorted that out and it ended up with the two of us racing each other, Sandy in his Mini against me in my Bedford van. I don't think you could say either of us won as such, it was more of a banger race than anything else, to see who could get the other off the road.

When you think about it now I suppose it really was quite dangerous, but when you're kids you don't think of the danger. We had no seat belts and we were flying around at 60 or 70 mph. We rolled the Mini once but nobody was hurt. Sandy was driving and I was in it with him at the time. It stopped on its roof. It didn't put me off in the slightest. It was all a laugh.

Competition in cars came with the autotests, when I was 16. We sold the trials bike and bought an autotest Mini. Obviously mum was going to be happier with that, wasn't she? It had four wheels instead of two and there were regulations to stick to. Autotests weren't that satisfying really, not unless they were the quicker ones. After a while, driving in first and reverse gears around cones can get pretty boring. But I was 16, driving a car and it seemed to me another step.

The next step was getting my full driving licence. I did my test a week after my 17th birthday. Driving wasn't a problem, I'd done plenty of that. But I had to go for lessons because I would never have passed if I'd used the techniques that I had learned up to that point! I had four or five lessons that week. I just crammed them in. I went to a proper driving instructor, a local guy called Joe Garrity who had taught my mother. He knew who I was and that I could drive a car so it was just a case of telling me what I should and shouldn't do. He never had to give me a flea in my ear because I took it very seriously. I was desperate to pass as all I wanted to do was get out on my own. I passed my test and then it was a case of 'Let's go'.

Keeping it in the Family

Passing my driving test was just the start of some real driving. It was great to have the freedom of the road and be able to come and go more or less as I pleased, but I also wanted to get into rallying. I was desperate to do the rallies. Dad was British champion and I'd been waiting for my first chance for some time. Racing never interested me. It had to be rallies. I went on the odd test with dad and that made me even more determined I was going to have a go.

I'd left school and gone to college at Coatbridge to do a one-year course in mechanical engineering. The course was tied up with the work I was doing at Archie's Autos, in Lanark. The trouble was that when I started rallying I was having to ask for time off college and the garage. They were really good about it at the garage but it became too difficult to dovetail everything so my father asked me if I wanted to go and work in the business with him. It was obviously going to be a lot easier to get time off and a bit of preferential treatment. I did the job properly, though. I went into an apprenticeship in plumbing and heating, so you could say I'm a fully qualified plumbing and heating engineer.

In reality, I was planning everything around rallying. As soon as I started I knew this was for me and even at that stage I set my goals quite high. I was just determined to do well. I borrowed a car, an Avenger 1600, from a guy called Davie Burden at the Coltness Car Club, in return for doing a wee bit of work on it. A guy called Barry Lochhead, who did a lot of work with me later on, helped me get the car sorted for my first event, the Kames Stages. It was a local farm track type of event which took in a small racetrack as well. We were flying straight away and were very close to leading the class with another guy, Geordie Gillespie, who was very quick at the time. And then of course we went off. We got stuck in a peat bog and it took us some time to get out. We finished 14th, first in class, so although it was an eventful start it was also productive and I had a good result to show for my maiden event. My co-driver was Gordon Gracie. He was much older than me, probably about 30, but he thoroughly enjoyed it. I think it was the quickest he'd ever been. That first rally convinced me I had a feel for it. I had no doubt I was on my way.

Dad didn't see me that day because he was away on his own event. In fact he'd let me get on with it and sort out everything myself. That was fine by me because I wanted to show I could do it. I didn't want it handed to me on a plate. He never actually taught me and only sat in the car with me halfway through the following season, when he was giving driving instruction and I took my car down to the forest for a bit of practice. I never asked anyone how to drive a rally car. It was just instinctive. It seemed to come naturally to me. You get into a way of doing it that is right for you. Barry helped me with the mechanical side, making sure the car was always bullet proof, which was a good thing! Maybe he would have said something if he felt I couldn't do it, but he wasn't that kind of guy. In any case he knew that was what I wanted to do and that I had the speed.

At the end of 1985 it was obvious that to make progress I would have to get my own car, so we sold the autotest car, put in a bit more money and bought a Talbot Sunbeam. I think it cost us £850. We took it to the Galloway Hills Rally and ended up in a tree. Hit it perfectly, though, right in the middle of the front of the car – put the engine back, broke the gearbox, did the prop shaft, bent the back axle, made a really good job of it. My co-driver was a guy called Colin Smith. He was an insurance man, which was probably just as well! I don't know whether he was put off by that little incident with the tree but it was the only rally he did with me.

Over the winter we spent a bit more money and an awful lot of time on the Sunbeam. One of the first jobs was to put in another engine. Barry was working for dad's firm, supposedly maintaining the vans, but in reality he was doing more and more work on rally cars. He loved it anyway. He had done some driving with a navigator called Derek Ringer. Little did I know then that Derek and I would be teaming up in later years.

We got the Sunbeam ready to do the 1986 Scottish Championship, starting with the Snowman Rally, up in Inverness. My father had seen that I had some speed but maybe not as much control as there should have been, so he managed to talk Ian Grindrod into sitting with me. Ian had navigated for dad as well as for drivers such as Henri Toivonen and Tony Pond. He knew his stuff and dad figured he would be a good influence. We were number one-hundred-and-something and did pretty well in our class. We managed to catch cars on every stage and that caused us our biggest problem. Just before we went into the last stage the rear brakeline burst so we had to carry on with front brakes only, and very little of that.

We'd been picking cars off all day and there was a guy in front of us in an Escort who obviously realised what was happening and was beginning to panic. I had told him there was no need to worry because we'd got this problem with our brakes and wouldn't be able to catch up. But about halfway through the stage we did catch him on a really narrow straight. He tried to move over but it was too narrow and we were right on his tail. He went over a crest and slammed on his brakes to pull up and find a lay-by. We came over the crest but couldn't brake and went straight into the back of him. We catapulted the poor guy into a ditch and kept going. He apparently got out of the ditch about five minutes later. I went to apologise to him afterwards and he was okay about it and told me not to worry.

We had a few dramas that year. My co-driver for most of the rallies was a guy called Nicky Jack and the pair of us became quite handy at emergency repairs. I suppose it was all part of the learning process. It was certainly a lot of fun and 18th overall in the Championship wasn't bad going. We must have caught somebody's attention because I was awarded the Jaggy Bunnett Flying Brick for being the hardest trier in the Championship. I'd actually won something in my first full season!

Although Nicky was my regular navigator in '86 I was joined by Derek Ringer on the Jim Clark Rally, which wasn't part of the Scottish Championship. He was clearly very good and we got on really well. He was involved in the co-ordination side in the Scottish, organising all the services and so on. He was very professional and always on top of things. He was about 15 years older than me so he knew rallying and he knew the forests. I asked him if he'd like to navigate for me the following year and he was all for it, even though it meant he would have to pack in driving.

Derek worked for Ferranti in Edinburgh. I never fully understood what he did but it was pretty complicated computerised stuff and he was obviously a smart guy. He was also able to get more time off work than Nicky could. At that stage there was never any talk about the long term future and what we might achieve together. Our attitude was 'Let's have a go at it and see where we get'. I hoped I would eventually get a works drive but there was nothing more specific than that.

The main thing was to keep progressing and having done the Scottish Championship I wanted to have a go at the National Championship. We got a front-wheel-drive Vauxhall Nova and managed to bring in some sponsorship, but basically we still had to pay our way. I had to do my share of work at the firm too, so there was no danger of getting carried away.

But the rallying made it all worthwhile and Derek and I struck up an excellent partnership. The good thing about him was that he didn't say a lot – and you could never go quickly enough for him. He just loved the buzz of speed and getting a good result. I haven't had as many navigators as some drivers but you hear there are those who keep trying to have an input into the driving side. I didn't want anybody like that. To be perfectly honest I wasn't interested in what anybody else was thinking. I was driving the car and nine times out of ten the driver is quicker and better at driving than the navigator. It has always seemed clear to me: the driver does his job and the navigator does his.

A lot was made of the fact that I was left-foot braking but I'd been doing that in the Sunbeam. We had a dodgy back axle and the wheel bearings weren't very good so it used to get a lot of pad knock-off. That meant I had to keep it pumped up with my left foot so I thought I might as well just use my left foot for braking. It wasn't a conscious thing, I didn't go through the process of figuring that this was the way it had to be done to get anywhere in the sport, it just seemed the obvious way. It was only when I had a front-wheel-drive car that people started raving about my left foot braking. I could still brake with my right foot but I got used to left foot braking and found it easier. There are top guys around, such as Didier Auriol, who brake with their right foot and can still win rallies. I think it's got to be slightly quicker with the left because of the split second required to shift your foot and I feel it gives you more options of control.

I actually competed in the Nova for the first time at the end of '86 on the Galloway Hills Rally and dad navigated for me. It was the first and last chance I gave him to partner me. We had three punctures on that one event, the only three punctures I had all year. As he wasn't driving I figured it had to be all his fault. Rest assured he got plenty of stick for that. But I have to say his advice and guidance at the time were spot on. He also had good contacts with sponsors and that was a big help.

People were taking notice of me because of dad and, I'd like to think, because they could see I was quick. They were constantly making comparisons between us, which was understandable enough. Being Jim McRae's son had its pros and cons. It was good because it opened doors quicker and more easily than if I'd not been the son of a famous and successful rally driver. But then when I made mistakes I was heavily criticised. It seemed I didn't get the credit I deserved when I did well because it was to be expected, yet when I went off I got hammered.

It wasn't a big problem, though. I certainly wasn't discouraged by the pressures or criticism. I was doing something I enjoyed and knew I was pretty good at, so I wasn't going to let anything else bother me. Dad didn't have to say anything because he could see I was taking it all fairly calmly so it wasn't anything worth getting upset about.

The word was getting around that I was quite hot and before the National season started I got the chance to make my debut in a World Championship event, the Swedish Rally. The organisers were prepared to back me, even though I was only 18. It was an offer I couldn't refuse and, if nothing else, had to be good experience in the Nova, which I could then take into events back home.

Ian Grindrod was talked into coming with me again but he was to regret it. We went out on the recce and that proved to be as eventful as the rally itself. We were on a stage, driving downhill in snow, and came to a blind corner. We weren't going that quickly but we suddenly saw a Saab coming the other way and there was no way we could stop. We had a head-on accident and it broke Ian's sternum. The Saab was full of dogs and they were thrown off the parcel shelf. There must have been about five of them, all quite small, but they were all okay. Ian wasn't so lucky. He was out of commission.

We had to find somebody to replace him and managed to get Mike Broad, who was co-driver to Russell Brookes, one of my dad's regular rivals on the British scene. Mike was another very good navigator but arriving late as he did he had to go into the rally blind. He hadn't done the notes or seen any of the stages. Not surprisingly, we had a few interesting moments on the event and became quite expert at digging ourselves out of snow banks. We didn't have any big accidents, though, and made it to the finish. We ended up third in class and 36th overall, which was a pretty good result considering we'd spent so much time in the snow banks!

I reckoned I was ready for just about anything after that but I had a few more interesting spills in the National. There was nothing too serious, though, and I knew I was showing the speed to get to a higher level. We often matched cars with far more grunt than our Nova. We finished the year as class winners and seventh overall.

That year I also had my first experience of the RAC Rally, when anything up to two million fans converge on the British forests. In the late '80s and into the '90s the rally still took in stages in the far north of England and the Borders. We also competed at night. Now World Championship events are standardised and much more compact. The Rally of Great Britain – I find it hard not to call it the RAC – has become in reality a Welsh event in recent years.

We took our Nova on to the '87 RAC and kept out of serious trouble. We took third place in our class after a really good fight against much more experienced drivers. It was a good finish to a good year and I was already looking forward to the day when I would have a more competitive car on the RAC.

The Nova had served me well. It was generally reliable and had given me the chance to clock up the mileage, which is what any young driver needs more than anything. I still had the Nova in '88, kept for the British Open Championship, a few Scottish events and the 24 Hours of Ypres. We didn't literally rally round the clock for 24 hours on that Belgian event but it was a good, long challenge and we covered a lot of miles before I crashed out. I also drove one or two other cars that enabled me to fast track my learning experience.

Peugeot were keen to give their backing to three of Britain's most promising young drivers in the National Championship and I was one of those they supported. The others were Warren Hunt, an Englishman, and Iwan Roberts, from Wales. I don't think they deliberately went for three drivers from three countries of Britain, they just wanted the three young guys of the moment. We were driving at a similar speed, and were all competitive and ambitious. They called us the 'Young Lions' and made a big issue of our rivalry. We were all capable of beating each other but generally I was the quickest and I won my class in the National.

I made another step up in power that year and competed in a number of rear-wheel-drive cars, including the Nissan that brought me my first win in a rally. We had set up a small motorsport business, buying, preparing and selling cars, and I was able to come to an arrangement to use a couple of cars we worked on, the Nissan and a Peugeot 205 with a 240RS engine. That was down to a friend of mine, Donald Milne, who first sold me the Nissan and then loaned me the Peugeot.

After that I got a deal to drive a Sierra Cosworth.

That was a strange year in the Scottish Championship because I honestly didn't set out with the title in mind. I was moving into other areas and just trying to improve my driving and generally gain experience. In fact, I had a woman co-driver for the Tweedies Daihatsu Stages. Her name was Alison Hamilton. It was a one off. The date was July 17, 1988, not long before my 20th birthday. And we won. My first victory – and with a female navigator. But more of that, and the lady Hamilton, later.

There was a lot of talk around that time of women in rallying. Louise Aitken-Walker had a Peugeot works drive and won a round of the National Championship. She was reasonably quick. The quickest woman of all time was Michelle Mouton. Now she was very quick. No other woman got close to her and no woman since has looked like emulating her feats.

There's no reason why a woman shouldn't succeed at World Championship level. You don't have to be physically strong. The physical requirement is general fitness and stamina rather than brute force, and a woman can be as well equipped as a man when it comes to that. Formula One is a different matter. You have to be physically strong to hold those cars and take the G-forces through corners on a Grand Prix circuit.

Any woman who was any good at rallying would find it easier to get support and opportunities, and progress quicker than a guy with the same ability because of the commercial possibilities. I suspect it's a mental thing with women in motor sport. They possibly see it as a man's game. They tend to be naturally more cautious than men and see danger more than men do. That's the only reason I can think of for more women not coming into rallying.

Another opponent that year was a Welsh co-driver called Nicky Grist, who partnered country-man Harry Hockly in a Nova. It's fascinating to look back and recall how the paths of certain people criss-crossed through their careers and eventually came together. Others you compete against drift out of the sport and you never hear of them again. At that time Nicky was just another competitor in the British Championship and I didn't really know much about him.

When Derek and I realised we actually had a chance of winning the Scottish we naturally went for it. Dad's involvement with Ford and the RED team helped me get hold of a Sierra Cosworth. My first event in a 300-plus bhp, turbo-charged car was the Border Rally, which we won by two seconds to take the lead in the Championship. We were second on the Kingdom Stages and first on the Hackle.

Our rival going into the final event, the Trossachs, was David Gillanders, an experienced guy with a good track record. But Derek had also been around for some time and his knowledge came into play on that event. He suggested we deliberately forfeit time to let Gillanders run ahead of us. That would enable us to see what we had to do and although it was a bit of a gamble I went along with the plan. As it happened, Gillanders went off so there was no pressure on us at all and we settled for second place. We had won the title and I was the youngest ever Scottish Champion. As I have reminded dad a few times since, that's one Championship he didn't win!

That success really was a bonus. I'd had a lot of fun and the privilege of driving some top class cars. I was always comfortable in those cars and against that opposition. I never had the feeling I might be taking a step too far or too soon. By that time I had no doubt I could go all the way in rallying. I knew I could beat anybody in the categories I'd been competing in and saw no reason why I shouldn't be able to keep moving up. Even then I honestly believed I could eventually win the World Championship.

The prize for winning my class in the National was the use of a Peugeot Group A 205 GTI on the RAC Rally. The weather was atrocious, apparently the worst on the event for 17 years. The snow and ice took a heavy toll. Eventually the engine went and we had to retire. It had been another good year, though, and I was already planning my strategy for '89.

It was a toss up between a Group A Peugeot and a semi-works Group N drive with Ford. In the end I went for the Ford, alongside dad in the RED team. I found a big rear-wheel-drive car appealing and the deal seemed to offer plenty of opportunities. Dad was going for the British Championship again in a Group A Sierra Cosworth and I was aiming for a class win.

With the benefit of hindsight, however, I think it would have been better for me had I gone for the Group A option. The Group N cars were fast but they were standard cars and they didn't really respond to an aggressive driving style, whereas the Group A cars did. I had my share of spills and incidents that year. An accident on the Sweet Lamb stage of the Welsh Rally was a case in point. I was basically going too quickly in a car not designed for that type of terrain. I went down a very fast hill into a dip and the suspension bottomed out. The car was thrown off the road and rolled, but I didn't consider it the major accident some people seemed to think it was. Derek and I were unhurt.

I managed to get my hands on a Group A Sierra Cosworth for the National Championship and a Group A Sierra XR4x4 to drive on the Swedish Rally. A works World Rally Championship drive was still some way out of range but that was my goal and here I had another opportunity to make an impression. I finished the first leg 10th and would have remained in the top 10 if it hadn't been for gearbox trouble. That would have been a major achievement for a 20-year-old. Instead I had to settle for 15th.

I also went to the Acropolis Rally that year, although I wasn't competing. Mind you, that didn't stop me testing my speed. My dad was there for Mitsubishi and I drove one of the chase cars, ferrying the mechanics to service points. It was the chance to learn something about another World Championship rally and have a bit of fun while I was at it. I had a bit too much fun for the team director Andrew Cowan, who didn't see the funny side of it when he got a repair bill of about £3,000 for the wear and tear on the car I'd been driving.

It didn't worry me because I wasn't paying, but Andrew's held it against me ever since. He still talks to me, but not about that bill!

I was back in a rally car – a Group A Cosworth – for the New Zealand event and achieved probably my best result of that year. I got some financial backing and Boreham supplied me with the car. Some guys from RED took their holidays to come out and look after us. It was my first experience of the rally but I instantly felt comfortable there. It's a driver's rally and one of the best on the Championship. It's fast and flowing and I built up my speed and finished fifth, which was a great result.

After that I was even more determined to drive Group A cars. The Group N Championship had gone out of the window by that time anyway and I felt New Zealand proved my style was better suited to Group A. I wanted a car that could respond to my driving and would be able cope with the strains. Ford took that on board and I had a Group A for the last three international events of the year – the Manx , the Audi Sport and the RAC.

We were looking good on the Manx, running third, ahead of my dad who had a puncture early on, but then we broke the rear differential on a couple of bad bumps and had to retire. It was a disappointment but it was my first opportunity to drive a competitive car against the likes of my dad, Russell Brookes and all those guys who were regular front-runners during that period, so it wasn't a wasted effort.

The Audi Sport marked probably the one and only time I can say I beat dad fair and square. I finished ahead of him in third place and he was delighted for me. If he was going to be beaten by anyone he would have wanted it to be me. It's like me now. If I'm going to be beaten by anyone I would prefer it to be Alister. I'm sure dad was pretty proud, but I was still a few years away from the stage where people stopped referring to me as 'Jimmy McRae's son'.

I had the same Sierra on the RAC Rally, which came to an alarming end for me in Kielder Forest. We had rolled the car the day before without losing too much time and were fighting, against, among others, Malcolm Wilson, and the Astras. It was dark, and unbeknown to us Franco Cunico, an Italian driving a Sierra, had gone off into a ditch and the back of his car was sticking out into the road. Neither Cunico nor his co-driver Terry Harryman had gone into the road to warn us to slow down and when we came around the corner their car was right in front of us.

I was straight on the brakes but couldn't avoid running into Cunico's car. Worse still, Terry was walking around the back of the car and I hit him. He was thrown onto the bonnet of my car and I thought, 'Oh, no!' He fell down between the two cars but I could see he was all right because he was trying to free himself. His leg was cut but wasn't broken.

In the confusion and fright of it all I didn't realise straight away that somebody else had been hurt. There were spectators standing on the bank and a young lad was caught by splinters from the shattered rear window. He was bleeding quite a lot and crying, and we couldn't tell exactly what had happened or whether anyone else had been hurt. Because it was dark everything was difficult to work out which made us even more anxious. We had to stop the stage and get the ambulance in. The car wasn't damaged so we could have reversed and continued, but obviously in those circumstances we didn't and that was the end of our RAC.

It had been a bit of a mixed bag of a season but Ford presumably thought I was worth supporting because I got a Sapphire – the car taking over from the Sierra – with RED for the British Championship the following year. Dad was beginning to back off a little, while Alister was coming through, driving a trusty Nova. It was the car most people used at the time to get started.

My season with the Sapphire couldn't have got off to a better start. I won the first rally out with the car, the Cartel. David Llewellin was the man to beat at the time. He was in a four-wheel-drive Toyota but had turbo trouble on the last stage and I became the youngest ever winner of a British international rally.

Shell and Pirelli helped us out a lot with their backing but we really did need that win because we were running the operation on a very tight budget, rally to rally. RED were building the cars but we were having to find the money to pay the bills. We picked up third place on the Circuit of Ireland after hitting a wall and breaking the front suspension. We weren't so lucky on the Welsh. We had quite a bad accident and wrote off the Sapphire.

Ford were in no rush to replace it so we were

left without a car for the Scottish. I had to use my own Sierra and came second. It wasn't a bad result in the circumstances but at a time when I wanted to be taking a step forward I was actually going backwards. We took the Sierra to the 24 Hours of Ypres and finished fourth, which really was a good result. Ford let us have a Cosworth for the Ulster but we lost a lot of time there and were only eighth. Llewellin had won the Championship. Third place on the Manx was nothing to get excited about.

I needed a bit of fun and had it on the Hackle round of the Scottish Championship. I used an old Escort RS 2000 and Robert Reid navigated for me. We won by more than half a minute.

Now I needed a competitive car and Ford supplied me with a Sierra Cosworth 4x4. I was second on the Audi Sport, the final round of the British Championship, but my attention was fixed firmly on the RAC Rally and my first chance on the event with a four-wheel-drive car. I had to make an impression if I was going to take that next step forward in 1991 so I knew I couldn't afford to waste this opportunity.

On the first day we clipped a gatepost in Chatsworth, one of the spectator stages, and broke the suspension. That cost us some time and then we went off in Yorkshire, damaging the side of the car quite badly. The only way we could hold the door shut was by putting on a sliding bolt from a farmyard gate. We also had to fix a plastic window to the battered car. We were presented with our next problem when a cylinder head gasket went. The RED guys changed it and back home in Scotland I set a series of top three times. We still had more trouble to contend with – gearbox and all sorts of things. We'd lose time and then climb back up. In the end we were sixth. I was the top British driver on the RAC.

It was the kind of result I'd been hoping for and I thought Ford would come up with a firm deal for 1991. I'd have everything in place, with no concerns about funding, well ahead of the new season. However, to my disappointment, they weren't prepared to commit themselves and didn't even seem interested. Nothing was happening. It looked as though it was going to be another year of trying to find sponsors from rally to rally.

That would have been absolutely no good for me. I couldn't go on like that if I was to get anywhere in the sport. I was relying on results to make sure I got backing for the next rally, but I knew I couldn't drive at my best because I was too inhibited. It was a vicious circle. I was concentrating on being careful and avoiding making mistakes rather than relaxing, driving naturally and showing what I really could do. The situation just didn't suit my style of driving.

It was a critical point in my career. I was confident that, given the opportunity, I could go all the way to the top in rallying. The problem was, there appeared no prospect of getting that opportunity. I had no idea what was going to happen or where to turn to next. All I could do was sit, wait and hope.

Into the Blue

The phone call came out of the blue. It was David Richards on the other end of the line. DR had been co-driver to Ari Vatanen when the Finn won the World Championship in 1981. Apart from my dad, Ari was my one true hero in rallying. He was exciting, daring. Perhaps I was subconsciously influenced by his style. DR went into management and my dad drove for him. He set up Prodrive, which has since become a massively successful operation in racing and rallying. The Prodrive factory has become something of a landmark on the M40, near the Banbury turn-off.

Back in that winter of 1990-91 DR was planning his rallying programme with Subaru. I'd never really spoken to him apart from exchanging the odd 'Hello'. He rang our home and spoke to dad, asking if we had anything sorted out which of course we hadn't. He said he'd like to fix up something for me with Subaru; he didn't have any sponsorship sorted at the time but was willing to commit to a programme and pay me a fee. I learned that was typical DR. He'd just grab something and go for it: he had a hunch and was prepared to back it, and wasn't afraid to take a risk.

I was delighted. His proposal was to run me in the British Championship but I was given hints that if things worked out well there might be an opportunity for me in the World Championship. And, for the first time, I would be paid for driving a rally car rather than having to find the money. I had become a professional rally driver. My salary that first year was £10,000, but to be honest I considered it a bonus. What really mattered was that I had a works drive and could concentrate on driving.

At that stage you couldn't really envisage what it would lead to but DR was obviously a go-ahead guy, a break from the mould. He struck me as a straight-up sort of guy who wanted to get things done. He had been working on a sponsorship deal with Rothmans and they eventually agreed to climb on board with us. We were up and running.

DR saw my British programme as a means of developing the Legacy for the World Championship, and presumably measuring my progress and potential. I certainly saw it as the chance to learn and stake my claim. Part of the agreement was that I would go to some of the World Championship events to drive the chase car and further my education. I didn't cause as much damage to the car this time. I could see real possibilities and wanted to get myself established in the team so I thought it might be wise to behave myself!

The British Championship was far from plain

sailing that year. I was still making mistakes and the car was new. We were down on power compared with some of our rivals and we had the inevitable reliability problems to contend with. But the Legacy was easier to drive than the cars I'd been used to and we got off to a great start, winning in Yorkshire. We had gone faster than Russell Brookes before he had trouble and lost a lot of time. There had been no pressure on me from the team to go for it in that first rally but the car felt good, so did I.

We won again in Ireland but things didn't go so smoothly in Wales. I had a couple of offs and a DNF next to my name. I got it right in Scotland and had my first win in my home international. It was a pretty good weekend all round for the McRae family. Dad was third in a Sierra and Alister eighth in the Nova.

In Ulster the gearbox broke and put us out, but our win on the Manx made up for that disappointment. Brookes was always good on the Isle of Man and Prodrive also brought over Francois Chatriot, the French champion and an asphalt expert. Everyone thought Chatriot would win yet we were ahead of him even before he made a mistake and went off. He finished second. Russell couldn't get near to us. It was a really satisfying rally and it took us within sight of the Championship.

We didn't have to push it in mid-Wales and I didn't. We finished third and that was enough to give us the title. I had become the youngest ever British Champion. Cue the champagne celebrations – but I ended up dripping blood as well as the bubbly stuff.

Derek Ringer was shaking the champagne bottle as I walked around the car towards him and he cracked me on the forehead with it. I was cut but nothing could have spoiled that day.

My stints in chase cars at World Championship events had also been well worthwhile. Sure, what I really wanted was to be driving the rally cars rather than the chase cars, but it was fun. I didn't have to do any real work and I was learning and picking up things all the time. That had to be of benefit to me in the future.

Prodrive were also keen to teach me how to be a modern rally driver. They impressed on me that I was a sportsman, not a chauffeur. That meant training properly, living properly and following a sensible diet. I've got to admit I've never been fanatical about following a so-called proper diet. I'm lucky in that I'm pretty slim and don't have to worry too much about my weight, but we're not Olympic athletes. As long as you're sensible and don't get stuck into the chips and fry-ups too much, I don't see a problem.

It's become a bit of a joke with me over the years, nipping round the back of the motorhome for a sandwich or a chocolate biscuit, but obviously I'm not going to be stupid. On an event you tend to eat little and often. Most importantly, you have to keep your fluid levels up, especially on the hot events. A lot of it is psychological. I think the trick is to do what is right for you. At Prodrive everything had to be done the right way. They were always looking at performance and ways of improving, which of course was very professional of them.

Another fun drive that year was in a TVR at Snetterton race track. My father was no longer a full-time professional rally driver and got himself involved in a number of ventures – including that race down in East Anglia. They had a spare celebrity car and asked me if I fancied a go. I jumped at the chance but had engine problems in qualifying, a couple of spins in the race and finished eighth.

The drive I was relishing even more was on the RAC. I joined up with Markku Alen and Ari Vatanen, which wasn't bad company to be mixing in. The two Finns were up there with the best and were genuinely good team-mates to be with. They'd done it all, had nothing to prove and certainly didn't have any problems welcoming me to the line-up. They didn't look down their noses at me, either. They had plenty to think about with their own rallies and left me to get on with mine. I had all the advice I needed from the engineers.

Derek and I made a good start and on the second day in Wales, went into the lead with a couple of fastest stage times. A spin in Hafren cost us time but we were still in a strong position as we headed for the Lake District stages. We were quickest on Grizedale One but got caught out on Grizedale Two where we rolled and lost a lot of time. Then in Kielder we went off and stayed off. It was a dismal end to our RAC Rally, but I'd shown my speed and overall 1991 had been a satisfactory year.

In 1992 we would be defending our British Championship and I would be going to a few more World Rally Championship events – this time to compete. My year began with the Swedish and almost a win. Ari was supposed to be the team's main challenger but he crashed on the first stage and I was more than happy to give it a go. I'd gained some experience on that rally, of course, and although no Briton had finished in the top six I was quite confident I could handle it. A puncture ended any chance of victory but I managed to take second place, beating the likes of Alen in the process.

The British Championship seemed low-key by comparison with the world events and that year the defence of my title was a relatively straightforward exercise. I won all six rounds, the Ulster rally by more than 11 minutes. But the highlight for the McRae family was definitely the Scottish rally. Alister was second and the old man fourth. He was very close to third but couldn't quite get back at Robbie Head and spoiled the clean sweep of the top three. We gave him a good slating for letting us down!

The closest rally I had in the British was mid-Wales, the last event of the Championship. I was pushed hard and got home just two seconds ahead of a works Nissan driven by a Finn called Tommi Makinen. I would be seeing a lot more of him in the years ahead.

One or two of the long established British guys were getting past their best and although it was a great season for me and for the team, I knew I was ready for more competitive action.

I had a sample of that on the Acropolis Rally, one of the hottest and roughest events on the World Rally Championship calendar. I faced a few problems but it's most unusual if you don't have any to confront in Greece. The stages there can be very tough on the cars and tiring for the drivers. Not surprisingly, I was able to improve on the re-run stages and reeled off a string of fastest times to make my way up to fourth by the end. New Zealand was a damp squib for us. I survived five stages before a piston failure put me out. Our other two cars went the same way.

That summer I also tried my hand on the 1000 Lakes, the most specialised rally of them all. It is fast, with jumps and blind corners that can catch out even the best drivers. You need experience of the stages to stand a realistic chance. Little wonder the Finns have dominated their home event over the years.

I had to start learning the stages the hard way. I rolled the car on the shakedown, leaving the crew with an all-night job to put it together again. When they took it to scrutineering they had to tell the marshals not to push on the boot lid because the paint was still wet. The stickers they put on started reacting and bubbling. That's how fresh the paint job was.

We had another off on the rally. I think we rolled seven times. We went through the tree stumps and smashed into a tree minding its own business. The tree wasn't too healthy after our visit but then neither was the car. The bodywork was completely destroyed, but the car landed on its wheels and as Derek undid his belts to climb out I said, 'Wait a minute, we'll be all right'.

He looked at me as if I was out of my mind and said, 'What? There's no way this thing's going to go again'.

So I fired it up and could see the worried look on his face. I put it in reverse gear, started moving backwards and he had to get in again, saying, 'Oh no, I don't believe it!'

Mechanically the car was perfect and we were able to continue, but you wouldn't have known what type of car it was! The guys patched it up as best they could in the limited time available and the next day we went off again, ploughing through more trees. This time we broke the rear suspension. Although we managed to get going again we had a long way to travel to service and the damage cost us quite a lot of time. We couldn't get the windscreen back in so someone brought us a couple of pairs of welding goggles from the service truck which we had to wear for the next couple of stages. Fortunately it wasn't too cold at that time of year but the midges were a real problem.

We made it through to the finish in eighth place, which wasn't bad considering the dramas we'd had along the way. I think DR wasn't too impressed with the first incident but after that he was almost laughing about it all. He was even helping the guys stick the car back together. What mattered to him was that we were setting quick times and he had to be pleased about that.

Not everyone was willing to forgive me a little exuberance that year. Not on the race track, anyway. Prodrive put me in one of their BMW saloon cars for a double header at Knockhill, a circuit in Scotland, and I qualified for the first race right behind Tim Sugden, one of the works drivers. I'd only had half a day's testing and even had to ask Tom Hunt, Prodrive's test driver and engineer, how to start.

He said: 'When the red light comes on just put it on the rev limiter. When the green light comes on slip your foot off the clutch and don't let off the throttle. If you do it will stall because it's a racing engine.'

So that's what I did and I got a cracking start. It was more luck than anything, to be honest. Then I thought to myself: 'Where am I going to go?' I went from 15th on the grid to eighth, right up through people jostling for position and along the armco barrier. My wing mirrors were scraping the pit wall and I just managed to get clear of the pit lane exit and back into the pack. I let Sugden go by but I think he had trouble with his head gasket and I finished eighth.

That meant I would be starting the second race from eighth place and I intended to get away as I had done the first time and try to get to the front. The red flag came out so I backed off and was hit by another car, which turned up inside me. I managed to get back to the pits but the front suspension was broken and I thought that was it. We didn't think there was enough time to get it repaired before the re-start but while the team were still assessing the damage, the heavens opened and it started pouring with rain. While everyone was debating whether it was going to be a wet or dry race our guys got to work on the suspension and fixed it. They put wet tyres on and sent me back out.

I didn't get such a good start this time and found myself stuck behind Matthew Neal. That was my inexperience of racing. I didn't know how to pass him. I tried everything. I was all over the back of him and he was blocking me every time. I could just about get to him down the back but then on the straight he'd pull away a car's length again. Then when he semi lost it I thought that since he'd made a mistake, I'd help him out. I punted him up the backside. He was stuck in the infield and I was away. I think I was the quickest on every lap after that and finished fifth. The first four were all grouped together and I probably wouldn't have been able to pass them – unless I punted them off too!

I'd had my fun but now it was payback time. The stewards disqualified me but Matt Neal and his old man, Steve, weren't satisfied with that and after the race they came stomping around looking for me. When I got back to the pits Tom came running to the car, opened the door and said: 'Quick, get out and get into the motorhome.'

Now for those who don't know let me tell you, Matt Neal is a big guy. He's six foot seven! But he wasn't really that bothered about the incident. It was his old man who was getting revved up and you wouldn't want to mess with him either. I think DR got the panic on when Matt's dad got hold of him and told him: 'I'm going to rip McRae's head off and shit down his neck.'

I kept out of the way and didn't give him the chance. Thankfully, it all blew over and now what happened that day is a good laugh. It was one of those heat of the moment things. I've spoken to Matt since then and he's fine about it. I'm not so sure about his old man, though.

I felt safer back on the rally stages and had an additional incentive to keep out of trouble on the RAC. Lombard, the sponsors, put up a prize of £100,000 to be awarded to any Briton who won the event. I was with the front-runners again and took the lead in Wales. I was first on the road the following morning but ran into trouble on the road section heading for Grizedale in the Lake District. A Range Rover appeared over the brow of a hill on my side of the road. I swung my car up a bank to avoid it but he caught my front and damaged the suspension. The steering and brakes were affected, and everything went downhill from there. I just couldn't maintain the pace and finished a far from happy sixth.

Derek couldn't do anything to humour me and didn't try. It's difficult for a co-driver to calm you down when you're like that. Sometimes it just makes it worse. Derek sat there and got his head down. He knew there would be another day.

We anticipated increasingly better days in 1993 because we were promoted to Subaru's World Championship team. My days of domestic competition were over. Prodrive were on their way up and a new sponsorship deal enabled them to stay in the ascendancy. If we were going to take on and beat the best we had to have the means to do so. DR hooked 555, one of British American Tobacco's Far East brands. That year the team replaced the Legacy with a more nimble car they called the Impreza 555, a smart way of getting around the cigarette advertising restrictions. The new blue livery became so distinctive that Subaru retained it after that sponsorship contract had run its course. Part of the agreement committed us to taking part in the Asia-Pacific Championship and the Hong Kong–Beijing rally.

I still drove the Legacy for most of the year and got off to a flying start in Sweden. I was leading the rally comfortably at the end of the first leg but had my advantage wiped out on the second morning by a broken driveshaft. I also had electrical problems. I wasn't the only driver to have trouble though, that's all part of the challenge and character-building in rallying.

The important thing was that I had stayed in contention and we came to the last stage with three of us in the hunt for victory, separated by just 17 seconds. I was second but naturally wanted to win and went for it. Unfortunately, I had a spin after a jump and dropped to third, behind Sweden's Mats Jonsson and Finland's Juha Kankkunen. It was still a fantastic result though and set us up for the next event.

That was Portugal, where we'd had plenty of drama in testing. It was a fairly dangerous test route, with the kind of drops you didn't want to have first hand experience of. We checked it out that morning and stopped at one corner which had a particularly nasty looking drop on the outside. Derek and I looked at it and gulped. It was the most frightening sight, the drop to the bottom of the valley seemed to go on for ever.

Two hours later we were driving along that stretch of tarmac again. We came downhill towards the corner and because I knew what it was like I wasn't pushing it. But just at that point the tyres went off and there was nothing I could do to stop us dropping over the edge of the cliff. The car plunged off the road, nose first, onto a smaller road below. I could see a tree at the side of the road and I just prayed it would stop us dropping down further, but it was a small tree and the car just snapped it in half. It was like a Roadrunner cartoon, with the car going off the edge of the cliff, stopping, turning, and falling straight down again.

We could see the ground coming towards us but luckily we landed on a small ledge, about 30 metres down. The car rolled over and stopped. There was another, bigger drop, all the way down into the valley so you can imagine how relieved we were. We didn't even dare to breathe. We slowly opened the door and got out of the car. It was the scariest moment I'd had up to that point in my career. I was shaken but unhurt. Derek though, wasn't quite so fortunate. The crutch straps had left their marks after the impact. He had severe bruising around his private parts and it was a bit of a struggle for him to climb up that bank! On the rally itself we ran well in the middle stages, setting a series of fastest times, only to slide off and get stuck. We lost several minutes and finished seventh.

I never expected to make the finish of the Safari Rally because Subaru asked me to drive the Vivio, a new little four-wheel-drive car they were trying to push on the market. I was told to make sure I got it through the rally but I knew that was being a bit too optimistic. I got it up to fourth place and as far as Mombasa before the suspension gave in, which I thought was pretty good going.

I was back in the Legacy and business-like mode for Corsica, where the tight tarmac roads up in the mountains leave very little margin for error or lack of concentration. I still had a lot to learn about a rally such as that, so fifth place wasn't a bad result. The Acropolis Rally definitely was a bad result – a DNF for me and my team-mate, Ari. We both went off and DR was not amused. He would tend to keep calm for so long when things were going wrong, and then he would explode. He thought I'd tried to go too quickly and let me know in no uncertain terms that he didn't approve.

There were always stories in the magazines and papers about his giving me rollickings, but I have to say that generally he was very supportive. This was all part of the learning curve. I was prepared to take it from him and just get on with my job, which was more than a lot of other people would have done at the time.

DR decided he would leave me out of the 1,000 Lakes, which was widely interpreted as a severe disciplinary measure and a warning as to my future conduct. I didn't see it as such a big deal, although I suppose it was a wee bit of punishment but it was probably the wrong way for him to handle it.

Finland is very much a specialist event, where you need experience to have any realistic prospect of going well, so he put Markku and Ari in, two Finns who were very familiar with the stages. I was busy enough, anyway. I was to go straight from New Zealand to Malaysia for a round of the Asia-Pacific Championship.

New Zealand, 1993, was and still is a great landmark in my career. I'd done the rally a couple of times and had gradually increased my pace so I went there genuinely believing I could win the event. It's not unlike a British rally so the conditions have always tended to suit me. I made sure I didn't make any mistakes on the first day and was fifth at the start of the Motu Road stage, on the second morning.

This famous and daunting test is very long, 50-plus kilometres, and very twisty. It demands total concentration and consistency all the way through. I was something like three-quarters of a minute quicker than Francois Delecour, who was very strong on the rally in a works Escort, and Juha. I'd gone from fifth to first.

The possibility of a win not surprisingly brought its pressures and then, when we were approaching the end of a stage, the oil light came on. A plug in the back of the cylinder head had screwed itself out, leaking oil. Fortunately we were able to reach the service, where the guys found the problem and put it back together again. We just hoped it hadn't done any damage to the engine. Again we were in luck and ready for a head-to-head with Delecour who was flying at the end and made it really hard. I had to fight all the way to hold him off which made the win even more satisfying. It was a ground-breaking World Championship victory for many reasons: it was my first, Subaru's first, the first by a Briton since Roger Clark's on the 1976 RAC Rally and the first by a Briton outside Britain. None of those facts was lost on me and of course I took pride in all of them. But the real pleasure came from the way it was achieved, beating a guy in a very competitive car, in a tense and close finish.

I knew I was capable of that and I think the team sensed it was coming as well. They had seen the speed and the performance were there, it was just a matter of time before I tied it all together. Everybody was delighted and yet it was all fairly calm and collected at the end. Derek was as happy as I was but he's not an emotional guy. It was strange, really. I think it was only when some of the other drivers started congratulating us that it began to sink in.

Being on the other side of the world also made it difficult to know what sort of an impact our success had back home, but we weren't conscious of any. We felt it was probably going to take something special in the RAC Rally and the Championship as a whole to do that, and those were my next major targets. I had broken through the first big barrier and now I was focusing on winning more rallies.

We won in Malaysia as we were expected to do, despite one or two big slides in a monsoon. Australia, in the World Championship, was going to be a different proposition but we weren't prepared for the tragedy that awaited us. Possum Bourne, a Subaru team-mate on the event, smashed into a tree, and his navigator and fellow New Zealander, Rodger Freeth, was killed. Rodger was a fun guy and when we were out one night on the recce he said: 'We are all here for a good time not a long time.' It was the first fatality I'd encountered on a rally and it was made the harder to take because Rodger was such a nice guy and we were quite good friends. The feeling we all had was one of numbed disbelief.

There was a lot of confusion as well as shock and sadness. There was talk of pulling our cars out but Rodger's wife Beverley said he would have wanted us to continue. In the end that was why we decided to carry on. Rather than undermine my confidence it made me even more determined to try all I could to win the rally. As a driver or co-driver you are obviously aware of the dangers and I have had a few frightening experiences during my career, but I never think or worry about getting hurt. You couldn't drive and compete properly if you did. In fact you would be more likely to have a bad accident if you went onto a stage in that frame of mind.

I drove on in a very positive fashion and had another terrific fight with Juha. He was regarded as THE man for Australia at the time so it was another big test for me. We were very close to him on the final leg when I made a mistake attempting to take the win. We half spun on a tight corner and the wheels dropped over a bank. I couldn't reverse back to the road so I drove further down the bank to try and turn. Instead I got stuck more and the more I tried to drive out the worse it got. In the end we had to dig out a tree stump to find a way back. By then we'd lost ages and dropped down to sixth.

We went up to China for the Hong Kong–Beijing Rally, which Subaru were always going to win. The only question was, which driver

would have the honour? I was confident it would
be me but Dave Richards decided it should be Ari.
DR felt that as Ari had been having a bad run he
needed a victory to boost his confidence, so I
would have to drive to team orders and finish
second. Needless to say, I wasn't too impressed
with that instruction. No driver is when he is told
he is not allowed to win. This was the first time
we'd done the event and I wanted the chance of
winning it. I wasn't used to being restrained in that
way.

The really annoying part of the whole business
was that Ari was psyched because he screwed up
early in the rally, went off and burst the radiator.
The car was overheating and he almost had to
retire. They managed to patch him up and get him
going again but we were country miles in front of
him by then. It didn't alter the team's plan,
though. We were ordered to back off and let him
catch us. You have to accept that it is a team
game, difficult and unfair as that may seem
sometimes, but from the point of view of the
manufacturer the driver is of secondary
importance. The priority is the car. The manufacturer is involved in rallying to sell cars and is
not overly concerned with the ego of a driver or
any other individual.

It was hard to go along with at the time and
disappointing not to be greeted as the winner of
the rally at the end of it. But it wasn't a World
Championship rally and I knew everyone realised
what had happened. According to the official
result I was second but to my mind I was the
winner, and I was comforted by that.

I'd also got the RAC Rally to look forward to and for my home rally I would at last be getting my hands on the Impreza. Any new car takes some getting used to and this was no different. It was a little nervous compared with the Legacy but it was a neater car, the engine had been improved and it clearly had potential.

Mind you, it wasn't a rally for raw grunt. Wales was more like the Arctic, snow and ice making conditions hazardous in a way the RAC Rally always had the knack of doing. It made for an exciting contest and I produced what had become my traditional charge in the Welsh forests. Juha was my closest rival and when he had a puncture, I was looking good for the victory the media had been grilling me about in the build-up to the rally.

In previous years I had left Wales in a strong position only to trip up as we journeyed north and it was something of a relief to come through Grizedale unscathed on this occasion. But Kielder still had to be negotiated and, sure enough, that huge man-made forest in Northumberland, which had mugged me in the past, was waiting to get me again. Bizarrely, a branch managed to work its way through the air intake and spear the radiator. It was yet another of those weird and not so wonderful incidents you have to contend with in rallying. They had been felling trees, branches were strewn around and one of them had been attracted to the Impreza. The engine over-heated and all the plastic parts melted. We made it to service and the engine was still running but there was no way the team would have been able to repair the car in the time allowed. I was still seeking my maiden victory in my home rally. Juha was in the clear and clinched a record fourth world title.

It was frustrating but not too much of a worry because I was getting closer to that win and I had no doubt it would eventually come. I was quick, still young and improving all the time. I felt the season overall had been productive and encouraging. I had finished joint fifth in the World Championship from eight of the 13 events. That wasn't bad when you consider the driver I shared that position with was Carlos Sainz, a double world champion.

Coincidentally, Sainz was to be my team-mate in 1994. The Spaniard had been recruited to replace Ari, who probably knew his best days were behind him. He was an inspiring driver in his prime and I was proud to have been his team-mate. He was a terrific guy to work with and I'm glad to say the team orders issue in China never soured our relationship.

I could understand the thinking behind DR's decision to sign Carlos. He'd been Champion only the year before and the feeling was that he would help us take another step forward. That was certainly my objective. I had a new, two-year contract and the assurance that I would be contesting every round of the Championship over that period. I felt I had finally arrived among the world title contenders and now I wouldn't be satisfied until I had proved I could be No. 1.

The Final Ascent

My life and career had changed so much in a few short years. I was part of a team planning a serious assault on the World Championship and earning the kind of money that gave me the opportunity to start ensuring my long term financial security. I joined the motor sport community in Monaco and have had an apartment there ever since.

Not unreasonably, most people regarded Carlos as the senior driver at Subaru and the more likely challenger for the Championship in 1994. He had the track record, the experience and the stature. His credentials were highly impressive and it was up to me to demonstrate mine. I had the speed and the commitment, now I had to put it together consistently and show I was also a contender to be taken seriously.

I can't say I achieved that in the first half of the '94 season. It got to the stage where you would have thought DNF were my initials. I was introduced to the Monte Carlo Rally that year, didn't enjoy it and have never liked it since. The changing conditions on the stages, from dry to wet to snow to ice, make it a nightmare for drivers. And then the spectators like to create a few extra hazards by shovelling snow on to the road. I appreciate the tradition and importance of the Monte and the atmosphere can be fantastic for the fans. I know because I've sampled it as a spectator. It's great. But as a driver I hate it.

Those fans caught me out in '94 on what was supposed to be a clear stretch of tarmac. Instead I hit the man-made snow patch and went off. After that it was just a matter of clawing back the places and trying to get a respectable finish. I managed to move up to 10th by the end but I wasn't sorry to get out of there.

Snow itself is not a problem. Sweden is a true winter rally and it has always been one of my favourites. You know what you are in for and if you make a mistake it's your own fault, not the spectators'. I could have done with the Swedish to make my mark after the Monte but at that time the Championship was organised on a rotation system and the event did not carry points in the title race.

Portugal looked more promising for me. I was running just behind Carlos when a fire put the car out of commission and me out of the rally. We were second in Corsica, going well on the asphalt, until we had two punctures. We repaired one of them but had to drive with the other and because of that we lost the car on a downhill section, breaking the suspension. We reached the end of the stage but the damage had jammed a bolt and we couldn't get it out, so our rally was over.

That was a setback but I was happy enough with our form and we confirmed that on the Acropolis Rally. I was leading from Carlos and felt confident. We went into a re-group, where the scrutineers could check the cars to make sure they were legal. We jumped back into our car to drive to the next service and as we went down the road the bonnet flew up and smashed the windscreen. The scrutineers had left the bonnet unfastened and we could hardly see a thing.

We managed to get to the service, which in those days was at the side of the road. The service time was taken off the road time we were allowed before the next stage. The guys removed the broken windscreen and prepared the surround for a new one, a job which took about ten minutes. DR told us to drive to the next stage and said he would speak to the clerk of the course to explain the situation to him. He felt sure the guys would be permitted to put the screen in there, because it was a safety issue.

We were still waiting for word back from the clerk of the course and as we were at the front of the queue to start there was a lot of agitated debate. Eventually the stage commander said it was fine to go ahead, so the guys put the windscreen in. All the other drivers had lined up by then and knew what was happening. They understood the situation, accepted what we did was fair and sensible, and had no problem with it. We did the stage and ended the leg neck and neck with Carlos.

The stewards held a meeting that night, discussed the case, and came to the conclusion that I had to be disqualified. I couldn't believe it. Nobody could. They said that we had not been given permission by the clerk of the course. Maybe we had jumped the gun a wee bit but we were given the all-clear by the stage commander. It was, after all, a safety issue and nothing to do with gaining a performance advantage.

Had we known what his decision would be, we would have driven the stage without a windscreen. We'd done that before. It was a terrible disappointment because that was a rally we could definitely have won. Instead I had just one point to show for my season, while Carlos was well placed to go for the Championship.

Things didn't get any better for me in Argentina. I went into the lead but then had a puncture and slipped down to fifth. I clocked four fastest stage times on the second leg before I hit a concrete culvert, breaking the front suspension. We drove on to try to get out of the stage because I felt sure it could have been repaired. The trouble was, we also damaged the sump. We drove the 12 miles or so on three wheels, lost all our oil and I have to admit, made a mess of the car. We had our fourth DNF in a row.

DR was fuming, not so much about the initial mistake but the fact I'd continued. He said I should have accepted there was too much damage and that my rally was over. But the instinct of a driver is to try to go on and get to the service. If you can get the car to the service you at least have a chance, then it's up to the crew. If they can't do anything about it then fair enough, you've tried your best.

My feeling about that and other 'rollickings' from DR was that to a certain extent he thought he had to be seen to be having a go at me. He was mostly very calm and just blew up now and then. He knew what I was like and that I would always do my absolute best. As a rally man and having navigated for Ari Vatanen he knew what it was like, he'd been in these situations himself. To be fair to him he probably tolerated more than other people would have done in the circumstances, although he did leave me out of the 1,000 Lakes again. I'd had a bad run and was getting stick from the public and the press.

This was the time when people were having fun calling me 'McCrash'. I can't claim it amused me but I could understand it and it didn't really bother me, I'm pretty thick-skinned. Yes, I crashed the car, but I was also driving very quickly and that was my way of doing it. I believe it's better to start with the basic speed and then learn to contain it. As a young driver you are more likely to get noticed if you're going for wins rather than fourth and fifth places.

Alternatively, there's the way Richard Burns has done it, starting steadily and gradually building up the speed. That's worked for him and my way worked for me. Tommi Makinen and I are often referred to as the two quickest drivers and he's also had plenty of shunts. I've had some pretty spectacular ones, but then when you are running at the front, you're with a top team and you're in the limelight, everything you do is going to be magnified.

Throughout that period I always believed I had

the backing of DR and David Lapworth, the engineering director of Prodrive. They obviously didn't like to see me go off and I knew that after Argentina they were getting seriously pissed off with me. If somebody's going to the absolute extreme of writing a car off in every rally then something has to be done about it. But they could also see the potential and didn't want me to lose the speed. DR said that he and Ari had made similar mistakes and he wanted to help me learn. He didn't want me to waste my talent and I had no intention of doing that.

It was time to start getting it right, though, and no-one had to tell me I needed a result in New Zealand. Considering everything that had happened that season I suppose any result would have been acceptable. I appreciated that I had to compromise a little because we had to finish. They weren't going to tolerate the DNFs any longer. I'd more or less been told that, although it didn't need to be spelled out.

But I liked New Zealand, I'd won there the year before and I knew the car would be good. When Carlos went out with a blown engine Subaru's hopes were pinned on me. I took the lead and effectively saw off the opposition on the Motu Road. I reckon all the other drivers protested about that stage because we had it canned and none of them could get anywhere near us. We won by miles.

Australia was another rally that didn't count towards the World Championship that year but it was a chance to maintain the momentum of New Zealand. I had another tremendous fight with Juha

Kankkunen, who was recognised as a specialist on the Australian event. This time though, we got the better of him. Juha piled on the pressure right to the end but we kept it together and stayed just ahead of him. It was one of those tight fights that makes winning feel even better.

San Remo, the Italian rally, was a new event for me so my priority was to get to the finish and gain some experience of the stages, especially the tarmac roads. I felt comfortable and we were able to run a controlled, consistent rally. Fifth place was more than satisfactory. People had got off my back, the team were happy with my driving and I was in a good frame of mind as we prepared for the RAC.

Yet again there was a lot of hype and conjecture about my prospects. I'd gone well a few times only to be disappointed and Britain was still waiting for a home winner for the first time since Roger Clark's 1976 victory. I was convinced it was coming. We had the car, I had the speed and I had the knowledge of the terrain. I believed that, given the bit of luck that had eluded us in previous years, we could pull it off this time.

Confidence is a big factor in rallying. It is in any sport, I suppose, come to that. You do go into certain rallies with slightly more confidence than you have on others. The RAC is one of them. Competing at home, in front of your own crowd, you definitely get that extra edge. I'm also conscious that a lot of foreign drivers come here beaten before they start. They simply don't have the self-belief that they can defeat me. Richard Burns has had the same kind of confidence on the event in recent years.

In 1994 my relationship with the fans really clicked. You could feel it growing throughout the rally as we took the lead and kept going. People often ask if you can hear the cheers and are aware of the following. Well, you can't actually hear the noise but you can see the excitement on people's faces, which is an amazing sensation. You can sense the atmosphere deep in the forests, and the fact that they have made such an effort to support you gives an incredible lift.

There was a lot of speculation in the build-up to the rally about team orders because Carlos had a chance of winning the Championship and that was clearly what Subaru wanted. Well, we weren't under team orders to help him and it wouldn't have made any difference if we were. Once I got well into the lead I had no intention of giving away my first RAC Rally win. In any case, Carlos was in second place and on course for the title, without any assistance from me when, he said, he had to swerve to avoid logs he claimed had been deliberately placed in his path. The suggestion was that British fans, angry that I might have to give up my win to help my team-mate become world champion, had decided to take matters into their own hands.

But there are so many bits of debris lying around in the road, I really don't know what to make of Carlos' story. Many of the stages are out in forests and it's normal for logs to be piled at the side of the gravel roads. Maybe there was a log there but I'm sure it wasn't put there by anyone. I might have clipped a log that was sticking out and flipped it into the road, which happens quite often. It's the same with rocks. It's amazing what a car's wheels, at speed, can pull out of the road. It's likely that's what happened there.

You might possibly get a deliberate act like that by fans in some of the southern European countries but certainly not by any British fans. I am absolutely convinced on that. There was no sabotage. If somebody got it in their mind they were going to sabotage a stage they wouldn't put a wee log out there – they'd put a huge log out or even a rock. If you really wanted to do it you'd make a proper job of it.

I've never known of any case of deliberate sabotage of that kind. You get fans throwing or even shovelling snow on the road on the Monte Carlo Rally and you can get mischievous kids causing you problems you haven't bargained for which happened to me on the Safari Rally in 1997. It was on a very fast section in a plantation when we were going over crests at 200-plus kph. We came over one of these crests to find a stone wall built across the road. It must have been a foot high and made of boulders. The spotter helicopter was just ahead of us but hadn't noticed it because it was in the dip, in the shadow of the crest. I braked to about 170kph but realised I couldn't stop in time. There was nothing I could do apart from accelerate again to try and lift the front of the car and clear the wall. I hit the rocks and we were launched into the air. I thought we were going to have a major accident but we got it all together and continued.

The helicopter saw what happened and I

radioed them straightaway to go back and check it out. As the helicopter swooped down, half a dozen kids ran from under the hedge. The pilot chased them across the field and away from the stage.

That incident was so close to putting us out of the rally, but we managed to reach the service where the guys had a lot of damage to sort out. Those rocks had burst the radiator, the front panel, the sump, everything. They did a great job and got us back out. We had no trouble with the car after that and won the rally. That's the only time it's happened to me and it was just down to a few kids having a bit of fun. It wasn't too funny for us though when we saw those rocks, or for Prodrive when they saw the damage. It must have cost them about £100,000.

The irony of the 1994 RAC Rally was that Carlos actually lost the Championship when he went into a ditch and spectators – British spectators – rushed to help him try to get his car out. When we heard Carlos was stuck we knew there would definitely be no more questions about team orders, so that wasn't an issue anymore. We were free to go and win the rally and we did so by a distance. This was the one we really wanted and now we'd managed to get it in the bag.

After such a bad start to the 1994 season the Championship was never really a proposition for me but I felt there were sound reasons to believe I could mount a genuine challenge in '95. Carlos was still my team-mate and would obviously be one of the leading contenders again. He had an impressive record of consistency and would want to make up for the disappointment of narrowly missing out in '94.

What I needed this time was a decent start to the year. The second half of '94 had been good and as long as I could sustain that level of performance into the new season I was confident I would be able to have a real go at the title. With only eight rounds in the '95 Championship I couldn't afford to throw away rallies and lose ground. So what happened? I had another bad start.

Monte Carlo was . . . well, Monte Carlo. It was one of those mishaps that make the event so infuriating. I was on dry-weather tyres when we suddenly came upon a patch of ice that took us by surprise. We went off and that was the end of our rally. That was more or less par for the course at Monte Carlo but next up was Sweden, an event I liked and one that usually proved productive. But not in 1995. All the Subaru engines failed. It was one of those freakish instances where a team can be put out just like that.

Two rallies, two DNFs. It had an alarmingly familiar ring to it. Worse still, Carlos had won the Monte Carlo Rally and he would win the third event, Portugal. I was third in that rally, which meant I was at least on the scoreboard but the trouble was that my team-mate had already opened up a gap and things were looking good for him. If I couldn't get some wins soon, I would be needing snookers.

We weren't particularly competitive in Corsica so fifth was about as much as I could have expected. Half the Championship season was completed and we hadn't really got started. The only consolation was that nobody had managed to break away from the pack. Results were being spread around. It was still an open contest and anyone who could find consistency in the second half of the year would be in the reckoning.

We had to fulfil our commitments in the Asia-Pacific Championship before world title business resumed and, after the struggles we had gone through, victory in Indonesia did me no harm at all. I headed for New Zealand, a happy hunting ground, looking to kick-start my World Championship campaign. Carlos couldn't join us on the trip as he'd had an accident away from the rally stages. He fell off a mountain bike, injuring his shoulder, and would have to miss at least one event.

Tommi Makinen had no intention of making life easy for me in New Zealand and had a strong start in his Mitsubishi. But he went off and I sensed the others felt it was my rally to lose. The Motu Road again gave me the advantage and I made sure I wasn't going to waste it. That win put me in the Championship frame and I was determined to stay there.

Carlos was back for Australia, although he reckoned he wasn't fully fit. As it happened he didn't have to test his fitness over the full rally. A branch went through his radiator and he retired. I had a Mitsubishi to contend with again but this time it was Sweden's Kenneth Eriksson. I spun on the last leg and, rather than risk throwing away what I'd got, I settled for second place. Kenneth wasn't in the Championship equation, so it had been another good rally for me.

With two events remaining, four of us were in with a chance of the Championship. Carlos was still there, despite his setbacks. His early form had given him points in the bank and they could still pay dividends. The other two contenders were Didier Auriol and Juha Kankkunen, of Toyota. No-one had been outstanding or dominant throughout, so the prize was up for grabs. Whoever produced a big finish would claim it.

The final rally would be the RAC and having won it the year before I was confident I could do so again. However, the penultimate event was the Catalunya Rally where of course Carlos would have home advantage. Juha emerged as the threat to Carlos and me in Spain but when he crashed it became a Subaru head-to-head. I was ready to fight my team-mate for the rally and the Championship. With one day to go the pair of us were well clear. Third was the Italian driver, Piero Liatti, in another Subaru.

The night before that final leg DR told us we were to maintain the one, two, three order. He explained there was a manufacturers' Championship as well as a drivers' Championship at stake and that he didn't want us to take unnecessary risks. It was never discussed and I certainly didn't agree to it. DR simply put his foot down, told me that was the way it had to be and that I would have to slow down.

I couldn't accept that because it was unfair. Here were two drivers with equal opportunity of becoming world champion and I felt we were both entitled to go for it. There was nothing in it.

Carlos was only seven seconds ahead of me overnight and I believed I could win. That would put me on top by five points going into the RAC. I could see the Championship looming and I wanted it – or at least a sporting chance of going for it. That didn't seem too much to ask. I tried to discuss the situation with Carlos but he was obviously going to benefit from team orders, so he didn't want to know.

At the start of that last day my mind was made up. I was going to try and win the rally. When Carlos realised I was going for it he responded and it was a real fight between us. He knew I hadn't agreed with the team orders and that I wasn't going to slow down. If he couldn't beat me he was going to have to trust the team to swap our positions at the end. It was a difficult situation for all of us but I was satisfied my action was justified.

I went into the lead and had every intention of staying there till the finish. The team were on the spot and felt they had to do something about it. Two of DR's right-hand men, Nigel Riddle and John Spiller, came out to the last stage to try and stop me before the finish board so that I would lose enough time for Carlos to win. Nigel was jumping up and down in the middle of the road. He must have feared for his life because there was no way I was going to stop and he had to leap out of the way as I flashed past him at about 100 mph. It's asking a lot when you're leading the rally and the finish is in sight. It was certainly asking too much of me that day. I was determined to go through with it and Derek was right behind me.

He told me to go for it and I did.

I knew they could still give the win to Carlos by holding us up and making us check in late, but that was the messy option and they had wanted to avoid that. DR was waiting for me and I don't think I've ever seen him as angry. And I hadn't even dented the car! He was in no mood to be humoured. He had the manufacturers' result he wanted but he wasn't happy because I had defied his team orders and everybody knew about it.

He asked me what I was going to do about it and I said: 'I'm going to check in and win the rally.'

That was obviously not the answer he was looking for and he said: 'I'd think very carefully about that decision if I was you.'

He also spoke to my dad and the threat was pretty clear. I think if I had checked in on time and won the rally my contract might not have been there for the following year – or even the following rally. It was a call I couldn't afford to get wrong. I had to think very hard about the consequences of confirming the win and blatantly defying DR again. Eventually my father persuaded me to go along with DR's instructions. We checked in a minute late and gave the win to Carlos.

It was gut-wrenching, one of the hardest decisions I've had to make in rallying. I would almost rather have just left the car where it was, walked away and not bothered checking in at all. That thought certainly went through my mind. The emotions were churning inside me. A lot of people seem to think I don't have emotions but that's because I'm generally not one to express them. I tend to keep things to myself but I can assure you I do have feelings and that day was the worst. You are there to do your best and this flew in the face of everything I, and the sport, were about.

Later, when I had calmed down and had a chance to consider all the possible repercussions, I realised that would have been a ludicrous thing to do. Yet in the heat and emotion of the moment that's the sort of thing that went through my head: 'Why the hell should I even check in?'

So Carlos and I went to the last rally of the Championship locked together and I was even more eager to put the record straight. I was going to win the rally and the Championship. I had been the moral winner, I believed, in Catalunya, which was Carlos' home event and one I had never done before. Now I was on home ground for the decider and I had absolutely no doubt I could win it fair and square. DR told me that if our roles were reversed in the RAC Rally he would again issue team orders, this time in my favour. But knowing Carlos and the way he felt after Catalunya and the fact that the Championship was at stake, I thought there was no way he would ever have gone along with that. I had to win it and that was fine by me.

Carlos and I fell out over the Catalunya episode. He claimed I'd not been honest with him but I never agreed with those orders and he knew that. He apparently admitted he would have done the same thing in my position yet he wouldn't talk to me because of what I did. The atmosphere in the team was terrible in the build-up to the RAC, so I decided somebody had to do something about it. I spoke to him and apologised for what I did. Okay, it may have been a bit tongue in cheek but there was no point in continuing with an atmosphere like that in the team. It wasn't fair on all the other guys involved. He accepted my apology and basically things were fine after that. There was no evidence of an undercurrent during the rally itself.

Overall, my relationship with Carlos has been all right ever since then. We became team-mates again at Ford and had another dispute over team orders there, but again we got over it and generally work very well together. I have no problem with his wish to do the best for himself. We're all in it to win.

But he did say at the time that I was immature in what I did. Yet he was the experienced member of the team and surely he should have taken it upon himself to speak to me first. I'd like to think that if I found myself in a similar situation with a younger team-mate I would go to him and discuss it with him, as well as with the team management, and try to make sure there were no misunderstandings. Somebody's not going to be happy at the end of it all, but at least everybody knows where they stand. Above all I think Carlos knew he was going to be beaten on the RAC Rally and that was nagging away at him.

The Championship was down to the two of us because Toyota had been thrown out, so Auriol and Kankkunen were no longer involved. Auriol was disqualified at Catalunya after his car was found to have an adjustable turbocharger restrictor, which was illegal. Toyota were banned for 12 months and their drivers found themselves on the sidelines. One of their drivers for 1996 was due to be Carlos, which probably didn't help his mood.

Toyota were definitely getting an advantage out of something. I've asked Nicky Grist, who was then Kankkunen's co-driver and is now mine, about it a few times and he reckons he didn't know anything about it. I've wound him up, saying: 'Come on, you must have known.' He says the only thing he noticed was that at a couple of tests before Catalunya they seemed to get an improvement in engine performance. He was told by his engineers it was in the electronics and they'd managed to find an edge. I thought: 'Mm, maybe. . .' but I'm pretty sure that if I sat in my car and had a 50 bhp increase I would know there was something dodgy. It just doesn't happen.

Anyway, with Toyota removed it was an all-Subaru affair so there was an enormous amount of attention on the team. My win the previous year on the RAC Rally and the prospect of a first British world champion created tremendous interest in the media and the support I received out on the rally, especially in the forests, was phenomenal. There were Union Jacks and St Andrew's crosses at every corner. People were jumping up and down. Carlos must have been psychologically destroyed in every stage. He could see my times, he could see my backing, but he couldn't see any Spanish flags.

We made a good start and went into the lead but a puncture cost us a couple of minutes and we had to play catch-up. Carlos had engine trouble, although he didn't lose too much time and he was still well ahead of us. We were on a big attack and closing on him when the front driveshaft broke in Kielder. We had to stop at the end of the stage and try to get the driveshaft out because it was flailing around inside the wheel arches and would have damaged the car as we drove to the service. So we grabbed hold of a log and used that to lever the wheel area free and make sure we could get the car to service.

I had usually gone well in Wales and that year was no different. We hauled Carlos in and took away his lead in the darkness and horrible RAC Rally weather. It was fine as far as we were concerned, though, and I felt quite relaxed about it all on that last morning. We had a long road section out and plenty of time to wait before service, so we stopped and had a coffee and a game of pool in a pub somewhere in mid-Wales. Everybody knows who you are in Wales so it was good fun and helped us pass the time.

We were certain that as long as we had no problems and made no silly mistakes the rally was ours. It can get to the point where you just know it's yours. Our times had been good throughout the event. If it hadn't been for the one or two problems we'd had we would have been in the lead by three minutes, so there was no question in our minds about the outcome. From the start we had the determination and that bit of anger as a result of what happened in Catalunya. If I needed any extra motivation, that provided it.

There's no such thing as a formality in rallying

so we still had to concentrate and finish the job. We had time in hand when we reached the last stage but you can't risk backing off too much. You have to keep going to within a couple of per cent of the way you have been driving, because it's when you try to change your pace and break your rhythm, that something can go wrong. You always have it in the back of your mind that anything can happen until you get to the finish, but we were both calm and felt we had it pretty much under control. I wasn't nervous and Derek never showed much emotion. That last stage did seem a lot longer than it actually was, but in the end it was all plain sailing.

It was a real family celebration right there at the end of the stage in the forest. Alister finished fourth in an Escort and mum, dad and Stuart were all there. We'd gone rallying for years together, mum bringing the sandwiches and the flask, and it was just so right that we were together to enjoy this result. It was a moment that made the effort, the uncertainties, the ups and downs, the knocks, the strains and the anxieties all worthwhile.

Subaru had dominated the rally, again taking the first three places. Carlos was second and Richard Burns third, securing the manufacturers' Championship. But it was the drivers' Championship that was important to me. I was Britain's first world champion and, at the age of 27, the youngest ever world champion. It is such a major hurdle for a driver to clear in his career, some guys compete all their lives and never do it or even get close to doing it.

There was inevitably some suggestion that there

might have been a different outcome if Carlos had not had his accident but you can't go through life worrying about ifs, buts and maybes. Everybody makes mistakes or has mishaps along the way. I had to concede Catalunya and still won the Championship which I believed I deserved.

Certainly it was a slightly strange season, with no-one able to string together consistent results. It wasn't easy for me after such a bad start, but then that two-year period had been a bit of a rollercoaster. There was no gradual build-up to that Championship success. Things went well for a while, then went downhill, then picked up again and all of a sudden it was there, the possibility of becoming world champion.

If anything the circumstances of that Championship made me even more determined to win it again and perhaps it would be even more satisfying to do so a second time. Back in '95 I saw no reason why I couldn't win it again the following year (but it is getting harder). We marked the achievement with due respect in Chester, where the rally was based, partying through to the following morning. I was on top of the world in every sense.

In fact there were quite a few good parties and celebrations in the subsequent days and weeks. I was given a civic reception in Lanark and handed the keys of the town, which was a great honour. The pride and pleasure were as much for my mum and dad as for myself. Lanark is our town and always will be.

At the Prodrive Christmas party I was amazed to be presented with the RAC-winning Impreza. DR knew I wanted one of my rally cars and sort of promised me one if I won the Championship. That car was obviously the one to have but I was led to believe it was being prepared for Sweden the following year. I also thought that Subaru would want their first World Championship-winning car, or maybe DR would keep it for a while. At best, I thought, I might get it at the end of the following year. So I had no idea they were going to give it to me at the party but there it was, all ready to go.

It's got pride of place back in Lanark now, along with another two of my old rally cars. I take it for a wee run once a year, just up the road and back. I need to get a silencer for it though. It's a bit too noisy!

I had another pleasant surprise at the 1995 BBC Sports Personality of the Year awards, taking second place. Earlier, at the hotel, I had bumped into Carl Fogarty – who eventually won four World Superbikes Championships – and we sat together during the programme. I thought there was no way we were going to beat Frank Bruno but he was third. Then they called me down as the runner-up and I said to Foggy: 'Do you want to go down there having beaten Frank Bruno?'

The winner was announced as Jonathan Edwards, the triple jumper who went on to win a gold medal at the 2000 Olympic Games in Sydney. Foggy and I gave each other that 'Who's he?' look. As I've said, I've never really been into other sports. Not that it was a disappointment to come second, I didn't think I would get anywhere near that. It just showed how far I'd come and how far rallying had come. That award made me realise what an impact my Championship had made on the general public, not just on die-hard rally fans.

Soon the parties were over and our attention was back to the hard graft of preparing for another season. I wasn't getting carried away with my own publicity and there was no danger of my going into 1996 assuming I could beat everybody. But I did think it was there to be done again and that was my target.

Partners

There was much optimism in the Subaru camp as we began the 1996 season, although I felt I had been handicapped even before a wheel was turned. The stupid system of rotation meant that this nine-round Championship would not be including two of my favourite events, New Zealand and the RAC. I wasn't alone in believing the schedule had to be standardised. There was to be an RAC Rally that year but the hundreds of thousands of British fans would be denied the drama and excitement of a title finale.

They would also be denied another chance of seeing their world champion. Our participation was the subject of much discussion throughout the year but ultimately DR pulled the plug because he couldn't get the go-ahead to run the car planned for the following season.

The confusion and wrangling somehow summed up the state of the Championship organisation at that time and should have left no-one in doubt that it needed to be sorted for the good of the sport.

Despite the loss of New Zealand and the RAC, we were confident we would still be capable of putting up a strong defence of our title. Toyota's expulsion certainly removed some of the most serious opposition, though my old team-mate did manage to get a drive. Carlos popped up with Ford. I certainly didn't think it was stitched on for us to win it again and I was right to be wary, because this was the year when Tommi Makinen and Mitsubishi really came to the fore. Tommi had gained the necessary experience to add to his undoubted talent and the new Lancer was clearly a very competitive machine.

Tommi got off to the perfect start, winning in Sweden. The conditions on what is regarded as the one true winter rally were strange that year. There was less snow than usual and our tyre studs caught us out at one point when we went off the road. The minute or so we lost put us out of contention and we had to settle for fourth place, but at least we had banked some points. The Safari Rally is a very different event but the result was the same. Tommi managed to keep his car in one piece to win, while we had rear suspension trouble and again finished fourth.

The Rally of Indonesia featured on the World Championship list for the first time in '96 and, having beaten Tommi in the Asia-Pacific event in Thailand, I was hopeful of chalking up a win on the title board. Tommi and I were miles ahead of the rest and when he retired it looked as if I was on my way to a much-needed maximum score. But you learn the hard way to take nothing for granted in this game. We had a problem with our

Me and Alister, aged four and one-and-a-half,
on our Dad's motocross bike.

Early driving lessons in the back yard!

Celebrating my 21st birthday with friends: (left-right) Willie Kirkhope, Tam Tweedie, Me, Robert Reid, Stevie Barr.

Fast-forward to my new family: Reilly, Alison and Hollie.

From checking out the wild life in Kenya 1992...

...to checking out my road in Australia in 1993!

Celebrating an important victory – the RAC Rally 1994.

Taking a moment out in my Championship winning year, Catalunya Rally 1995.

The day I swapped seats with Martin Brundle at Silverstone, 1996.

Derek Ringer and I being initiated as Maasai warriors in Africa!

1,000 Lakes, 1996, after we slid down a ditch on a fast section of the road.

Argentina in 1996, a difficult year after the Championship success of 1995.

intercom, which effectively left me to negotiate the next stage of the rally, without notes. I rolled the car and our near-certain win went out of the window.

The team were dismayed but try to imagine how I felt! The only way to vent my frustration was to go out and win the next one, the Acropolis Rally. I got off to a flying start, was out in front and resolved to stay there. Tommi launched his attack towards the end, as I expected he would, but I knew what I had to do and made sure I had just enough in hand. It was a big win, one we badly needed. Now we had to keep it going.

I should have sensed that wasn't going to happen in Argentina even before the rally began. I smashed a car in practice and then managed to throw myself off a motocross bike, messing about in a wheelie competition at a service area on the recce. That gave me a pain in the back and some of the organisation – or rather the lack of it – on the event was a pain in the backside.

The crowds were enormous, both out on the stages and at the service areas. On the first stage we hit a photographer who was at the side of the road and although he wasn't seriously hurt we both could have done without the fright. Worse was to come when we struck a huge rock, breaking the rear crossmember. We reached the service still leading but the work the crew had to do on the car inevitably cost us time penalties.

It was a mad enough rush to get us out of service but it was absolute bedlam in that place.

One guy ran in front of the car and ended up on the bonnet, but he was perfectly all right so we checked out of service at the time control, three minutes late. There were all sorts of reports about what happened, some suggesting we ploughed down at least three people. That was nonsense, I hit only the one guy. The problem was that it was such a crush there, with so many people milling around, they were pushing each other and falling over. The crowd-control was almost non-existent, it was a complete mess.

We were still on course for what would have been a useful second place when we rolled it. I caught the inside of the corner, which was very sandy, the car dug in and turned over. The car itself wasn't too badly damaged but we landed quite heavily on the bonnet and that broke the camshaft. It was the end of the rally but it wasn't the end of the Argentine affair by any means.

We got hauled up before the FIA, motor sport's Paris-based governing body, over the incident at the service area. There were lots of stories about the FIA supposedly gunning for me and rumours that I could receive a lengthy suspension. It was also reckoned by many that the timing of the hearing, which coincided with the recce for the 1,000 Lakes, was deliberate. I don't know if that was the case but certainly the FIA gave off that air of 'We're the bosses and you will appear in front of us'.

I didn't believe I deserved a ban but then I didn't think I should have been punished in any way, so I was not at all impressed with a £50,000 fine. They made out I was the guilty party but I didn't agree. In my opinion the blame lay with the organisers and the FIA because they were supposed to control the service areas. There was an inexcusable lack of control by the organisers, who simply hadn't got their act together. It was typical of a lot of rallies at the time. They fail to do their job properly and the driver gets blamed when something goes wrong. It wasn't my fault yet I was the one who had to cough up £50,000. I felt very hard done by and still maintain I shouldn't have paid for what happened that day.

On top of that, of course, we missed part of the practice for the Lakes, the rally where you need experience of the stages more than any other. Without the knowledge of those jumps and bends it is very much a journey into the unknown. The whole thing had a snowballing effect and I suppose it was no big surprise when things didn't work out for us on the rally. I made a mistake on a fast section of road and slid down a ditch. I tried to carry on but the car wasn't having it and packed up on me.

That was another sore point with DR. There were a number of times when he went public about our differences and that was one of them. He suggested the Championship had come too early for me and made other statements like that. It was an up and down relationship with him, one moment he was building me up and praising me, the next he was knocking me down again. But then that reflected the way it was going for me at the time. I was having very high finishes or DNFs, so I could sympathise with his point of view. I take my hat off to him for being as patient as he was. You can take only so much before you have to let it out. Yes, there were occasions when I wished he'd not been so open with his opinions and taken me into the motorhome for a private chat. But to be fair to him he did do that in Finland and overall I have no real complaints about him or our relationship.

Much has been made of the downside in '96 but I was by no means at my lowest ebb that year. It wasn't as bad as '94, when we really did have to pull something out of the bag and get finishes. I still had some decent results in '96 but of course because you are the Champion everybody expects you to be up there all the time, so when you don't finish rallies and get good results, the fingers start pointing at you. I suppose I was paying the price of fame. I was high profile and the expectations around me had also risen.

For all the stick I got, Prodrive actually liked to cultivate my 'rebel' image. I wasn't a rebel at all, I just like to be myself and do my own thing. But when I lived up to the image they shouldn't have complained, should they? I wasn't into extreme sports so much as outdoor fast sports although I suppose I was more of an action man than most of the other top guys around at the time. A lot of them were getting a bit past it!

Outdoor sports don't come much faster than Formula One and that summer – on my 28th birthday to be precise – I was given the chance to drive a Jordan Peugeot Grand Prix car at Silverstone. In an exchange stunt made possible by our sponsors, Martin Brundle, the ITV commentator who at the time drove for Jordan, tried his hand in my Subaru rally car.

It became more of a PR and press event than I

would have preferred. It would have been better if I'd been able to do a proper test to find out just what I could have got from the car. Even so, it was great fun and both Martin and I did pretty well. I got within a couple of seconds of Martin's time in the Jordan, and he got within a couple of seconds of mine in the Subaru.

The respective merits of racing drivers and rally drivers have long been the subject of debate in motor sport circles and I am often asked who I believe to be the better. I don't think you can give a straight answer to the question but what I would say is that I have a great deal of respect for Formula One drivers. I would never try to put them down or underestimate their abilities. But it is impossible to say whether, for instance, Michael Schumacher is better than me or I am better than him.

I do think, though, that a rally driver would make quicker progress in Formula One than vice versa because when you are going round a race circuit, lap after lap, you are bound to learn every line and corner and improve your times. In rallying you have the chance to look at the stages on the recce and make notes with your navigator, but you have no high-speed practice. The first and only time you drive through the stage flat out is on the rally itself. That's the big difference between the disciplines. Maybe after a year or two the drivers would end up at the same level, but the Grand Prix driver would need that time to make up the ground. It would take him longer to reach the top level in rallying.

Safety standards and measures in Formula One

have advanced significantly over the years. You'll see many high-speed accidents in Formula One and thankfully serious injuries are very rare. There aren't so many high-speed accidents in rallying because you can't afford to go off some of our stages. If you do you are in the lap of the gods. You won't find many barriers, gravel traps or run-off areas up in the mountains. When you have precautions like those it can make a huge psychological difference to your driving and your willingness to push yourself to the limit.

Much as I enjoyed that drive in the Jordan it didn't give me any ideas about switching to Formula One. It was probably the best driving experience I've ever had or am ever likely to have. But there would be so much to learn before I could become half-decent in Grand Prix racing, and I couldn't settle for that. I haven't mastered rally driving yet and maybe I never will. No driver can claim to be the master of what he does and that he will never be beaten, but at least I have reached the top of my sport and that, for me, is the satisfaction. If I went into Formula One I would be starting at a very low level, facing a long, steep climb and an awful lot of hard work.

Another pleasant trip that year took me down to Buckingham Palace to receive my MBE from the Queen. It was further evidence that people were taking notice of our sport and what I had achieved. Rallying demands so much of a driver's time and attention that he tends to be locked inside his own little world. I was very focused on what I had to do and tended not to concern myself too much with what was going on in the outside world. It was very satisfying, though, to know the outside world was taking an interest in what we were doing.

It was in my best interests to finish the 1996 World Championship with a flourish. Fourth place in Australia was nothing exceptional, especially as Tommi won again to confirm that I'd lost my title to him, but after a couple of DNFs it was a welcome result. The show returned to Europe for the last two rallies, San Remo and Catalunya, and if I couldn't win the Championship I could at least finish second.

The Italian event came down to a battle between Carlos and me. I was under pressure from DR not to make a mistake because the manufacturers' title was still at stake, but as we prepared for the last stage Carlos was within striking distance, so I pushed a bit more and won by quite a comfortable margin in the end.

It was an exciting finish again in Spain, but this time it was a domestic affair, with my team-mate, Piero Liatti, providing the main opposition. I could appreciate Subaru were anxious that we didn't throw it away because again they had their own objectives and I patiently tracked Piero for most of the rally. But it was also important for me to beat Carlos to that runner's-up spot in the drivers' Championship. The team agreed with me so there were no orders to hold station. I went past Liatti to win by seven seconds.

Derek and I had wound up the season in style, with two excellent wins, which was quite remarkable since it had already been decided that we would be parting company after Catalunya. I'd been put under a lot of pressure from DR to make the split because he felt Derek wasn't putting enough into it and controlling me in the way he would have liked. Not that I was the type of person to be controlled, but DR was making Derek half-responsible for our results because we are in the car together. My view is that it's the driver who generally has to be the strong character to be where he is. Certainly the co-driver should be a strong character also and exert some influence, but if he tried to have too much influence that would have a negative effect on me. Derek never really tried to rein me in and I always stood up for him because he was a very good navigator. He was brilliant at his job and never missed a note. It suited me that he kept quiet and let me get on with it. I respected him for that.

But towards the end he was getting a bit of hassle at home because we were away so much. He had a family and things were becoming difficult. It was a problem which built up over the years. It seemed he was losing a wee bit of interest and becoming a little negative about things. I think DR could see that and he suspected it was having an effect on his driver.

Derek and I never had a fall-out but it got to the stage where I wasn't enjoying it so much. You're together for most of the day so you have to enjoy it. Instead it was becoming boring and hard work. Derek did say it was maybe getting too much and that he wasn't sure he wanted to continue for a lot longer. It wasn't a sacking, our partnership had just run its course. DR wanted me to have a new co-driver and I didn't support Derek as I would have done previously because he wasn't as committed as he had been. I saw DR's point. You need someone who is 100 per cent committed and enthusiastic. Derek wasn't happy about it but sometimes hard decisions have to be made. We talked it over but I had made up my mind.

When Derek and I parted it was a bit sour, which was a shame because we had been together for a long time. We had achieved a lot together, reaching the pinnacle of the World Championship. I've spoken to him now and again since then and it's been fine between us. I'm sure, though, that he feels hard done by, but then partnerships can end with someone unhappy. Since our split he's navigated in the British Championship and done other bits and pieces, which is probably more to his liking anyway. He wanted more time at home, for himself and his family, and now he has that.

DR told me he wanted me to take Nicky Grist as my co-driver. Nicky had partnered Juha Kankkunen to World Championship success and had also navigated for Malcolm Wilson. When Toyota were thrown out of the Championship Nicky was left without a full programme so DR asked him if he wanted one. I was aware of him and what he'd done but didn't really know him. He struck me as being pretty sharp. He was always there, an in-your-face type of guy with quite a strong character who was prepared to stand up for what he believed. Everybody got on with him and seemed to respect him. DR tied things up and arranged for us to meet in Dublin, where Nicky happened to be at the time. We had a chat, drank loads of Guinness and agreed to give it a go together.

I have to say I haven't regretted the decision to team up with Nicky. When he comes to work he's spot on. He's very professional, very meticulous, but he's also such a bubbly character that he's fun to have around. Work's work and play's play, but there's no reason why you shouldn't enjoy your work. That's the way I've always looked at it and it's good to have someone who has that attitude as well. You need that because you spend so much time together, someone you can have a laugh with and go out for a beer with. We train together and do a lot together outside the car.

Derek and I were completely different people, whereas Nicky and I are more alike. Derek was a quiet guy and kept his opinions to himself. Making general conversation wasn't easy. I'm not really a chatty type of person either and when you've got someone like Nicky Grist with you there are times when you have to turn it off, otherwise he'd never stop! You can be tired out at the end of a day with Nicky next to you.

Nicky is a lot stronger than Derek and when he does start getting on his high horse it ends up in an argument rather than an 'Okay, you're right, I'm wrong' type of reaction. It's good that we have a relationship where we can have an argument and thrash things out. It strengthens the mutual respect and makes you think about the other guy's opinion rather than just going about the job with blinkers on.

Having Nicky on board gave me the lift I needed going into the 1997 season. His enthusiasm rubbed off on me. The atmosphere in the car was really good. There was a buzz and I realised I'd needed that extra kick. Nicky provided it.

If it was time for a major decision about my partner in professional life, I had to come to an even more important verdict about a partnership in my private life. I realised it was time to make things up with my ex-girlfriend and commit myself to marriage. So that autumn I flew out to Canada to convince Alison Hamilton I was ready to settle down. Yes, the same lady Hamilton who had been my co-driver when I won my first rally, back in 1988.

We first met on Lanimer Day when we were 14-year-olds. She was a farmer's daughter from nearby and a friend of a girl I knew. She was still an ugly duckling then and I wasn't really interested, but by 1987 when I bumped into her again, we'd both changed. I was out with one of my best friends John Hamilton, Hammy, who happened to be Alison's cousin. Alison and I started going out together and had some good times.

The trouble was that as the years went by, Alison thought we should be spending more time together, but I wasn't ready for that. I wanted to get on with my career and hang around with the guys. I was happy being single, free to do what I wanted. Marriage was the furthest thing from my mind.

I think we met too young. Alison wanted a serious relationship but I wasn't ready to make that commitment. The lifestyle was too good to give up. There were so many other opportunities, so many things happening and I didn't want to let go of that. She was very frank about her demands so in the end the only answer was to go our separate ways and that's what we did in 1994.

She went to Canada and I missed her. There was always a strong attraction there, so when she came home in November of the following year and called me, we went out for dinner. We had a good night and I would have liked a relationship with her again, as long as it was an open one. Alison still wouldn't go along with that and I can't say I blamed her. Most girls wouldn't have agreed to it. I was just being selfish and only thinking of what suited me. So off she went to Canada again.

I stayed in touch though, ringing her up a few times. Then in November '96, I flew out to Canada and made the commitment she insisted on. I didn't propose to her as such. I was warned not to even turn up in Canada unless my intentions were honourable! So I knew exactly where I stood and agreed to her terms. She came home and we were married before my 29th birthday, on July 14, 1997.

The wedding was at the Popinjay Hotel in Rosebank, which is down the Clyde Valley from Lanark towards Hamilton. It was more nerve-racking than any rally I've been in. I was in full panic mode that day, just trying to get it all right in my mind. It seemed to be going okay right up until the moment when I was actually standing in front of the minister. Then everything went – my mind went blank, my legs went weak, my whole body went numb. I'd never known anything like it. But somehow I managed to blunder my way through the ceremony and Alison and I became man and wife. Our honeymoon was interrupted

by a rally. We went to Fiji for four days on our
way to New Zealand, then went to Canada on our
way home.

*　　*　　*

Alison McRae

When we first met Colin was too busy playing
with the other boys to be bothered with me. Girls
weren't allowed to play with boys then, but it was
a very different matter when he grew older. He
stalked me for months. Hammy told me he used
to come to every Young Farmers do I was at,
wanting to see me and ask me out. I didn't fancy
him at all. I wasn't interested. I had other fish to
fry.

Then, when I was driving to Ayr for a night out,
a car came up behind me, flashing and beeping. It
was Robbie Head, Hammy and Colin. They ran
me off the road and into a lay-by. Colin jumped
out and got into my car. I told him to get out but
he wouldn't be put off and he kept chasing me.
After a couple of months I gave in and let him
have my phone number. I thought I'd be really
horrible to him and then he wouldn't pester me
any more. On our first date he took me to
Knockhill. I didn't know what it was about but he
said his dad was driving a car or something and
would I like to go with him. He was very nice. He
even held an umbrella up for me in the rain, so I
couldn't really be horrible to him.

On another of our early dates somebody came up

and asked him if he was Colin McRae, because obviously the family was well known in the area. He said he wasn't. He never liked any fuss or attention. I noticed, though, that his face started twitching as he told that wee white lie. So now I always know when he tells lies!

I worked for my father on the farm, driving tractors and doing a multitude of jobs. We kept sheep and sold turf. The sheep kept the grass trimmed and well fertilised. But then I fell out with my dad and went to work for a socket screw manufacturer. After that I went to college and took up hairdressing. Colin would be off at weekends rallying so I wanted a job which I could do in my own hours, while he was away.

There was never any question of my getting involved in the rallying on a regular basis. I had no urge to do it. That rally I did with him, when he had his first win, was just a one-off. When the speedo showed 240 I thought it was mph! I didn't actually call the notes, just the junctions. But I did have the route and road maps. Even though we won we didn't kid ourselves we were a winning combination. We would never have stayed together if I'd been his co-driver.

After a number of years it did become more difficult to stay together but I don't agree with Colin that it was because we were too young when we met. The problem was that he became well known very quickly and was away more and more. Every week I used to think he was going to ask me to marry him and I put pressure on him to do so, but he didn't want to be tied down. Looking back now I can appreciate what it must have been like for him. What young guy wouldn't be tempted by all those gorgeous promotions girls? I was terribly upset when we split.

But looking back I'm sure that was the best thing that could have happened to us at the time. And it was a very definite split. I punched him and knocked him out! It was in Corsica in 1994. He was having a bit of a hard time in his career and I wasn't happy about the way things were between us, so I decided enough was enough.

Then he won the RAC Rally later that year. I was sitting at home, on the windowsill, watching on television, and it was breaking my heart. When we were younger I used to hang about the garage with him, helping a wee bit on the car, and he would say, 'One day I'm going to win the RAC Rally'. It was a goal we had shared and then when he won it I wasn't there. By then I was a mobile hairdresser and everyone knew I used to go out with Colin. People would say, 'Did you see Colin on the telly? Did you read about him in the paper?' I was hearing this six or seven times a day and in the end I couldn't take any more. I decided I had to get away from Lanark and the further the better.

I could have gone to Australia or New Zealand but I thought, why should I go there when two months down the line he's going to show up for a rally. So I went to Canada because there are no rallies there and I wasn't going to see a rally car or bump into a rally driver or hear or read anything about rallying. I went for eight months on an exchange programme.

I came back home to my mum and dad, in November, 1995, when Colin had just won the

World Championship, and of course he was everywhere. He was on television, all over the papers, and you can image what it was like in Lanark. I thought to myself, 'Am I ever going to get away from him?'

But since I was at home I thought I ought to try to get hold of him and congratulate him on winning the World Championship. So I phoned his home and he was in. We had a chat and arranged to go out for dinner. We had a great night and I thought maybe we would get back together. He talked about going to Spain and hinted he'd like me to go with him, but I couldn't because I had appointments.

I couldn't face being around and not seeing him so I made up my mind to go back to Canada for good. I got the immigration papers, a house, a wee hairdressing salon, a car and a dog. I was determined to settle down and make a new life for myself in a place called Black Diamond, near Calgary.

Then he started phoning me. At the beginning it was once a month, then twice a month, and then it was sometimes twice a week. I thought: 'He's missing me.' He said he wanted to come over and stay with me but I told him: 'No, you're not. This is my nice clean country and you're not coming over here.'

And then, in November, '96, I got another call from him and he asked me what was for dinner on Tuesday night. Again I told him I didn't want him to come over, but this time he wouldn't be put off. I made it clear to him that there had to be a firm commitment, and he agreed. I came home at Christmas and we were married the following summer. It's been bliss, well, most of the time. Mind you, he's not around most of the time!

Changing Times

The 1997 season seemed like a fresh start in so many ways. I was happy and relieved I'd sorted out my private life, which put me in a good frame of mind to concentrate on my job and the World Championship. Teaming up with Nicky was another timely boost and I quickly felt comfortable with him on board. It was as if I had a new lease of life.

There were even welcome changes to the Championship. The rotation system, which just about everyone agreed was ridiculous, was scrapped so that we had a proper, 14-rally calendar that the public could understand and follow. Bringing the scoring system into line with Formula One was another positive move for competitors and spectators alike. It meant 10 points for a win, six for second place, four for third, three for fourth, two for fifth and one for sixth. People would find that easy to follow, especially so because they were used to it in Grand Prix racing. These were steps towards standardising the World Rally Championship, a process that has continued since then and has been necessary to establish the sport as a major global and television spectacle.

The mood in the Subaru camp was upbeat. We were confident we had a competitive car, a car capable of bringing back the Championship. Nicky and I hit it off straight away and I had no doubt we would be in good shape to win rallies. The one factor you can never be certain about though is reliability, so we were just hoping for a decent share of luck in that department. If we could finish rallies the points would mount up.

It was no great surprise to me that fortune didn't smile on us in the Monte Carlo Rally. Some things don't change! We had an accident there but we also proved to ourselves – and our opponents – that we had the pace to compete for the Championship. Fourth place in Sweden put us on the scoreboard and effectively got us on the move.

Next was the Safari Rally, a car- and heart-breaking event that supposedly doesn't suit my style of driving. I don't suppose there would have been gasps of amazement if I had trashed my Impreza and joined the distinguished names on the list of retirements. Makinen, Sainz and Eriksson all went out on this gruelling and unforgiving terrain.

To a certain extent you are at the mercy of fate and we had a scare or two along the way. Broken wheels are typical of the problems you face in Kenya. So are battered shock absorbers. We had both handicaps to cope with and did some running alterations to the suspension to get the best out of the car. We also had an electrical gremlin to see off but by then we were in control of the rally. We had pulled ahead of Richard Burns and then maintained a steady pace without taking too many risks.

That might not be my favourite way of winning but it was satisfying to show I had the discipline to do what was required in the circumstances. I think it proved I was learning from experience and some of the disappointments I'd suffered in the past. I had no intention of throwing this one away. There are many ways of winning and for me the priority is always the result. It is all about winning. That win confirmed we were very much in business for the Championship that year.

The pattern of setbacks and surges had been established and we had to kick-start our campaign again after a blank in Portugal, where the consequences of an engine vibration put the car out of commission. Fourth place on the Catalunya Rally served to generate the momentum we needed as we headed for the island of Corsica.

We lost time through the wrong tyre choice in the wet but at least we avoided the kind of incident Tommi encountered. He hit a cow and disappeared about 120 feet down a mountain. He was fortunate to escape serious injury but it was another reminder that security and safety standards have to be monitored and upgraded constantly. The trouble is that it is difficult enough controlling people on some events, let alone animals.

My main concern on that rally was to catch

Carlos and the two-wheel-drive Peugeots, driven by Francois Delecour and Gilles Panizzi. I managed to squeeze past Delecour and moved up alongside Panizzi, but with only one stage and 20 miles left I was still seven seconds down on Sainz. It was raining again, which didn't bother me greatly but I don't think Carlos fancied it too much. I wasn't over confident, you can never afford that. I just felt the opportunity was there and I was going for it. The conditions were tricky but I judged it pretty well and we beat Carlos by eight seconds.

That is the best way to win, taking it in a shoot-out on the very last stage. The excitement built up and built up towards the end and then it was a sprint to the line. To pull it off like that was great for everyone in the team. It was a real thriller. Over the years I've earned a reputation for being able to do that on the last stage and I think it has worked to my psychological advantage. When I draw up close to the leader, as I did to Carlos on that rally, you sense he is already half beaten in his mind. I'm conscious I can exploit the situation – especially against Carlos! They tell me we had a great party that night. We've had a few of those over the years and it's difficult to remember one from another in precise detail – the definition of a great party.

We had already had engine trouble that year but it wasn't the only bone of contention and source of frustration for me. David Lapworth, our engineering director, and I had a difference of opinion, which developed into a battle, over the Impreza's wide-track suspension. In theory the idea was sound. From an engineering point of view it made sense because it improved the traction, but in practice I didn't like it. As a driver you are sometimes prepared to sacrifice a bit of performance to make the car easier to drive because if you have confidence in it you are able to drive it quicker. I was second to Tommi in Argentina, and although the Mitsubishi was obviously a good car I thought I would have been able to compete with him much more aggressively with narrow-track suspension.

Driver–engineer arguments are not uncommon in rallying and it's good to have dialogue about the development of the car. Any engineer will tell you he needs the input of the driver and I have always tried to contribute as much as possible. I like to think I am respected by engineers and mechanics as a very good test driver and that my opinions carry some weight. But I really had to push my case with David on that issue and it became quite a running battle through the year. He dug in his heels yet eventually I won the fight and we finally got the car on narrow-track for New Zealand.

Of course, cars and components are changing all the time. The evolution of transmissions, tyres and so on has created significantly different cars today. The cars have reverted to a wider track but that doesn't mean to say David and like-minded engineers were right all along. At the time I was more comfortable and quicker on narrow-track than on wide-track so I was right to insist on it. The team had to work hard to change the car but I was convinced it was worth the effort.

Before New Zealand I had to retire on the Acropolis Rally when I broke the steering, but recovered with the victory we and the sponsors required in China, even if it wasn't a World Championship event. The Far East had been something of a happy hunting ground for Subaru and Prodrive and now we had the boost of this win as we made for New Zealand, another productive rally for me in previous years. What was more, I had the narrow-track car I had been fighting for and I was also a married man. Alison and I had our four-day honeymoon in Fiji on the way to the rally.

We got away to just the start we were looking for in New Zealand, building up a good early lead. Better still, as far as our Championship prospects were concerned, Tommi went off. I had little doubt we were on course for a maximum score until another engine glitch stopped us in our tracks. A win was less likely in Finland but points would have been welcome. Instead engine trouble sabotaged our plans once more.

We felt our luck might change in Indonesia. We were wrong, but not for the want of trying. Monsoons and mudflats are to be expected here and again we made an excellent start, stretching away from Tommi. The stages were unbelievably slippery and we slid off, hitting a tree and bursting the radiator. We were able to get out of the stage onto the road section but then had to find a way of botching up the holed radiator.

Normally we carry a can of resin in the tool kit to plug holes but for some reason we didn't have any with us that day. We parked at the roadside, wondering what to do, when Dom Buckley, a former rally driver who was running a motorsport business, asked us if we'd got any chewing gum. We said we had and he told us to chew the whole packet and stuff it in the hole. We also scraped up mud from the side of the road and stuffed that in as well. We needed to top up the water so we used a helmet to scoop water from the river. You can't imagine what that helmet smelt like! The engine didn't survive much longer but you have to try all the tricks in the book and some that aren't, it's all part of the adventure and challenge of rallying.

If we were to have any chance of the Championship we had to produce a big finish and hope Tommi and Carlos would slip up. There were 30 points up for grabs, in San Remo, Australia and Britain. I believed I could do it if I had it in my own hands to do so, going into my home rally, but to put myself in that position I really had to be thinking in terms of winning the next two.

The San Remo Rally turned into a tense event right to the end but I felt throughout that we had the pace to get the job done. We had to make up time after a tyre came off the rim and it was my team-mate, Piero Liatti, who led at the end of the first day. We launched our attack on the second day, setting a number of fastest times, and took over at the front early on the third day. Although Tommi and Carlos weren't that far behind, it was clear Subaru had the upper hand. Piero and I traded the lead before team orders were issued. I slowed down on the last stage but he didn't slow enough and had to clock in late to give me the win.

Piero was obviously very disappointed, especially in his home country, and having been on the rough side of team orders, I could appreciate his feelings. But the important difference in this case was that only one of us had a chance of winning the Championship, and it wasn't Piero. We both understood the circumstances and accepted the team's instructions. It was a great result for Subaru and for me.

I went to Australia with my title hopes still alive and my confidence high. I was third in the Championship behind Tommi and Carlos and it was still a long shot, but I had nothing to lose and everything to gain. A win for Tommi in Australia would have wrapped it up for him so our plan was straightforward, we just had to go for it.

We were comfortably on schedule for the victory we needed going into the final day and with Tommi in fifth place our prospects for the Championship were looking good. The downside of leading the rally is that you are first on the road, which means you clean it and make it easier for the drivers following you. Having got ourselves into that position we didn't want to throw it away so it was probably no surprise we lost a little of our rhythm and had a spin. Tommi was understandably keen to finish it before we got to Britain and worked his way through the order, leaving it to the last stage. I knew Tommi would be charging so I had to step it up. He made a mistake, I did enough and the ten points were mine. We'd wrapped up the manufacturers' title for Subaru and taken the drivers' Championship to the wire, even if the odds were still stacked heavily in Tommi's favour. Carlos was out of it and I was still 10 points behind. I had to win at home and rely on Tommi tripping up or finishing outside the top six. That would leave us level on points but give me the Championship on a greater number of wins, five to his four.

Again my target was simple, it was all or nothing so I had to win. On the face of it Tommi's task was even simpler. He needed only one point. But he had to decide how hard he could afford to push – or rather how much he could afford to back off. That could make it far more difficult. The pressure was on him. He could only lose the Championship.

I needed my two team-mates, Liatti and Eriksson, and perhaps the two Ford drivers, Sainz and Kankkunen, to beat Tommi, but Kenneth's engine went and Piero rolled it so that made life easier for Tommi. I did all I could, winning my third home event in succession – we skipped the non-Championship rally in '96 – ahead of Juha and Carlos. But Tommi, who to be fair had been struggling with flu, managed to make sure of sixth place and the single point he required. He'd successfully defended his title, I'd missed out on my second by one point.

Considering the engine problems we'd had that season it was a satisfying effort. We'd won five World Championship rallies and made a contest of it when Tommi must have thought it was going to be a formality. For Nicky it was a great first season as my co-driver and we both felt that as a partnership we could only become stronger.

We would be driving for Subaru again in 1998, despite a lot of stories that had been linking us with Ford. They did make inquiries about my availability and whether I would be interested in joining them, but I was still under contract with Subaru and at that stage I was content to continue with the team. We had finished '97 strongly and naturally hoped we'd be able to carry that form into the new season. The car was likely to be good, Nicky and I were working well together and we reckoned that as long as we had reasonable luck in terms of reliability, then we would be in with a good chance.

By now you will be familiar with my feelings about the Monte Carlo Rally and I figured any points from there would have been a bonus. The first half of the event was typically frustrating, our progress not helped by the problems we were having with our tyres. They worked much better on the dry tarmac and we surprised ourselves by coming through to take third place, behind Carlos, who was back at Toyota, and Juha, in an Escort. Tommi had gone off, so all in all it was a good start to the campaign for us.

With Sweden coming up next we were in good spirits. Again though, our tyres weren't as effective as some of the opposition's so another third place would have been a good result. We were up to fourth and closing on Carlos when we realised we had electrical trouble. The voltage started to drop as we approached the longest stage of the rally, which meant it was not so much a matter of if but when we were brought to a halt. It happened about six kilometres into the stage. As if to rub salt into the wound, the relief car ran out of fuel! Tommi bounced back with a win so it was clear we would have to see off the usual suspects if we were going to mount a serious challenge for the Championship.

The tyre debate raged right up to the Safari Rally, an event notorious for shredding rubber. Pirelli concentrated on trying to give us a tyre that wouldn't puncture rather than opt for anti-deflation mousse, a compound developed to serve as an automatic emergency repair solution in the event of a puncture and enable you to carry on, though not at maximum speed. They felt such tyres would become unbalanced in the African heat, which in turn would affect the handling of the car.

In the event, tyres were the least of our concerns on that trip. Nicky, Piero, his co-driver, Fabrizia Pons and I had a lucky escape when the helicopter bringing us back from testing north of Nairobi hit a telephone cable. Fortunately, the cable didn't catch the rotor blade. It snapped and we came down without crash-landing.

I should have known then that this wasn't going to be our rally. We were strong and running well, with Tommi in our sights, when suddenly the oil pressure started to drop, the temperature shot up and we knew the engine was about to give up on us. To make matters worse for Subaru, Liatti's car went the same way on the very same stage. For one reason or another, it was a Safari Rally to forget.

Richard Burns claimed his first win on that

event and put his name in the Championship frame. We were stuck on four points and couldn't afford to lose more ground. We had to get back on track in Portugal.

We appeared to be doing just that, taking the lead on the first stage, but we had a bit of an engine problem before the end of the day so that 'here we go again' feeling came over us. To our relief we got through that. The worry for every competitor was the lack of crowd control and it was especially bad on the last stage of that first day, with people wandering onto the road and standing in ridiculous places. The police and marshals didn't have a clue about keeping order. I had a couple of hairy moments and we were all lucky no-one was seriously hurt. Little wonder there were warnings that Portugal could be struck off the World Championship calendar the following year.

We had a puncture on the second day and had to cope with the disadvantage of running first on the road, yet we reached the final stage of the rally still holding the lead. We knew Carlos would pile on the pressure and it seemed an age before the times came through at the end. When they did we were confirmed as winners. We felt we were in business again, as long as we could maintain a reasonable degree of reliability.

But then we had a rude awakening in Catalunya. Not for the first time, we struggled for grip and simply couldn't find the performance to compete with the front-runners. It was all we could do to reach the top 10 before we had to retire. It was obvious the other major teams had made significant steps forward and we had to get our act together – quickly.

The whole team needed a lift and, after successfully appealing against disqualification at the end of the first day in Corsica, we got it. Rain made the going tricky but, despite an early puncture, we were comfortable enough and it was a relief to be competitive again. Then we were told we had been excluded because our tyre tread was below the minimum legal requirement. We pointed out that the excessive wear was as a result of the puncture and, quite rightly, we were reinstated.

We were never really under threat after that and had our second win of the season. Better still, Carlos was forced to retire and, to our amazement, we found ourselves at the top of the Championship table. If we could string together a few results we had to be in with a good chance of the title.

We ought to have extended our lead in Argentina. We were well ahead in the event, outpacing Tommi, until we hit a wall with a rear wheel and damaged the suspension. Nicky and I had to resort to some pretty crude DIY work, using a rock to knock the car back into some sort of running order. Although time penalties put us down to fifth place, we at least salvaged a couple of points when many might have given it up as a completely lost cause. We had lost our lead in the Championship to Carlos but were only two points back in second place.

We more than made up that deficit on the Acropolis Rally. It was a tough, close encounter all the way through. Even when it seemed Didier

Auriol had the victory within his reach we kept up the pressure and it paid off on the penultimate stage. Didier had an engine problem which cost him time and we were right there to take full advantage. We were fastest on the last three stages and had our third win of this topsy-turvy Championship. We were also five points ahead of Carlos.

New Zealand had served me well in the past but this time I had to settle for two points. It would have been nice to celebrate my 30th birthday as leader of the World Rally Championship but I had ample consolation – a two-year contract with Ford.

There had been speculation about my future for months and at one stage I was linked with at least four teams. Seat were very ambitious, as were Peugeot, although they were not in a position to give me a full programme in 1999. In the end it really came down to a choice between Subaru and Ford, and eventually I decided I needed the new challenge.

I think it must have been obvious to most people that I was ready for a change. There had been the frustrations since I'd won my World Championship with Subaru in 1995. We'd had a lot of mechanical problems in those two and a half years and that was certainly a factor that influenced my decision. So, too, was the money Ford were willing to pay me. Three million pounds a year is big money, up there with some of the better-paid Formula One drivers. It gave me the chance to secure my family's future – very much on my mind because our first child was due later that year.

But it wasn't only a financial decision. I think the money would have come, anyway. Ford were launching a new, very exciting project and I relished the prospect of being in there at the start of it. Their rally car from 1999 was to be the Focus, voted Road Car of the Year. It was being built and prepared by Malcolm Wilson's M-Sport operation, which was based in Cumbria. Malcolm was planning a new factory at Dovenby Hall near Cockermouth, and the facility would be second to none.

It was a bold move by Martin Whitaker, Ford's Director of European Motorsport, and like-minded executives to take the World Rally Championship programme out of the company's direct control and entrust it to Malcolm and his specialist team. But I agreed with them that it was a necessary step and it provided further proof of their commitment to the project. This was a serious effort, with all Ford's resources behind it, and they wanted to build it around me.

Ford had first approached me the year before. My contract with Subaru was for '97, with an option for '98. Ford wanted me to join them for '98 but DR wasn't willing to let me go. Martin went on record as saying that if they had been able to sign me for '98 he was sure I could have won the Championship for them with the Escort.

I knew what Malcolm had done and how he had built up his team so that didn't require any hard sell. I was confident the car and the running of the team would be right because Malcolm knew the business. He had been there as a driver and now ran a successful team. The only doubt in my mind concerned the commitment of the Ford Motor Company, because previously it seemed rallying was just a bit of a sideline to them and never their main motor sport activity. That was the part Martin had to sell more than anything. He had to convince me that the Ford Motor Company were 100 per cent behind it. He did that and now Ford are behind it more than they have ever been behind any rally programme.

Martin and Malcolm felt I could drive the Focus project forward and speed up the development process of the all-new car. I had a good reputation as a test driver. I didn't mess around. The time scale for the new car was limited so it was important that we got on with it. They were also very keen to have a British driver and obviously they had to be satisfied the performance would be there. The plan was to sort out the car and make a breakthrough, perhaps winning one or two rallies in the second half of the first year, then be in a position to mount a challenge for the Championship in 2000. All in all I was convinced it added up to precisely the challenge I needed at that stage of my career and I went for it.

There was no fall-out at Subaru and we parted on good terms. That was something I wanted to make sure of because motor sport is a small world and you don't want to burn your bridges. DR was disappointed to lose me and so was David Lapworth. They pushed very hard to keep me but I had been there a long time – eight years – and there was a danger we were all getting too set in our ways. I felt I had to have something fresh and DR acknowledged this was probably the right time for all concerned to make the split. DR and I had had our run-ins but that happens in any job. As I've said all along, he tolerated a lot, it built up inside him and when it did come out it was with a bang. That's why everybody knew about it and yet, for all the public explosions over the years, he did say he would have me back. That was good to hear as I didn't want my relationship with Subaru to tail off or turn sour. It had been a great relationship and I wanted to remember it for the good times and the great achievements we'd had together, the wins and above all the World Championship. They left the door open for me and I appreciated that.

My father had been acting as my manager and he took on the responsibility of negotiating my contract with Ford. In a position like that you need someone you can trust and who better than your own dad? It was really a natural progression from the early days. He was always there, pointing me in the right direction. He's not a pushy person and it was always up to me to get off my backside and go out and do it. Then, if he saw I was committed to it he would help me. He had always negotiated his own deals and he ran his own business, so he had the experience and the expertise. He knows rallying, rallying knows him, and having him there to take care of my affairs has given me the peace of mind to concentrate on the driving. He also looks after Alister's interests.

I was comfortable letting dad do the negotiating with Ford as it's a lot easier for someone else to put a price on you and haggle for it, rather than doing it yourself, although I don't think there was much haggling in this case. If you go in with a figure in mind it's very difficult for the employers to knock you down too much. Subaru had wanted to keep me and were prepared to more or less match the money, so in the end it wasn't really the issue.

As well as his management role, dad also does my gravel notes. He drives the gravel car through the stages an hour or two ahead of us, at a slower pace, checking the lines, noting if there are any rocks on the road, whether there are any slippery stretches of tarmac or any changes in conditions from the recce, and marks them on the notes. Again, you look to someone you can trust to do that and dad is just the man. He's probably got more experience than any other guy doing the job. It's a very important one, the more so on certain rallies.

Dad nearly packed it in at the end of the 2000 season. It is a big responsibility and means getting up at an unearthly hour. But he decided, at the age of 57, to give it one more year and then look at it again. I didn't persuade him. I left it to him and was very happy with his decision.

Gravel car crews have been look-outs for police speed checks on the road sections. I've never been done for speeding on an event but one or two rally drivers have. The way rallies are organised now there's plenty of time for the road sections so it's not really a problem. It was far more fun in the good old days, when you raced from the end of the stage to the service and then to the next stage.

Nicky supported my move to Ford. He was

equally excited by the new venture and was satisfied with his new deal. We officially signed for Ford on my birthday, August 5, at the company's technical development centre in Dunton, Essex. After all the rumours and soul-searching it was good to put that piece of business to bed and switch our minds back to the work we still had to do for Subaru. We were determined to finish our relationship in style. There were four rounds of the Championship remaining and we were only three points behind Carlos.

Finland hadn't been one of my more productive rallies in previous years and my luck wasn't about to change. We were quickest on two of the first three stages only to suffer a rear suspension failure after clipping a tree stump. Tommi's win on home ground lifted him to joint second with me and we were set for a three-way battle for the crown.

Tommi gave himself a great chance of making it a Championship hat-trick by winning in San Remo, where we did well to finish third after a terrible start. The handling of the car wasn't right on the first day and a puncture didn't help matters but we were able to get the hammer down on the second day and at least we managed to nudge Carlos into fourth place.

If I was to have a realistic opportunity of pulling off the Championship in the last round, the Network Q Rally of Great Britain, I had to go for another Australian win. That seemed almost impossible as we stumbled from one problem to another on the first two days, but somehow we hung on and, in an all-or-nothing effort, we stormed into the lead with just two stages left. We'd knocked the stuffing out of the rest but then, on one of the most demoralising days of my career, we had a turbo failure and were relegated to fourth. Tommi admitted we should have won yet nothing could console us. Our Championship bid was over and there were a few tears shed in the camp that afternoon.

Tommi won from Carlos, leaving them to fight for the title on my home rally. Carlos was angry that Tommi had escaped a time penalty after a jump start on the Langley Park super special stage, but he knew that a win in Britain would make him Champion. I envied him that chance. I felt so down after what happened in Australia that my immediate reaction was to say I didn't even know if I could face my home event. But you get over the setbacks – you have to – and I resolved to give the British fans a show in my last drive for Subaru.

The hype leading up to the Network Q was incredible. With a Finn and a Spaniard going for the Championship, the British media seemed intent on building up the rivalry between me and Richard Burns, who was to replace me at Subaru the following season. I'd had a fantastic following for a number of years and there was a great deal of interest in the fact that another Brit was coming through. Everybody was eager to see us go head to head. It was, and is, great for British rallying to have two drivers among the top guys in the sport and I enjoy it because we have our own wee competition. There's always the debate as to who is the best British driver and I quite like all that. Of course, I've no doubt who it is!

But certainly Richard is now a very good driver, up there with the very best, and he was becoming pretty quick by the 1998 Rally of Great Britain. That gave me a little more edge for the event. I wanted to leave Subaru and Prodrive on a high and the way we started made me feel confident we would. We managed to avoid the oil that tripped up Tommi on a Mickey Mouse stage and put him out of the rally, and took the lead on the first day.

Richard went on the attack on the second day, in Wales, but we responded and it was building up to the battle of the Brits everybody had been talking about. The fans loved it and so did we. But then, suddenly, the fight was over and Richard was left in the clear to take his first home win. Our engine went sick on a road section and our stomachs sank. The crew pounced on the car at service and discovered a piston had gone. So was our rally and so was my time with Subaru. We were all distraught. It was the end of a very bad run of reliability problems. We could have ended the year with two wins and the Championship. Instead, we were left with nothing and an awful empty feeling. At that moment I knew I was right to be moving on – it was time to start a new chapter in my career.

Bad as I felt, I still had sympathy for Carlos at the end. All he had to do was finish in the top four to win his third Championship and he was little more than 300 metres from the line when the engine of his Toyota expired. I can imagine what he must have been feeling. It hits some people more severely than others and I'm sure it hit

Carlos pretty hard because he'd been trying for a long time to win the Championship again. It can be so cruel.

Coming after three days' hard work and concentration makes it even worse. A Formula One Grand Prix only lasts around an hour and a half, so when you've been toiling for three days and even nights, it's very hard to take it if something goes wrong right at the end. No wonder he and his co-driver Luis Moya were so devastated they did a Basil Fawlty on the car. Tommi had given up on his title and was packing his bags to leave when he heard about Carlos. Tommi was Champion for the third year on the trot.

I have never hidden my admiration for Tommi and he deserves the success he's had, but I did feel it was unhealthy for the World Rally Championship that one man should have been able to dominate the title for so long. We had to show the public that it was an open, unpredictable contest. The onus, though, was on the rest of us to do something about it. I, for one, was anxious to get to work with my new team and new car and try to do something about it.

There was another new responsibility I had to start getting used to that winter – fatherhood. Hollie Jane was born at the William Smellie Memorial Hospital, near Lanark, on 17 December, 1998. We liked the name Hollie and it was a coincidence that she arrived a few days before Christmas. Jane is Alison's middle name. No parent needs me to tell them what an experience the birth of your child is. I had wanted changes in my life. Now it would be changed for ever.

Focus of Attention

There is no such thing as a close season in rallying because no sooner have we finished one World Championship schedule than we are testing in preparation for the next, which starts barely a couple of months later. The period between the '98 and '99 seasons was even more hectic and important than usual.

Ford had already been working flat out to produce the Focus and well into the autumn there had been a great deal of speculation as to whether it would be ready in time for the opening round of the '99 Championship, the Monte Carlo Rally. But Martin Whitaker, Malcolm Wilson and his team insisted all along that they would not have to wheel out the trusty old Escort again, and sure enough we made it to the south of France with the Focus.

By the time I officially joined the team the car had already been given its first test run, appropriately enough by Malcolm. He had a long association with Ford and I can image how he felt when he took out his new baby for the first time. I had my first chance to try the car just a few days after I signed off at Subaru. I drove about 50 miles at Millbrook, Bedfordshire, where the car was built. At that time Malcolm did not have his facilities in Cumbria ready to undertake such a massive job within the time-scale.

It obviously wasn't a full test, more of a systems check really, but I was happy with what I'd seen and had no doubt the car had potential. There was a good feeling within the team, as well. Everybody was so enthusiastic. There was a real tingle of excitement. I sensed straight away that I was getting the new lift I needed. Everything about this was a fresh experience, I had a new team and car, they had a new driver and car. There was also a lot of attention from the media and the public. This was a massive venture for all concerned.

I wasn't the only new driver. Juha Kankkunen had been expected to stay with Ford and partner me, which would have given us a strong and experienced line-up. But apparently he wasn't too happy when he heard of the deal I'd signed with Ford and I could certainly appreciate that and sympathise with him. If it happened to me I would rather forget it than drive for a lot less money than a younger driver was being paid. It is especially understandable when you've got a record like Juha has. I didn't speak to Juha about it, that was between him and Ford, but the upshot was that he decided to leave the team.

Although there would have been a positive side to having a guy like Juha as team-mate, I think it might also have created one or two problems having two top-line drivers at that time. When so much is new you need a definite No. 1 driver who calls the shots, decides on the car specifications and so on. If there are two of you trying to do that it can make things difficult and hard work for the engineers. We had a lot of ground to cover in very little time so we could not afford to pull in different directions. We had to get on with it which meant a lot more work for me but I was pretty used to it by then. I had enough experience to cope with the demands.

Juha's departure left the team looking around for my team-mate and I discussed the situation with Malcolm and Martin before it was decided to opt for a squad system rather than name one specific partner. Thomas Radstrom, the experienced Swede, was to do the gravel rallies and Simon Jean-Joseph, from Martinique, would take the asphalt events. Petter Solberg, a promising young Norwegian, was to have a few rallies to further his education and help develop the car.

Another newcomer to the camp was Martini, who joined us as major sponsor. They had a terrific reputation and pedigree in the sport, notably through their success with Lancia, and it was a coup to have that distinctive red, white and blue livery on the Ford Focus, as well as their financial backing.

We went to Norway to get stuck into some serious testing the week after my run at Millbrook and the workload for the team was unbelievable right up to Monte Carlo. With the benefit of hindsight you might say that we would have been better off with Juha alongside me in that first year, but I'm not sure. The biggest problem was that we simply didn't have the time to do all the work and testing that was required.

We had a 14-rally programme and at that stage the team was still quite small so we didn't have the luxury of a separate test team and test driver. Since then the whole operation has been upgraded and we have to continue expanding to compete at the highest level. Look at the way Citroën have approached it. They settled for only four rallies in 2001 but had already been running the car for more than a year. It was no surprise that they were able to lead an event straight away. Everybody in the Ford team was under severe pressure that winter of '98-'99.

We had another problem that I wasn't aware of until just before the Monte Carlo Rally. Ford had produced a water pump that was larger than the standard version and they had repositioned it in the engine bay to make the cooling more efficient. The team felt they had the freedom to do that and had been negotiating with the FIA for confirmation of that right. They were under the impression they had a verbal agreement to that effect.

Then, on the night before the event started, I was told of the extent of the problem. The following morning our car failed scrutineering and at midday, less than two hours before my scheduled start time, we were formally excluded for having an illegal water pump. We were, however, allowed to compete under appeal and were confident our case was sound. At the time I wasn't particularly aggrieved that the team hadn't told me what was going on because there was nothing I could have done about it anyway and they were convinced they were doing nothing wrong. In fact I'm sure the FIA and Ford were in the process of sorting it out.

The trouble was that when everyone else got wind of what was happening the pressure was on us and the FIA. Engineers from other teams were pointing fingers, so the FIA had to be seen to be doing something about it. I know Martin was particularly angry that Toyota were among those doing the pointing. They had been banned for a year over their illegal turbocharger and it did seem like a case of the pot calling the kettle black. Martin and Malcolm were adamant that Ford had not sought to cheat.

We had to put the politics and controversy out of our minds and concentrate on the job, which we feared was going to be difficult enough. Here I was with a new team, driving a brand new car – and on the Monte Carlo Rally, at that. So what happened? On the fourth stage we set the fastest time. It was amazing. We were also fastest on the final stage of that day and finished the leg sixth overall. It was a tremendous boost for the whole team, especially after all the flak we'd been taking.

We completed the second leg with another fastest stage and were fourth. On the last day Nicky and I had a problem with the rear driveshafts and had to force them back in before recording another fastest stage time. We were up to third and we held our place to the end. We hadn't dreamt of making the podium in our first rally with the car and I don't think anyone in the team could really take it in. It was quite an emotional occasion.

I must admit my emotions were running high when our appeal was thrown out and our result scrubbed. It was a shock and felt like a kick in the teeth after we'd done so well. I had been led to believe the business of the water pump would be sorted out, but instead the FIA said they had to apply the letter of the law. The affair led to my first run-in with Martin. It didn't take long!

In the heat of the moment, when you've just been disqualified from a result like that, you are likely to say things you might later regret. A journalist asked me for my reaction and I gave the wrong answer as far as Ford were concerned. I said I was disappointed in Ford and M-Sport and blamed the engineers for making a mistake. I felt the team had been incompetent. Ford had designed and built the car and there are definite rules and regulations you have to abide by. I merely expressed my feelings.

Not surprisingly, Martin rang me as soon as the story appeared in print. I told him I didn't know who was telling the truth about the matter and who wasn't. He explained that the FIA had not been straight with Ford, so it wasn't entirely Ford's fault. I could appreciate that. He also made it clear he didn't need his No. 1 driver having a go at the team: I'd made my point but I had to be a bit more diplomatic in future. Well, you learn from experience, don't you?

I'm not sure it was such a bad thing for me to

let off like that. It showed them I cared and that I took the job very seriously. I can be hard on the team because I am very straight. When you want to win and somebody makes a mistake that prevents you from winning, you are going to be hard on them. I call a spade a spade, that's the way I've always been. You can't be diplomatic when it comes to things like that. I'm not really a PR person anyway. I say what I think and I believe people respect you more for that.

What got to me was the fact that nobody had been up front with me about it all. It was as if it had been swept under the carpet. To a certain extent that is a general problem in rallying, the driver tends to be kept in the dark but he's the first guy who is going to have to comment when things go wrong. The team should make sure the driver knows the whole story when it becomes clear the stuff is going to hit the fan, but instead, they seem to prefer to keep it to themselves and let the driver get on with the driving. There is a lesson to be learned there. A team should make sure they have proper lines of communication from top level to the driver, then if something such as the water pump business crops up again, they can mark the driver's cards. It seems a pretty obvious precaution to me.

Perhaps I should stress here that I haven't made a habit of having run-ins with Martin. In fact, that is the only real one I've had. He has also said he wanted the emotional and human element that I brought to the team. The Ford TV commercial I did with my dad reflected that policy. The advert featured us when I was a kid and then later, when

I joined Ford. I don't know where they found the youngster who played me as a kid but the likeness was amazing. They did a brilliant job on the advert and the feedback from it was tremendous.

A couple of computer games I've been involved with have also been very popular although I didn't know what to expect from it when we first discussed the idea. I'd seen a few rally and racing games on computers that were pretty rubbish, so I insisted that if I was going to put my name to anything we had to get it right. I think we have and, again, the response has been really good.

I sensed more recognition after the advert and computer games came out, and especially so following the release of the commercial. The reaction I got was incredible. I noticed the difference when I walked down the street or into a restaurant. Suddenly, instead of the odd person recognising me, lots of people were. It just goes to show the power of television.

It's fair to say I tend to bottle up my emotions and then just explode. A bit like Dave Richards was with me. I believe I am generally a fairly tolerant, patient and fair person and as long as people are doing their best you can accept it if something goes wrong. In a rally environment people are working under pressure, against the clock, often in very difficult conditions and circumstances, so you have to be understanding and pull together. It is very much a team effort.

Sometimes I can be less patient with fans who want to approach me at the wrong time. Drivers still have a job to do at a service area but some people don't seem to appreciate that. You might have a bit of a panic on and the last thing you need is a fan who thinks he's the only person who's asked you for an autograph that day when he's probably the 1000th. Don't get me wrong, I'm proud and privileged that I've had such a loyal and enthusiastic following over the years and there's nothing like that support to give you a lift. It's important to make time for fans whenever possible because without them there wouldn't be professional sport. But on an event it's very difficult, as I'm sure other drivers will agree. We are there to work and perform to the best of our ability, which is ultimately what the fans want to see. We try to give them commitment and entertainment on the stages.

We often have signing sessions before an event and I try to give the fans what they want then. I've also got a website. The queues we get for autographs in Britain are staggering and I must say I feel sorry for some people who wait for hours and then leave disappointed because we've run out of time. The only way to make everyone happy, would be to make signing autographs a full-time job – but you wouldn't have time for the driving!

Ours was hardly a happy camp after our disqualification from the '99 Monte Carlo Rally. The team were faced with a frantic schedule to redesign and build the engine bay with a standard pump before the Swedish Rally. There was even talk at management level that we might just roll the car over the ramp – to avoid paying a fine for not competing – and then retire. It really was that desperate a scramble to get the cars finished and sent over to Sweden in time.

It is to the team's credit that we not only made it to the ramp but well beyond. Unfortunately our engine gave in with a head gasket problem on the second morning, but at least my team-mate Thomas kept going to finish third. This time the result stood, which was what the team needed after all the hassle and pressures of the previous weeks. The car was beginning to confirm the potential we thought it had and I reckoned it was time Nicky and I had something to show for our efforts, as well.

Next was the Safari, a rally we shouldn't really have been thinking of winning because we'd done no testing on rough terrain. But that year we were still allowed to use the rally car to practice, which was a definite bonus. We were also confident that the car was basically very strong. Although we'd had the odd problem with steering racks and things like that, the main chassis had been sound. On the recce we had silly wee niggles, which could have cost us time on the rally, but the car never broke. It was as strong as a tank. It was all very reassuring and even before the start of the rally we were reasonably confident.

On the first day we hit a rock the size of a sofa. It bent the suspension quite badly but we managed to get out of the stage. I've absolutely no doubt that if it had been the Subaru or the Escort we would have been out of the rally. It was one of those situations where you're waiting for the accident to happen and the damage to be done. Instead the Focus just bounced and kept going.

Nicky couldn't believe it, either. He said: 'Is it okay?'

I said: 'Yeah, it seems to be all right.'

It wasn't 100 per cent but we were still going. Some of the other guys weren't so lucky and a few of them did drop out. It was very rough but the Focus never gave us a problem. We built up a huge lead and then just made sure we didn't do anything stupid. We had our first win in the car, in only our third outing. It was a fantastic achievement for the team and yet I can't say it was a big surprise because the signs were so good on the recce. We genuinely sensed it could happen.

Mind you, we still celebrated the win in style. After the prize presentation at the HQ hotel we all ended up in the pool – with our clothes on. We had to get a taxi back to our hotel on the other side of Nairobi and the driver wasn't too keen when he pulled up and saw us standing there, dripping wet. Eventually, when he realised who we were, he threw open the doors and we piled in – all 13 of us, plus the trophies. He wouldn't even let us pay!

If that win wasn't such a shock to the system then the next one most certainly was. Our cars were still overweight and Portugal is a much faster rally than the Safari. I thought we were in for a reality check on this one. But we attacked from the start and it paid off. The stages aren't technical tests so you can push 100 per cent. We set the pace on the first day and left the rest to try and catch up. The downside was that we had to run first on the road for the following two days, so we lost time from that point onwards, but we'd pulled out enough of a lead on the first day to be safe. We did just as much as we had to and no more. Again, apart from one or two minor incidents, the car ran well and we made it a second successive victory.

I had to believe there was a possibility we could actually win the Championship. The plan had been to perhaps pick up a win or two towards the end of '99 and go for the Championship in 2000. But with two wins from our first four rallies in the Focus, we couldn't ignore the prospect of a bid. We were in second place, just two points behind Tommi Makinen. That said, I wasn't over confident. We'd had our wee problems and got away with them but we wouldn't always be so lucky. The team – the engineers and the top people – were all realistic about our chances.

Even so, and again with that marvellous benefit of hindsight, the worst thing that could have happened to us was winning those two rallies so early on. The team knew we still had an uphill task and yet, perhaps subconsciously, we did relax a little. It wasn't obvious complacency and it certainly wasn't arrogance. It was, I suppose, just a natural human reaction to such an incredible start. It could have happened to any team.

We went to Catalunya with a lighter car, which was essential to make an impact on tarmac. After making a reasonable start we were up to sixth halfway through the first day when we had a problem with the turbo anti-lag system, which slowed us down. We lost nearly six minutes over two stages so our rally was effectively over. We decided to stay on for another day and use it as a test, which was a useful exercise, and our times were competitive. That was what kept us going when we weren't getting the results. Had we been messing around, struggling to get into the top six and then breaking down it would have been really soul-destroying.

That unscheduled test sent us to the Mediterranean island of Corsica confident of a good result from another tarmac event. The two-wheel drive Citroëns put victory out of reach for the regular front-runners but I was third going into the last stage, where bonus points were on offer as part of the TV package. I missed a gear, half spun on a corner and missed out on a podium place. Fourth still kept me in the Championship frame, six points down on Tommi, but with a long way to go.

Argentina was pay-back time for the Safari Rally. Right at the end of the test we hit a rock in the road and broke the pin that goes through into the upright. No-one could understand it because it wasn't a bad bump. The pin was sent back to base to be checked but there was nothing that could be done before the rally and we started with the same specification. We were fastest on the first orthodox stage but on the second we hit another rock and the same thing happened. The car tipped on its side and although Nicky and I hauled it back onto its wheels, the front suspension was too badly damaged for us to continue. We discovered that we had been supplied with a batch of faulty pins. Needless to say, the specification of the pin was changed for the Acropolis Rally.

We required a high finish in Greece and we looked to be on our way until the gearbox gave up on us. In the circumstances, we were relieved to be able to tell the tale. We were on a charge on the second leg but were just a bit too brave for our own good. There are a few moments in your career that stand out as the lucky ones, and this was definitely such a moment.

We were in sixth gear, turning slightly right, over a jump. I couldn't see the road on the other side of the jump so I had to get the line right. I didn't. We were too quick over the jump and landed on the outside edge of the corner. The car slid down the edge of the road on the sill, smashing it right into my seat. There wasn't a lot down the other side, just a long drop, but amazingly – and to our great relief – the car bounced back onto the road. We had the shakes until the end of the stage.

There was a lot of unsophisticated pulling and banging at the bodywork at the service and we were still hopeful of claiming a high position. Clearly, though, we'd used up our ration of luck for one rally and there was nothing left to get us through the next stage. We lost a gear on the road section and then on the stage the box simply didn't want to know. We were out of the rally.

The optimism of the spring was fast evaporating and the rest of the season slid downhill. We started with a blinder in New Zealand, trading fastest times with Tommi. We got ahead and I felt sure we were going to win, but the engine, which had cut out a couple of times early on, got worse and worse until it eventually stopped. We couldn't work it out. It seemed an electrical fault of some sort. Every time I started the engine and put it in gear to drive off, it stopped and wouldn't go any further.

The helicopter took us out of the stage and the mechanics went back to get the car. It started up and they drove it all the way to Auckland. They also drove it all the next day trying to find out what had happened but the car just went on and on. It wouldn't stop the way it had on the rally but finally it started cutting out again and they traced the problem through the wiring. It was a broken wire.

All retirements can be frustrating and infuriating, especially when you're running well and smell victory. But generally mechanical failure is easier to take than your own mistake. If it's not your fault you don't feel guilty, it's not your one slip that has cost the rally for the entire team. Of course we're all human and no-one's perfect, but as a driver I accept my responsibility and it hurts when you blow it.

The breakdown in New Zealand was just one of those things that can go wrong in a highly sophisticated car. The wiring cost a fortune. It's the best material, aircraft spec material; but you can have the best of everything – parts, designers, technicians and engineers – and even then, there is no guarantee of reliability. You will always ask yourselves if you could have done more and you're always learning from experience. Ultimately, though, you have to take it on the chin – and come out fighting for the next one.

The '99 Championship was no longer a realistic

target for me, especially as Finland was the next one on the schedule. It's still the hardest rally of all because it is so fast and you need to know exactly where you're going on the road. The other point is that a lot of the faster events have gone, so you are at a disadvantage in Finland.

Malcolm Wilson felt my reticence on the stages showed in my driving on the first day. He told me to try and relax and not over-drive, and it was good advice. I was more positive and confident on the second day, setting fastest times and moving up to fourth. We even entertained thoughts of perhaps making the podium. Then, on the penultimate stage, the engine started to go sick. We dropped down to sixth and would still have had the consolation of a point – as long as we made it to the finish. We couldn't afford to push because we had a failing piston but then we didn't need to as we had a big enough advantage over the next car. Well into the stage our car went slower and slower, until we finally stopped in a cloud of steam only 600 metres from the end of the rally. It was another sickener.

We were now 25 points behind Tommi in the title standings but figured we could still pick up a few good results before the season was over. The first World Championship China Rally was a step into the unknown for the other drivers, while we had been there a couple of times previously. And, having won the two non-Championship events, we were favourites in the eyes of most pundits. We were familiar with the stages and conditions, although it wasn't one of the more difficult rallies to learn.

I just hoped lightning wouldn't strike twice. On one of our earlier trips we went to the Great Wall to combine a bit of sight-seeing with some training. My dad, Nicky and I were up on the Wall and Bernie Shrosbree, our fitness coach, was in full action-man attack on one of the towers. He had climbed halfway up when a storm suddenly started raging around us. The thunder and lightning got more and more terrifying, then a huge fork of lightning hit one of the conductors on the wall and it felt as if someone had given me a massive slap at the back of the head. I knew I had been hit by lightning because I'd seen it coming. That was it. I thought: 'Bugger Bernie. Time to get out of here!'

It rained long and hard and some of the stages had to be cancelled. In our pace notes we had a 'don't cut the corner' warning about two kilometres into the first stage, but when we came to it we got stuck in a rut and weren't able to take a wider line. Everyone else had taken the same line and got through okay, but we hit a chunk of concrete and it broke the suspension. I think it was just about the shortest rally I've ever had.

We were parking our broken car at the edge of the road when Thomas came around the corner and did exactly the same thing. Our cars were parked almost bumper to bumper. What was that about lightning striking twice? Subsequently improvements were made to the crossmember area and we never had that problem again.

It was our fifth DNF in a row and at that point we started looking ahead to the following season. There were three rallies left in '99 but any slender chance of the Championship had gone so the priority was to get the car right for the 2000 Monte Carlo Rally. We were effectively testing for the rest of that year.

We encountered more engine problems at San Remo where we were reasonably quick until we had a water leak and a bad misfire. We dropped out of contention but decided to put the mileage on for development purposes. When we rolled down a bank our work was finished for another rally.

Australia, one of my favourite rallies, came to an even more dramatic and abrupt end. We were flat in sixth on a long right-hander, landed heavily over a jump and the steering locked up. Nicky and I were just passengers as we slammed into a tree. The team reckoned we'd gone from 160 kph to zero in 10 metres and 1.3 seconds. Fortunately the car struck the tree at its strongest point and we were relatively unscathed. I got a bump on the head and Nicky had a sore ankle. Had we hit the tree at a slightly different angle it might have been very nasty. It was a frightening one and we were very lucky it wasn't THE BIG ONE.

We had more 'Battle of Britain' headlines as Richard Burns and I headed for Cheltenham and our home rally, but in truth our car was never on the pace and simply didn't pose a threat to the Subaru. We changed the engine spec but it didn't come off. We were fighting a losing battle when we hit a bale by a gate-post just after the start, breaking a window. That wasn't a problem but it was a sign of things to come.

We went off in darkness on the Myherin stage in

Wales and hit an Escort that had crashed on a run earlier in the day. It was a fast, uphill section, and I made a mistake you should never make. My eyes followed the tree line and, especially at night with your lights on, that is asking for trouble. The trees pull you into them and before I could react I was leaving the road. A lot of the drivers said they'd had the same experience but just managed to catch it in time. We didn't. Nicky's side took the impact and both wheels were ripped off but we were able to walk away. The driver of the Escort, a Pole called Janus Kulig, was long gone.

It was a miserable end to what had become a wretched season. After those two early wins, we'd retired from the last eight rallies. Our Championship had gone pear-shaped. There was a lot of talk at the time that maybe Richard, who had again won the British event, was getting the better of me and that I was cracking under the pressure but that was not the case at all. There were mechanical reasons for our disappointing showing and when you have so many problems you perhaps do try even harder.

Behind the scenes I left the team in no doubt about my disappointment, but then they had been stretched trying to cope with the excessive workload. The basic problem was the one we were all aware of from the start – a shortage of time. Doing 14 rallies, the testing and the development work with a brand new car is a tremendous challenge and extremely demanding. All the work on the car, the engine, the transmission, the weight and everything else was ongoing and it was very difficult to get on top of it.

The comforting thought was that we would surely be able to reap the benefit of all the effort and the painful lessons, in the 2000 World Championship.

I was to have a new team-mate for that season. The team abandoned the squad system and appointed another recognised front-line driver, my old side-kick Carlos Sainz. I was consulted on the choice and supported it. I had been shouldering the responsibility for testing and reckoned now was the time to have someone with Carlos' experience on board to take some of the pressure off me. Two heads are better than one and two voices are louder than one. There were occasions when I felt my opinions might have brought a more positive response if two of us had been doing the shouting. Engineers have their ideas, drivers have theirs and they are not always the same.

From a personal point of view I had no problem at all about Carlos joining us. What had happened between us previously was history as far as I was concerned. That had all been smoothed over. I knew from our time together at Subaru that we had similar preferences in setting up a car so we were bound to push in the same direction in terms of development. That, I thought, ought to accelerate our progress and ensure we were competitive.

Carlos was obviously going to be a rival as well as a team-mate but again I had no concerns about that. His ability, experience and knack of getting results had to be respected. But I was fairly confident that I was going to be quicker than him and, despite some of the incidents in '99, I believed I was making fewer mistakes and knew how to hold a winning position. I felt any competition would be a positive factor rather than a cause for worry.

If you want to win the World Championship you have to beat everybody. Tommi had just won it for a fourth time in a row and it was about time somebody took it off him. If it was to be a Ford driver I intended it to be me.

My Greatest Escape

Any driver will tell you he always wants more from his car and I have heard it said of me that I'm never satisfied. It's the nature of the beast, I suppose. I certainly pushed for improvements to the Focus in preparation for the 2000 Championship, but then the entire Ford team were intent on raising our game. Any slight step forward can be crucial. Subtle aerodynamic changes were expected to give us a little better performance, although the car was still heavier than we would have liked and engine development was a constant process.

It was difficult to know precisely where we stood in relation to the other teams but I reckoned we were up there in the top three. Even when you are not the outright quickest you might have the better package over the season. I felt that with a fair wind we had a good chance of cracking it this time.

Points from Monte Carlo would have been the perfect send-off and we were ready to bank four of them for third place, behind Tommi and Carlos, as we took to the last stage. We were on an uphill section when the engine just popped and that was it. Gutted again! And people still ask me why I don't like that rally! I was reasonably happy with the performance of the car but that didn't seem much of a consolation at the time.

Sweden had been kinder to me over the years and the event didn't let me down when I needed it. We ended our depressing run of nine DNFs with third place after a terrific fight with our former team-mate Thomas Radstrom, driving a Toyota. I'd almost forgotten what it was like to finish a rally, let alone stand up there on the podium.

Off and running? We ought to have known better. Subaru were too strong for everybody else on the Safari Rally so we would have settled for another third place, our position on the second day. But our hopes drowned and we had only ourselves to blame.

We had to negotiate a water crossing a second time and the gravel crew reported that it was quite a bit deeper than it had been on the earlier running of the stage. We heard that spectators had dammed the river to raise the level of the water and with it, the spectacle. Other teams reacted by fitting snorkels to their cars but for some reason we didn't. When we went through again the water flowed over the bonnet and was sucked straight into the filter, choking the engine. It was a crazy, avoidable retirement and to add insult to injury we did the cars behind us a favour by getting stuck and blocking off the deepest part of the crossing.

They had to steer to the right of us, where the water was only half as deep.

We began the first full day in Portugal with a promising surge, only to be slowed down by a power steering failure. Gearbox gremlins gave us our next headache but it was the oil pump that ultimately put paid to the engine and our chances. It was retirement No. 12 from 13 rallies.

That latest setback inevitably fuelled speculation about my future. My contract with Ford was due to expire at the end of the year and I clearly wasn't enjoying the catalogue of DNFs. I was linked with Peugeot and a return to Subaru, where DR hinted he would like to pair me with Richard Burns in a British 'dream team', but I wasn't looking to leave Ford. I was looking for a winning car and I still believed Malcolm and his people could provide it.

Catalunya reinforced that conviction in the best way possible. We won a thriller, edging out Richard and Carlos in a tense finale. We were separated by less than 10 seconds at the start of the last leg but lost 10 seconds even before we entered the day's first stage. We had a problem with the clutch and the crew set about changing it at the service. We were allowed only 10 minutes and our late departure cost us a 10-second penalty. Even then, the mechanics hadn't had time to finish the job so Nicky and I had to do that ourselves.

We were down to third place so we needed to get on with it as I wasn't interested in anything less than victory. We shot clear of Richard by seven seconds but he retaliated and we led by just

1.1 seconds with two stages remaining. Carlos wasn't out of it, either. He was 5.5 seconds down on me and, in front of his own fans, wanted to prove a point. On the penultimate stage I extended my advantage over Richard to 5.9 seconds. Carlos couldn't quite keep up the pace so we were left with our little 'Battle of Britain' in the north-eastern corner of Spain. Richard and I had identical times on the final stage and that was enough to secure my win.

It was a great rally and, for us, a great result. We would have taken any kind of win after the poor run we'd had but achieving it like that made it even better. That's always the best way to win. Richard had come a long way, there was no doubt about that, but I felt I still had the edge on him and that rally confirmed my belief.

It looked as though Richard and I might have a return bout in Argentina, where he had a storming second leg to take the lead. We were only 12 seconds down in third place, despite a heavy landing at a water splash that damaged the sump guard. The following morning the oil pump belt snapped and the engine blew. A small stone had worked its way into the car's internals when we were dragging the broken sump guard on the ground.

The Acropolis Rally made up for that disappointment, even if Carlos wasn't overjoyed for me. It was another rally that turned into controversy over team orders. This time it was Carlos who had to accept defeat. We dominated the rally from the start and were leading by a country mile going into the final day. I was 48 seconds clear of Carlos, while Richard, in third place, was more than two minutes further adrift. There was absolutely no danger to us so Malcolm implemented team orders, which was the sensible decision to make. The stages were hellish rough and having put ourselves in such a strong position there was absolutely no reason to take any risks. He told us to make sure we didn't break the cars and hold station.

Carlos didn't want to know. He argued against the directive and made it clear he wasn't happy about it. The team assured me everything would be sorted out and before we started on that last leg I went to Malcolm and asked him if he was sure Carlos would obey the orders. He told me not to worry and there wouldn't be a problem so I didn't bother speaking to Carlos directly about it, even though Catalunya '95 must have been on his mind. There was no need for me to do anything except drive to instructions.

I did just that and Carlos passed me. But again I was assured I would win the rally so I wasn't tempted to speed up, which of course I could have done. I would have looked the stupid one had I gone quicker and broken the car. By then we were even further ahead because Richard had dropped out. It was management's job to manage. I was aware they were talking to Carlos about the situation throughout the day and before one of the services they went out to meet him on the road section to talk to him, away from prying eyes. I didn't know how the conversation went and I didn't speak to Carlos at the service area, but then that's not unusual. Drivers see one another, but generally we're busy doing something. It's more usual for the co-drivers to communicate, exchanging times and various pieces of information.

We reached the final stage and I figured the team would have to do something pretty soon. The rules had been re-written since '95 and it wasn't possible to drop time on the last road section, as I had done at Catalunya. So Carlos just HAD to slow down on that last stage. But he kept up the pace until the final possible moment, then stopped and dropped more than two minutes. He had obeyed team orders and had made his point. There was actually some debate as to whether he had stopped before the finish, but I was confirmed as the winner and the team were hugely relieved.

Of course it wasn't a satisfactory way to get the job done and it was all the more annoying because the drama was totally unnecessary. The Catalunya incident inevitably came up in the inquest and Carlos had a go at me, saying that a driver of my experience shouldn't have reacted as I did. He claimed this was a different situation because it was much earlier in the season and titles weren't at stake. He also claimed that he was always going to obey orders. But he was far more experienced than I was and what he did was just as bad.

That did our team and rallying no credit. If he had done what he'd been asked to do it would have looked like a clean, straightforward one-two for Ford. People may say it goes against the spirit of sport to order drivers to back off and not go for the win, but I believe that in certain circumstances it is justified and reasonable. It is a team game and when you've done your work over the previous two days, building up a commanding lead, you are entitled to hold on to what you have. You'd be crazy to throw it all away.

He came up to me at the end to shake my hand, but I wouldn't, because that was the treatment he gave me in Spain. I told him: 'That's what happened five years ago in Catalunya and you didn't shake my hand there, so why should I shake your hand now?'

I'm not particularly proud of my response that day, but it was how I felt at the time. There wasn't a big row or anything, just that frosty exchange. There was a bad feeling between us again after that. The team tried to bring us together but for about three rallies we didn't really speak and I certainly didn't feel it was my place to sort it out. All he had to do was apologise, as I did to him after Catalunya, but he wouldn't budge. He's very Latin in that way. He never did apologise properly but we gradually got to the stage where we realised we had to get on with the job and get back to normal, so that's what we did. After that our relationship was fine again. These things happen in rallying as they do in all walks of life and there's no point in allowing ill feeling to fester for ever.

There was plenty of travel time for all of us to reflect on the Acropolis as the next stop was New Zealand. We were up against it because of problems on the first day and although we climbed up to second place and pushed hard on the second and third legs we couldn't catch Marcus Gronholm in his Peugeot. He was into a strong run that announced him as a Championship contender. Richard, who retired with electrical trouble, still topped the standings, but only by four points from Marcus and eight from me.

Marcus and the Peugeot were too fast again in Finland but our second place there seemed almost like a win. The experience of the previous year stood me in good stead and we had revised pace notes to help us. We had a terrific fight with Harri Rovanpera and beat him to those six points by just over three seconds.

We had yet another second place in Cyprus, which replaced the rally in China on the calendar. This time, though, the man ahead of us was Carlos. He led from the start and we decided on the last day there was no point in taking risks, so we settled for another Ford one-two. Marcus' retirement left me only two points behind him, in second place, in the Championship. Richard was third and Carlos fourth as we all anticipated a tight finish to the season.

We felt our chances were very good. Marcus was having an excellent first full Championship and his car was strong and competitive. But his lack of experience on some of the later rallies suggested he might have his work cut out. Richard had lost ground through one or two setbacks but he was capable of bouncing back and you could never write off Carlos. After winning the Championship for the previous four years it looked as though this was one too many for

Tommi and his Mitsubishi.

Marcus might not have been at his most comfortable or effective in Corsica, but Peugeot were still the quickest, with Gilles Panizzi and Francois Delecour dominating the event and ultimately having to drive to team orders! So third or fourth would have been a decent result and I was running fourth, sandwiched between Carlos and Richard, at the end of the first leg.

Corsica is quite a difficult rally, with lots of potential danger in the form of rock faces and low walls. You have to be neat and tidy and it calls for a little more precision and care than most events because there is less margin for error. A driver's natural inclination is to try and take every last inch to improve his time, but in Corsica it's wise to resist that urge. You have to discipline yourself to take a slightly wider line and be happy to come through unscathed. Road conditions are often mixed – wet and dry – and that makes driving more difficult. A few drivers were caught out this time and had spectacular accidents. They included Freddy Loix, Tommi . . . and me. Freddy and Tommi escaped unhurt. I didn't.

Carlos and I had traded times on the opening two stages of that second leg on Saturday, September 30. We'd made one or two changes to the car to try and find a bit more speed but couldn't make any significant difference to the performance. We were already considering our strategy for the rest of the rally and felt that third was the best we could realistically have hoped for.

Feo-Col San Quilco was the next stage. It was a

new stage but we had covered it twice on the recce and there was nothing especially tricky about it. It was just going to be another stage. Nothing significant was reported by the gravel crew and the roads, damp in the morning, had dried completely. It should have been straightforward and it looked that way when we came to around the midway point. I don't think we were driving particularly quickly. We'd tried quite hard on the previous stage and hadn't made an impression so we decided it wasn't worth the taking risks.

I don't remember much of what happened next. What I know is based largely on the accounts of other people. It was a very fast, long lefthander and I didn't pick up the braking point because it was almost one corner and we had a short straight in the notes. I realised there was no way I could brake so I had to try and turn in early to scrub off the speed. But the road was narrow and we hit a small rock, jutting out of the bank. The car turned over, through a hole in the little wall on the outside of the corner. I remember seeing the hole in the wall and it was pretty unlucky that we should have gone off just at that point! When you know the accident is coming all you can do is brace yourself. It all happened very quickly.

The next thing I remember was being stuck in the car, upside down. We had fallen into a ravine. I've heard various estimates of how far we fell, which range from 15 to 30 feet. But I didn't have a clue where I was because the car was so badly smashed around me. I was in and out of consciousness. For some reason I thought I'd ended up with my head down in the pedals, in the footwell. I couldn't work out where I was. I could hear Nicky but I couldn't see him because the roll cage was around my head. My helmet was jammed and I was trapped. He was telling me to hang on and that he was going to find someone to get me out.

I could smell petrol and that worried me. You can stay in a crashed car for as long as you have to, that in itself is not a problem. But the fuel was a big worry. The engine was steaming hot and, because of the position I was in, I didn't know where the smell was coming from or whether the tank was leaking.

Apparently I was in there for 40 minutes. I remember Nicky being there a lot of the time and I can remember rescue people being there. I also remember nothing really happening and that I couldn't move. I was bleeding from the side of the head. I couldn't see the blood, but I could taste it. At first I thought I might choke on my blood, but once I realised I could clear my throat, that wasn't a concern. I had difficulty breathing because my chest was being pushed in and somehow I had been forced halfway into the back of the car.

Those 40 minutes now seem like five minutes. In a situation like that your body shuts down. But at the time it seemed to last for ever. The body really does react in strange ways. I was still drifting in and out of consciousness when the rescue people started cutting. I remember trying to tell the guys to cut here and cut there, but I didn't have a clue what they needed to do. I was aware Nicky was there, talking to me. I think dad arrived close to the end and it was Bernie Shrosbree and Nicky who eventually got me out.

I wasn't aware at the time, but I was told later that the rescue people seemed to have given up. They were sitting and looking, maybe trying to figure out what to do next. They had started cutting but couldn't move anything. I gather they kept going on about the smell of fuel and were worried about using their equipment and being stuck down there when the thing caught fire.

Bernie got right inside the car and managed, through sheer strength, to bend part of the cage that was jamming me in. He pulled it away from my chest and managed to release me. They had to carry me up the slope to the road. I can't remember who carried me, I think it was the rescue guys and Bernie. It's all very vague. I believe they tried to put me on a stretcher down in the ravine but couldn't get it up the hill, so I had to walk as best I could with their help. Once I'd got out of the car the last thing I wanted was to be tied down to a stretcher. I was so happy to be free of it. I think I was then put onto a stretcher, lifted into an ambulance and driven down the road to the helicopter.

Then my memory really goes. They must have given me some painkillers or something as I remember getting into the ambulance, but I don't remember the helicopter at all. The next thing I remember was waking up in hospital in Bastia. I stayed in overnight. They did all the X-rays and checks, cleaned me up and kept me in for observation.

My main concern was that I was all alone. I

wondered where everybody was. I expected to find everybody there but they weren't. It was a strange, lonely feeling. I was on my own, in a hospital bed, in a single room for what seemed like days. I suppose it was no more than half an hour but when you are in that situation you get a weird, uneasy feeling. I knew I had been in a big accident but I wanted to see people and ask them what had happened. Then people started arriving. I can't remember who was there first. I think it might have been my father and mother, but I was still dosed up with drugs so I can't be sure. I was coming and going, in and out of consciousness, all the time.

The following morning I was flown to Edinburgh by air ambulance and taken straight from the airport to see Glen Lello, a leading facial surgeon, at Murrayfield Hospital. My cheekbone had obviously taken a battering but there was so much swelling he wasn't happy with the X-rays. He was also worried about the eye and the eye socket, so I had to go home for a week and wait for the swelling to go down. It was still a bit painful but other parts of my body – chest, shoulders and back – were more painful than my face.

It was more than a week later that I had the operation on my cheekbone and eye socket. He said my cheekbone wasn't just fractured, it was like a packet of cornflakes. They took all the small fragments out and threw them away before re-aligning the cheekbone. I've got a scar on my face where they put a big hook through to re-align it and there's still metal in there. The surgeon said it was up to me whether I left it there but that he would take it out if I wanted him to. If it wasn't giving me any problems, I could leave it.

He knew what I did for a living and asked me when I reckoned I'd be fit to drive again. I told him I intended being at the next rally, San Remo, which was three weekends after Corsica. He shook his head then said: 'Okay, I'll do my bit.' I think a lot of surgeons would have said 'No way' and that would have been the end of the matter.

By the time I'd had the operation, the San Remo Rally was only 10 days away. He said his biggest worry about me going to San Remo was the risk of another knock. Even the bumps on the road could dislodge the cheekbone.

It was because of the Championship that I wanted to do San Remo. If there had been no chance of winning the title then maybe I wouldn't have bothered, but I was determined to be there. I did no testing or training before the rally; in fact I did as little as possible. I had no flashbacks to the accident, but then I couldn't remember a lot of what had happened so none of that came back to me. It still hasn't.

I thought it might jog my memory if I saw the car, so my dad and I went down to Cumbria before San Remo. I just wanted to know what happened. The in-car camera had stopped and there was a problem with Nicky's connection in the intercom so I couldn't hear the notes. It wasn't a case of having to know what went wrong, but I would have preferred to. The accident nearly killed me and I wanted to know what the reason was. I wanted to know why.

I knew it was going to be bad but I've never

seen a car so badly damaged in my life. Dad was a bit shaken when he saw it again. He hadn't been able to see the extent of the damage when it was lying in the ravine. There was no way you could have climbed back into the seat because the car was so badly smashed in. All the other accidents we'd had and thought were horror shunts were nothing compared with that one.

It didn't jog my memory, but it didn't put me off the idea of going to San Remo either. Any thoughts about packing it in had gone soon after the accident, although I remember thinking as I was being dragged away from the car: 'That's it, I'm never getting back in a car again. I don't need to do this.'

I was so relieved because I'd thought I wasn't going to get out of the car. I really did think: 'This is it; I'm going to die.' So when I did get out I thought: 'I've got my Championship; I've got the money; and I've got my family. Why get back in?'

These thoughts were still flashing through my mind when I was in hospital because it was such a traumatic experience. But the horror of the accident didn't last long. By the following morning, the Sunday, all I wanted was to get myself sorted out and back to business. It was a severe accident but it would have taken more than that to make me stop rallying; I'm not a quitter. It wasn't a case of worrying what people might think of me, I wanted to get back in because I was still capable of winning rallies and I wanted the chance to try and win the Championship that year.

* * *

Nicky Grist

You have to say that was the biggest accident we've had because of Colin's horrible predicament and the fact that it was by far the scariest. We drove 500 yards up a hill and after a series of corners, came to a third gear left, to a second right. I called the notes and as we went into the third left, I thought: 'My God, we're travelling!'

He must have misheard and went into the corner in fourth. He realised he was going too quick and tried to react but he clipped the rock face on the inside and the car started to roll. There was a gap between a bridge parapet and the wall on the outside of the road and we went straight through it. Then there was a big impact with a tree on Colin's side, which spun us round. We hit the bank at the back and dropped down into the ravine, onto the roof.

When we came to a stop, upside down, I said: 'Col, are you okay?' He said nothing. I grabbed his arm, and still nothing. He was unconscious. I was disoriented because of the darkness and because we were upside down. His side was open but he wasn't moving. Apart from the confusion, I was all right. I lay on my back and kicked the door and forced a big enough gap for me to be able to slide out.

Colin started to come round and I could see that the roof had been smashed in and wrapped around him. He said: 'Get me out, get me out.' It was quite frightening. I couldn't work out how bad he was because of the way he was trapped. I don't think he was aware of any danger of petrol at that stage. I think it was the shock of not being able to see anything that really worried him.

I couldn't see his face properly, only one of his cheeks. I tried to push down on the cage but there was no way I could do anything to get him out. I told him I would have to go and get help. I climbed up the bank, about 18 feet, and ran down the road, maybe 500 metres, to a radio point. In my broken French I told them they had to stop the stage and that we needed an ambulance and a doctor. There were three other guys there, spectators. I pleaded with them to help me. They went back with me to the car and tried their best. I thought maybe we could do something with the car jack, anything. The back window was smashed and we managed to get the jack out.

Then I realised there was a smell of petrol. There was also a pool of water from a small stream that ran through the ravine and that sort of half washed away the petrol. There is always the possibility of fire in an accident involving a very hot rally car. But the fortunate thing about the underneath of the car facing skywards was that it reduced the risk of fire.

It was a very bizarre and eerie situation because here we had this awful, desperate scene in the ravine and yet from the road you wouldn't have known there was anything down there. We'd gone straight through that gap and there was no visible sign of an accident. If both of us had been trapped it could have been ages before anyone realised. It doesn't bear thinking about what might have become of us. I think three or four rally cars passed before the stage was stopped.

The rescue services arrived after 15 or 20 minutes and I didn't seem very efficient. That started to panic Colin. They seemed reluctant to start using their cutting equipment and didn't know what to cut. They eventually started but seemed absolutely useless to me. I tried to tell them they had to push down on the roof bar from the inside. Colin had been there for 25 to 30 minutes and I was aware that 'Golden Hour' medical reaction time was running out. That first hour is vital in getting the person checked, put on a drip and taken to hospital. But all of a sudden the rescue work stopped.

Fortunately Bernie Shrosbree arrived with the doctor, physio and Jimmy. I told them the rescue people were doing nothing. I told them they had to chop off the steering wheel. It was a panic situation for me but at the same time I was trying to calm down Colin. He was telling them to get rid of his helmet strap because his helmet was trapped. A guy was trying to cut the strap but he was cutting downwards, towards Colin's throat. I stopped him and did it myself.

Bernie and I took over. I stood on the roof from the inside and he used all his strength, pulling from the outside. We managed to give Colin just enough room to get out. There were six or eight of them in the rescue crew but they didn't get him out, Bernie and I did. Colin had been trapped in there for about 45 minutes. The medics had got a stretcher, like a cradle, down to him but they were faffing around so I told our doctor to take control. He put a neck brace on him and checked him over. Colin walked to the back of the car and they put him onto a stretcher.

That was such a relief. The worst part was the feeling of helplessness because nobody was taking control. At one point a guy stood on the floor pan of the car when we needed to be pushing from the inside. I thought they were incompetent. I had cuts and gashes but that was mainly from trying to rescue Colin. I didn't really notice that until afterwards. You don't when the adrenaline is pumping. Thinking about it later, the tree pushing the seat back probably saved Colin. Or spared him greater injuries, anyway.

*   *   *

Bernie Shrosbree

I was with Malcolm, back at service, when the message came through on the radio that Colin had crashed and was trapped in the car. There was an air of panic about Nicky. He was worried the rescue wasn't being co-ordinated properly. I went up there with Jimmy and Martin Wilkinson, Colin's head mechanic, and took the physio and doctor with me.

When we got there my initial impression was that everything was fine. The rescue people were there and presumably in control. Then Nicky came running up the bank saying Colin was still in the car. This was nearly 45 minutes after the crash. From my background in the Marines and working as a team player I was horrified to see the lack of co-ordination between the rescue service people and the medical people. The problem – which has been rectified since – was that too many people didn't know who was in charge.

There was a fear factor with the petrol so you had the guy cutting but not knowing whether to carry on or stop. And all this time Colin had been trapped, hanging upside down. I was concerned that he had banged his head and there was bleeding in the head. His head must have twisted inside his helmet. He was drifting in and out of consciousness but what was going through his mind when he was conscious, trapped in that environment, is difficult to imagine.

I was standing and kneeling in water as I tried to work out what to do. The car had landed on the lip of a waterfall and water was cascading down to Colin's side of the car. Fortunately the level of the water was low because of the time of year. If it had been in flood they would both have probably drowned.

The team involved in the rescue had the cutting equipment but not enough skill in reading the situation. They weren't cutting an ordinary car. Nicky had to coach them on where to cut because this car had roll cages and all the stuff you don't see in an ordinary road car. They didn't understand that. So they were worried they were going to cut things in the car that would make it cave in and crush them all to death. And all the time there was the smell of petrol, so it added up to a very difficult and anxious situation. They were nervous and I could understand why.

That was the reason Nicky and I decided to take action. We took lots of risks because Colin should have had a neck collar put on before we moved him. We could have broken his neck or his spinal cord. But everything was so entangled that wasn't possible. I asked Colin if he was all right and he said: 'I'm all right, I'm all right.' Because we got that response we set about getting him out.

Nicky went inside the car and pushed the bottom of the car and I pulled away the tangled metal. Colin actually pulled himself out and then collapsed on me. He said he was fine but then I saw his face. His head was blue and twice its normal size. To see a friend and colleague in such a bad way shocked me. His head had swollen so much because he had smashed his cheekbone and the blood was flowing to one side of his head. It was a massive trauma of bleeding. The pressure could have killed him. He could have drowned in his own blood because he had blood on his lungs, as well. There were all sorts of horrific possibilities.

Colin McRae is a very lucky man to be alive. You can't put an exact time on how much longer he could have survived down there but I don't think he could have gone much more than 15 minutes before he would have died.

Probably the main thing that kept him alive in Corsica was his conditioning. Colin is never going to be the guy who wakes up every morning and wants to go out training, but he has become much more conscious of the importance of fitness. He's been biking quite a lot and we've noticed the difference. He's still got work to do on the cardiovascular side, but we're getting there. I can only look at Colin McRae in admiration for the way he came back after being trapped in that cage like that. Malcolm said he had never seen a car like it.

That's why I did everything I could to get that guy back for the next rally. The doctor told him he didn't advise it, but certain people have that exceptional desire that comes from within. You've either got it or you haven't: the clenched fist approach, the grit and the hunger. You have to have that to be a champion in any sport, and Colin McRae most certainly has it. He could have taken the easy way out and missed a couple of rallies, but he said: 'I want to get back in that car.' And you knew he would.

We've all learned from what happened that day. The FIA have. They said it would never happen again, that changes would be made and they have kept their word. There is now a proper medical team that understands everything and the whole rescue operation has been revised. In the event of an accident a helicopter carrying a team of cutting guys who know what they have to do is flown to the scene. There is also an emergency button in the car to call for assistance and alert the services.

* * *

Jimmy McRae

I was still doing the gravel notes and got the message that there had been an accident. When I came back to the service area Malcolm Wilson took Margaret and me in and said Colin was all right but he was still trapped in the car and he was sending their doctor, physio and everybody up there. I said I was going, as well. I went in the recce car with Campbell Roy, who was co-driving for me, and got them to follow us in the Galaxy because I knew exactly where it was. Margaret stayed back at service. I didn't want her to go up there.

I must admit when I got there and he was still in the car after all that time and nobody seemed to be doing anything, I thought the worst. That's the first time I've ever felt that. It was probably the worst moment of my life. I thought that if nothing was happening it wasn't going to be good news. They had cut the cage and done one or two things but they were just standing around talking. I don't think they were trained for a job like that.

At first you couldn't really see Colin because of the way the roof had been pushed in. You couldn't work out where he was or what he was doing. The first thing I said was why couldn't they lift the car and take the weight off the roof. Colin was unconscious at that stage. His head was up in the cage, which had come down and jammed his helmet. They couldn't get his head out of the helmet. They'd even cut the straps of the helmet but still couldn't move him.

It wasn't until Bernie moved in that things happened. He just used his sheer, brute strength to pull the cage back. He managed to spread it and Colin was able to get out of his helmet. When I saw him coming out I thought: Oh, dear. Because he had been upside down for so long his face was enormous. It was red and bruised and there was blood and . . . It was just the worst thing imaginable. They put him down and gave him oxygen. Then they got him out of the gully, into an ambulance, down to the helicopter and away. It was a bad day but it could have been worse. It could have been a lot worse.

I never think to myself that he should quit and I would certainly never suggest to him that he should. It's his life, his career and it's what he wants to do. When he got back to Scotland he was black and blue and looked as if he'd gone twelve rounds with Mike Tyson, but all he could talk about was getting into the car again for the next rally.

It's the same with Alister. He had a big one after Colin's. David Whitehead, the Hyundai team manager, left a message on my answer phone to say he'd had a pretty bad accident, a sixth gear, 100 mph job, but Alister and his co-driver were okay, just a bit of bruising. Before I picked up the message Alister rang and said: 'I'm all right.' I said: 'What do you mean, you're all right?' So he explained and then, of course, I picked up the earlier message. This is what they do and any decisions about retirement have to be theirs.

* * *

Margaret McRae

You just know there's something going on when you're in a service area and suddenly things go very quiet. And the first thing you think is: 'It's one of mine.' So many times, of course, it's not and in time you can become a little blasé about it. But when I heard it was Colin it was a horrible feeling. Your first instinct is to get to him and be with him, but Jimmy wouldn't let me. I was just glad I was in Corsica. It would have been worse being at home, so far from it.

This was the first time I'd been to Corsica. Henri Toivonen, who once drove for the same team as Jim, was killed in Corsica and I'd never been there because of that. I went this time after Alister's girlfriend, Tara, had enthused about the scenery and told me what a wonderful place it was. But when we got there she said I was awfully quiet and seemed not to be myself. I told her I wasn't happy, that I just had a strange feeling about the place.

A couple of nights before, I had a dream that one of the boys was in an accident. I told Jim about it and when Colin had his accident Jim said he couldn't believe it. Probably the dream made me feel uneasy, I don't know, but it was all rather weird.

It was a huge relief when I finally knew it wasn't as serious as it might have been. I was pleased I was there for his sake and I was pleased I was there for Alison's sake. Alison was at home. She said she knew that when I spoke to her I would tell her exactly how things were, whereas other people phoning her maybe wouldn't have told her exactly the truth. I think Jim spoke to her first, told her there had been an accident but that Colin was all right and on his way to hospital. We would find out what was what when we got there. David Richards was very kind and laid on his helicopter and pilot to fly us over the Bastia.

There's no point in my wishing the boys would give up rallying because I know they are going to keep on driving as long as they are happy to do it. Thinking that way would be wasted energy. It's better to accept this is what they are doing. We used to go rallying as a family when Jim was driving and we had a lot of fun. I know how much the boys enjoy it. But I won't be going to Corsica again.

*　　*　　*

Alison McRae

I was at home but I'd missed a couple of calls earlier in the day because I was out. It was Sharon, Nicky's wife, who spoke to me first. She wasn't in Corsica either but she'd heard there had been an accident. She said they were both out of the car but that they'd taken Colin to hospital. Then I spoke to Jim and he asked how much did I know. I thought: 'How much is there to know?' He said he was going in the helicopter to the hospital but that it was fairly bad. Then Nicky phoned me and said Colin wasn't very pretty. His face had taken a lot of the impact but he was conscious and would be all right.

Rallying is Colin's life; it's our life; but I don't like watching him rallying. I hate going on to a stage. If I go on a rally I very rarely watch the stages. I stay in the service area, listening to the radio. There's too much time waiting for his car to come around. On more than one occasion I've stood waiting and he hasn't come around. I get a sick feeling. It's terrible. I sometimes think I've had enough and wish he'd give it up. After Corsica I thought: 'We don't need this any more'. But how can I stop him? We discuss the dangers but there's no point in asking him to stop.

* * *

Malcolm Wilson

I was with the guys at mission control when we heard about the accident and I have to say I found it hard to understand why he was trapped, knowing the strength of the car. But I thought that as long as there was no fire or anything like that then he was going to be okay. I must admit, though, that when I saw the car the next day it was one of the biggest shocks I've ever had. We never envisaged the car could be so badly damaged in the roof.

The roof was hit above his head. The impact must have been incredible. We've done nothing with it since then. It was just a freak accident and wouldn't have mattered what we'd done to it. That's the worst accident I've had as a team boss. It was only when I saw the damage that I realised how lucky Colin was. Our rally cars had a bar behind the seats which we took out when we were looking at the weight issue. The fact that the bar wasn't there any more probably saved his life. Had it been there, it wouldn't have allowed the seat and his body to be pushed back the way they were.

I'll never forget the day Jimmy and Colin came

down to the factory to look at the damaged car. I didn't want them to see it, to be honest, but Colin was quite adamant he wanted to see what had happened. It was very strange. I still have this image of Jimmy shrinking six inches when he saw the car for himself. The first words he said were: 'Bloody hell, Colin, the Hyundai's got that bar behind the seats. If it had been Alister his seat wouldn't have gone back.' It was just another bar in the roll cage to strengthen it, which we felt wasn't necessary and we didn't compromise the safety of the car when we took it out. Quite the opposite as it happened! We would never build such a bar into a car in the future.

Colin was fine when he saw the car but then that's Colin. He just wanted to see it and to know what had happened. The impact and tremendous amount of pressure pushed and broke the seat, forcing everything back. The whole thing was amazing. I don't worry about it affecting him psychologically. It was probably a good thing, mentally, that he came back for the next rally, although I thought it was too soon. But he's very determined and it didn't surprise me.

Colin has had his offs, sometimes when he's been leading rallies, and we've spoken to him about this, about the need to be more disciplined in certain situations. I think we have seen a change in this direction and he is a more complete driver now. But Colin is Colin and his speed and style are what make him special. Everyone knows that if he doesn't have problems he's going to win. If I had the choice of any driver out there I would still take Colin.

The public relate to him. He's straightforward, he's got no airs and graces. He's happy when he's winning, he's not happy when he's not winning. He can be difficult when things are not going well but then he's not the only driver like that. It's particularly hard to take when you know you're the best and you're not winning.

* * *

I wasn't worried that I might have another accident at San Remo, even though the terrain is similar to Corsica. There are a number of big drops and it is quite dangerous. My only concern was that any sort of bump might be enough to dislodge everything that had been done to the cheekbone. All my other thoughts were about the Championship. I still had a real chance with three events remaining. I was third, four points behind Marcus and two behind Richard. If I could get something from Italy I was sure I would be fit enough to give it a real go in Australia and Britain.

Nicky didn't really say anything about getting back into the car and seemed pretty relaxed about everything. You can have the worst accident of all time but get out unhurt, while on another day you can have a very simple accident and hurt yourself. Nicky walked away from the Corsica crash. You can't afford to panic. If you are in this kind of job and you start to worry it will affect your performance. You're going to make a mistake and that can result in an even more serious accident. Nicky is very professional and went about his work as he always does.

It was only when I started the San Remo that I realised how tough it was going to be. It wasn't the cheekbone or the 14 stitches, eight of them inside my mouth, that bothered me. I simply didn't have the energy to drive as hard as I usually do. I was soon drained. But once I'd started I felt I had to carry on; I couldn't give up. Bernie and the guys did a great job on me to keep me going and I think they were the ones who really got me through it. They came up with all sorts of vitamins and concoctions to give me a little more energy, and even oxygen now and then when I was really feeling it.

But it was worth it because it worked. The car wasn't fully on the pace and I drove sensibly. We weren't the quickest but we weren't far off Carlos. We finished sixth, one place behind Carlos, and scored the best point I've ever scored. The team were delighted because they had supported me in my decision to go to San Remo. They could have urged me not to but the decision was left totally to me. There was a deserved sense of achievement all round.

I was sure there would be no psychological problem getting back into the car and driving the stages at competitive speeds. Although it was a pretty horrible crash I'd had all sorts of mishaps over the years, in cars and on bikes. You fall off, get a few bumps and bangs, and get back on again. It depends on the individual. It might be a big deal for someone who couldn't cope with it mentally, but for me it wasn't a big deal.

A point would have made the difference to my Championship campaigns in previous years and this time it left me just one down on Richard, who retired at San Remo. The not so good news was that Marcus picked up three points so he was six ahead of me. It could have been worse but I knew I would have to go for wins in the last two rallies.

The surgeon still wouldn't let me do any training before Australia so, although I felt stronger than I had at San Remo, I was nowhere near fully fit for the penultimate event. The big danger was a build-up of blood pressure, which could have caused serious damage to the eye, so I had to keep my blood pressure as low as possible. That meant a lot of sitting around doing nothing. The drugs had worn off so I did feel fresher for Australia and the long journey wasn't a problem for me at all.

We made a solid enough start and I was comfortable with the pace. I felt that as long as I could maintain that pace for a couple of days I would be in a position to push hard on the last day. Then, out of the blue, the engine popped. We got out of the stage and tried to get to the service, but we had a piston failure and the car stopped altogether on the road section. It was a real sickener, particularly after all the effort we'd put in. Our Championship was over and it was very much in Marcus' hands. Richard had only an outside chance.

I have to admit I wasn't really up for a big finish in Cardiff, the new base for the Rally of Great Britain. The spark had gone out of me and I still wasn't feeling great anyway. I found it difficult to get stuck into the recce and all the boring bits and pieces involved in the build-up. The one thing that did keep me going though, was the latest round in the McRae v Burns 'Battle of Britain'. There was a lot of stuff written about Richard taking over from me as the country's No. 1 driver and going for the Championship, but what people say about who's the top Brit doesn't bother me; in the end, the results speak for themselves.

Once I got into the rally I was surprised how well I did because I wasn't anywhere near full fitness. But the excitement and power of it all can do amazing things. The adrenaline starts rushing and you find the strength to rise to the challenge. By the end of the first full day we were in front and we built up a good lead on the Saturday.

That afternoon we were on a second run of the stages, which were in a terrible state. There had been so much rain, they were very rough and rutted and I got caught in the ruts. I went into a corner slightly slower than on the earlier run because the gravel crew had marked a boulder on the outside of it. The sump guard hit the crown of the road and lifted the car out of the ruts. We rolled and although the car landed on its wheels the radiator was too badly damaged for us to be able to continue.

You can always say you could have been a bit more cautious with any accident and we could have set quickest times even if we had gone slower. But I don't think we were too quick, it was just that the road was so badly rutted. The win was there to be had and for us there was no point in settling for anything but a win. It would have been a tonic for everyone if we had finished the season with a win, but that's not the way it turned out.

Marcus didn't have to win the rally to get what he wanted. He was happy to take second place behind Richard and with it the Championship, a terrific achievement in his first full season. It had been five years since my Championship win, far too long as far as I was concerned, but I was still convinced we could do it with Ford. I confirmed that belief by signing a new two-year contract. My objective for the winter was to regain my fitness and then come out of the blocks flying in 2001.

Friends and Rivals

Rallying, like Formula One motor racing and a number of other sports, is a travelling show, with the same people pitching tent every two or three weeks through the season. You can spend more time in your working and sporting community than you do at home. It makes life considerably easier if you can get on with those around you and I'd like to think many of the regular drivers in the World Rally Championship are friends as well as opponents. I sincerely believe I don't have any enemies in the camp. I suspect it can be slightly different in racing circles because there the drivers come into close contact out on the track and feelings can run high – as I discovered after my infamous altercation with a certain Matt Neal. It's probably just as well I took up rallying rather than racing.

I certainly regard guys like Richard Burns, Tommi Makinen and Carlos Sainz, some of my sternest rivals, also as friends. We mix easily and have meals together fairly regularly during a recce.

That's quite normal in rallying, even for drivers from rival teams. But I don't think any driver at this level can say he has a really close friendship with another driver, for no reason other than the fact that we usually only see each other in a working environment, at rallies. When an event is over we go home to our families and friends, in different parts of the world. We live separate lives: our public lives and our private lives.

My situation is a little unusual in that one of my early rivals was my father and one of my current rivals is my brother. My dad was, for obvious reasons, a great influence on me and my career. I watched him when I was a boy and grew up wanting to emulate him. I didn't have to look far for my first and biggest hero. He was right there at home.

The only other guy I regarded as something of a hero was Ari Vatanen, who made his presence felt on the British Championship scene at the time my dad was competing. Ari was such an exciting driver to watch. He was one of those guys who made you get to the stage in time to watch him because he was such good value. I take it as a compliment when people say they see something of Ari in me. I think we do have a similar attitude to rallying and like to give the fans what they want to see.

Later, of course, we were team-mates at Subaru and it was a terrific experience to work with him. He's a top guy too and likes to live his life. He's great company and it's always good to see him when he pops up on the scene. He's been using his personality and communication skills in a very different sphere recently, as a Member of the European Parliament. I reckon that's where the comparisons between us end. I certainly don't have any plans to go into politics!

Of the current front-line drivers I would say Tommi is not only one of my better friends but also my main rival – the best of my opponents. I think we are very similar in terms of ability and style. Tommi's record speaks for itself: world champion four times in a row. He can be naggingly consistent when he has to be, clinging on for a result when things aren't really going his way, but then capable of producing that extra two or three per cent when it's needed to win a rally. It's that extra speed when it comes to the crunch that marks him down as a special driver.

Of all the guys I have competed against, Tommi is one of the quickest and hardest to beat. Strangely enough, though, we went into the 2001 season never having really found ourselves in a head-to-head situation all the way to the end of a rally. Either he had a problem or I had a problem and the big fight to the finish failed to materialise. I think we'd both relish the chance to battle it out and hopefully it will come. As I have long stated, I would back myself to beat most of my opponents in a last stage shoot-out, but taking on Tommi might be a different matter. I certainly wouldn't be so confident I could beat him every time.

Tommi is not a particularly outgoing person and, if anything, comes across to the public and media as quite timid. In fairness, it should be said that is largely because his English isn't brilliant and English happens to be the language of world rallying, as it is in most other global sports. He is a fairly normal, down-to-earth guy who is perfectly happy when he is allowed to just get on with his job. I suppose he's not dissimilar to me in that respect. He doesn't go in for the hype and all the high-profile stuff that comes with the job, but he is a true competitor. He wants to drive as quickly as possible and win as many rallies and Championships as possible. Unfortunately for me and the other drivers, he has the talent to do so!

He comes from a farming background, as many of the Finnish drivers seem to. From a very early age they drive tractors and other vehicles and work with machinery, which makes them natural drivers and mechanics. The Finnish roads are very fast and give them a good training ground for learning to drive rally cars, enabling them to build up a high level of car control and commitment, which in turn breeds confidence. When you are armed with all those qualities you are entitled to believe you can take on drivers anywhere in the world.

The Finns always appear very focused, and quite aggressive in a controlled sort of way. They always seem to be like those giants taking over in the World's Strongest Man-type competitions. They stay quite cool in the heat of battle. You don't often see a Finn getting revved up as, say, an Italian might. I suppose that can sometimes make them appear to be quite dull. They do their job and, win or lose, show very little difference in their emotions.

Tommi is definitely not one to show much emotion. To be honest he's never been any different when we've been out for a drink, as we have done occasionally after rallies. I've never seen him really let himself go. Mind you, there is this theory that he could be in a permanent stupor. Just joking, Tommi! I have a lot of respect for the guy. Anyone who can pull off four World Championships in a row deserves everybody's respect.

It may be no surprise to hear that Tommi is very competitive away from the rally stages, as well. He's another bikes fan and we've been out riding together in Finland. It's always more fun to be out with someone who's good and I can assure you Tommi is very good. He tried to hammer me the first time I went out with him and really made me work. But I knew he would and so I was prepared. We had a tremendous scrap. We keep saying we'll have a return in the UK but we haven't got round to it yet. We'll manage it some day and I'll make sure we do, because I've got to get my own back.

Another regular contender for the World Championship is Carlos, one of my team-mates at Subaru and my partner again at Ford. He won the world title in '90 and '92 and can never be disregarded in the contest. I have had my run-ins with him but you can't knock him as a driver. It's not just about being the quickest driver. You need all sorts of qualities to be successful and Carlos has enough of them to be a formidable competitor. He is one of the most consistent drivers at the top level and always seems to be there to pick up the pieces. Add to that the ability to produce a winning performance, which he still has, and you understand why he remains such a strong challenger.

If Carlos has a weakness it is possibly a lack of confidence. I think Tommi, Marcus Gronholm, Richard now, and I have a lot of confidence in our ability. If you are confident you are more relaxed when you are driving and more likely to let the car work for you rather than try to force it. Perhaps Carlos doesn't have so much natural ability and has had to work at it harder than most. Malcolm once made a point about my over-driving in Finland in '99. That was a lack of confidence because I didn't know the roads so well. It's a classic example of how important confidence is to us all. If you have to work at it harder then it will take you longer to build up the confidence. That, I believe, is the situation with Carlos. He definitely works harder at it than Tommi and I, and even Marcus, need to.

In motor sport your team-mate is your first rival because he has the same equipment. Therefore, he is the driver you can be measured against most accurately and the first man you must beat. Occasional tension and friction between team-mates is almost inevitable. We do this for a living and there is a lot at stake, but despite our few bust-ups, Carlos and I do actually get on and we work well together. We share information and compare notes. Between rallies we occasionally discuss things on the phone. It's in the interests of both of us to pull together, particularly if we want changes to the car or we want the team to address a certain problem. We have no big secrets or factions in the team. There's never an issue of that sort and the atmosphere is good. Carlos and I are relaxed together and we occasionally socialise after hours. I'm quite comfortable with him now.

But Carlos will always be Carlos. He does like to have things done his way and no-one else's. He can be rather selfish in that sense. He complained about me in Catalunya, saying I was immature, and yet he did exactly the same thing to me on the Acropolis. That's the selfish side of him. It's probably the emotional, Latin side. Carlos is not merely a star in Spain, he is a megastar, and he doesn't like to be beaten. Some people accept defeat, others don't. Carlos doesn't accept it as well as I do. I'm not a bad loser at all, despite what some people may think. If someone is good enough to beat me then I say good on them, I don't have a problem with that. Carlos is very different.

At the end of '98, my last year with Subaru, I took part in a rallysprint in Madrid, Carlos' home city, and the two of us made it through to the final. Before we faced each other in the final Carlos came up to me and said: 'Colin, you have to let me win.'

I said: 'Excuse me?'

He said: 'You have to let me win in front of my home crowd.'

I told him: 'I didn't come here to finish second, Carlos.'

That's the way it was left and I beat him. He didn't come and congratulate me. That's Carlos. It tells you something about his character and his pride. That's how important it was for him not to be seen beaten in front of his own people. I wouldn't dream of asking another driver to let me win in the UK. Not even jokingly. But Carlos is a very proud person and it hurts him to lose, especially in Spain.

I do believe I have a psychological advantage over Carlos. I'm confident I would beat him nine times out of ten in a straight fight, the sort of situation we had that day in Madrid. That's the difference between Tommi and Carlos. Against Tommi I wouldn't take it for granted that I was going to beat him. The very fact that Carlos asked me to let him win showed he was worried he couldn't win. I wasn't.

Carlos doesn't throw tantrums or have major dramas in that way. He is normally fairly calm and level-headed. He is very serious about his work, very professional and very committed. It's good to have him in your team because he is so experienced, knowledgeable and focused. He pushes for the things that need to be pushed for and works hard to improve the car. I have no hesitation in saying Carlos is one of the best team-mates I've ever had.

The only other four-times world champion in the history of rallying is another Finn, Juha Kankkunen. He won his first title in '86 and his last in '93, so I didn't have the opportunity to compete against him when he was at his peak. By the time I was climbing to the top Juha was tailing off a bit. But you just have to look at his record to realise he ranks as one of THE drivers of all time.

Again, you can see the influence of his Finnish background. There is a cool, focused determination about Juha. You are left in no doubt that he is there to do business and not to mess around. He's probably been more consistent than Tommi but not quite as capable of that explosive, decisive pace that is required when it comes to the crunch.

He has never been at his best on asphalt and in later years that weakness did count against him. When he was at his height he could compensate for that because he was good on gravel and had the knack of grinding out results, but in more modern rallying you can't afford to have such an obvious weakness. Teams have used tarmac specialists to suit their own needs and priorities but a driver who has ambitions of winning the individual Championship these days must be more of an all-rounder.

Juha was due to be my team-mate when I joined Ford at the start of the '99 season but evidently wasn't happy about the disparity in our salaries and decided to leave. In the circumstances it might have been an awkward situation, especially as the team needed clear, single-minded direction. On the other hand, we might all have benefited from his knowledge and experience. From a personal point of view it would have been interesting working with a driver who had achieved so much in the sport.

Finland's amazing list of World Championship winners goes back to Ari, in '81. And since my success, in '95, it has been a Finnish whitewash. Just when Tommi's run of four titles ended, up popped another of his countrymen to claim the crown. Marcus Gronholm pulled it off in his first full Championship season, which is a fantastic accomplishment by any standard.

It also serves as an example and inspiration to

other drivers who struggle to get the drive they crave and perhaps begin to think their chance will never come. If you have the determination as well as the ability, it's amazing what you can do and Marcus has provided emphatic proof of that. He had been around for quite a long time waiting for a break and then, when Peugeot obliged, he made the most of it.

I remember Nicky and me talking about Marcus a couple of years ago, when he'd gone off for the umpteenth time and seemed to be going nowhere except into ditches. He was obviously pretty quick but he had a lot of accidents and was around the scene for ages without really making an impression. A lot of teams looked at him but weren't prepared to take what they considered a gamble. At that stage it was understandable because you certainly wouldn't have rated him a potential world champion.

Even when he got the Peugeot drive he made a few mistakes at the start and although it was clear he had a very good car I don't think many people would have backed him to win the Championship. I certainly didn't. Even when he began to chalk up some good results most people thought he wouldn't be able to keep it together. His inexperience of certain rallies and the pressures of going for the Championship were expected to prove too much for him. Not a bit of it. He drove in a cool, relaxed style, kept his nerve and eventually won it well. All credit to him. Much as I was hoping to be Champion again in 2000, I think Marcus' win was good for rallying and for all those drivers out there striving to make it to the very top of our sport.

We were joined at Ford for the 2001 season by another very experienced driver, Frenchman Francois Delecour. And there the comparisons between Francois and the rest of us end. He is . . . different. I didn't know him well before he came to Ford but his reputation as something of an eccentric preceded him and from what I have seen of him so far at close quarters, I can believe the tales about him. He is a character. He is good fun and highly entertaining.

I was quite intrigued to find out for myself what he was like because we had heard all sorts of stories from his colourful past. There was the one about his not wanting anybody else in the motorhome when he was eating, so everybody else had to get out. And then the one about his throwing beds out of hotel windows because he wasn't happy with them. Apparently when he's in those moods he's not to be messed with. He was in trouble with the authorities for riding a bike on stages before a rally and has had his own share of bust-ups with team officials. It really is some CV.

There may be more madcap incidents to come and certainly it wouldn't surprise me. There's definitely a wee bit of daftness there. We saw a glimpse of his temper in the 2001 Cyprus Rally, when he lost time going off at a corner and, in a fit of pique, yanked the gear knob off. But then you need variety in life and it's good to have one or two out-of-the-ordinary people around. If it works for him that's the only thing that matters, and there's no doubt that Francois can be quick. He is good on tarmac and gravel, although he tends to be a little inconsistent, which can count against him over a season.

The one Frenchman to have won the Championship is Didier Auriol. He is nothing like as explosive or expressive as Francois, but then I can't claim to know him well because he's very quiet and keeps himself to himself. There is no doubt that he is capable of being very quick and giving anybody a good fight on a stage. When the weather is to his liking and the wind is in the right direction he can be up there with the best.

The trouble is that he is the kind of driver who needs everything to be perfect for him to produce those times. Most drivers – including Carlos – will drive around a problem and make the best of a less than perfect job. But not Didier. According to the WRC grapevine, Didier has been known to demand his seat be moved one millimetre because it wasn't quite right for him. He has a reputation for being generally pernickety. Every driver likes to be as comfortable as possible but I suspect it's a psychological thing with Didier. You can't always have the car absolutely perfect. Sometimes you have to take what you've got and simply get on with it.

Perhaps there's something about the French temperament. They can be rather highly-strung and I'm not sure that's an advantage when you are driving a rally car. Gilles Panizzi is a tarmac expert and can be very good on rallies he knows well. But he is so intense, driving along with his eyes popping out, you do rather worry he might crack at any moment.

Driving on tarmac is actually easier than driving on gravel. If the car is right, the tyres are working well and you know the road, you shouldn't have much of a problem. You are basically driving to the limit of the tyres. On gravel the tyres don't have a limit because you're sliding all the time anyway. It's far more in the hands of the driver. The ultimate test for a driver, of course, is to turn it on anywhere. Gilles is hot on tarmac and makes a living doing his own thing, but aiming for the Championship is a different matter.

I think I can safely say Britain has one of the strongest representations – if not the strongest – in the World Rally Championship, with three drivers among the very best. When I won my first rally at this level it was hailed as a major breakthrough because British drivers had made little impact on the world scene since Roger Clark. But I now have more than 20 wins, as well as a Championship, to my name and Richard Burns has also claimed victories. I have absolutely no doubt that my brother Alister would be Britain's third current winner, given a car competitive enough to get the job done. A lot of countries must envy the strength of our challenge.

It's fair to say Richard has surprised a lot of people – including me – the way he has come through to the sharp end of our sport. He was always a steady fourth or fifth type of driver. He was dependable but never particularly outstanding or exciting. He had become rallying's Mr Consistent. He was regarded as a good No. 2, the man who would give you a good solid performance and get you a result. But he didn't win rallies and in all honesty he didn't look as if he was going to win rallies.

And then, all of a sudden, he started to put in

blinding times. There had been a steady improvement in his form and obviously he was still learning, but the leap he made from Mr Consistent to Championship contender was amazing. He confounded all of us. Now he's right up there fighting it out with the best in the business and I respect him as one of my toughest opponents. He has the ability and the confidence, and the big results have started to come his way.

Some people in the sport believe he has peaked but I don't go along with that. It gets harder to make significant strides once you reach a certain standard but you can always work on your weaknesses to keep inching forward and become a more complete driver. He has had to cope with some bad runs over the last couple of seasons, just as I have, and I think he's got the strength of character to do that. We were both able to show what we could do in the 2001 Rally of Argentina and no-one could get near us. Winning that was satisfying enough for me after 11 months without a victory, but beating off a charging Richard in the process made it even better. And then following it up with another win at Richard's expense in Cyprus. . .

I still feel I have the beating of Richard in a head-to-head fight. We come back to the comparison with Tommi. I'm more confident I can get the better of Richard when it's down to a sprint finish. I look forward to a few more battles with him in the future. It has been claimed that I stopped Richard from joining me at Ford, but that's not true. I have a feeling he didn't want me to go back to Subaru while he was there. I would have no problem being in the same as Richard.

Drivers don't really talk among themselves about who's the best in our business. It's just not done. But I do phone up Richard now and then when I've had a few too many beers and feel in a mischievous mood, and tell him I'm quicker than him. I like to wind him up. He reckons I must love him because I only ever call him when I'm drunk! He's never tried to get his own back yet but he'll probably get me back a cracker one day. Richard is the only one I wind up like that. Carlos would be too easy to rev up. It wouldn't be as satisfying and he definitely wouldn't appreciate it. Richard can actually see the funny side of it.

People try to build up the rivalry between Richard and me, which is fair enough. I like that bit of edge. It makes things more interesting for both of us, especially when we come round to our home rally. But it's no more than rivalry. It's certainly not hostility. In fact, we're both quite amused when people try to stir things up between us. I've got a lot of time for Richard. He's a decent chap who likes a laugh and a bit of fun away from the job. We'll have a drink together after a rally and enjoy each other's company. Apart from the fact that he's English, he's okay.

The other Brit I rate is an even closer mate and he's a Scotsman: my brother Alister, of course. It has been tough for him to get the opportunity he deserves because he is called McRae. His father was five-times British Champion and his brother has been world champion – that's some double act to follow. The name has undoubtedly held him back and denied him the chance of good drives.

In my case the name might have helped. It got me recognised and it opened a few doors for me. But for Alister it has been a hindrance. It would seem he is one McRae too many. If he was called Smith he would have had a competitive car long before now because his driving has merited it.

It is very difficult to know exactly how well Alister could do and I realise people may think I am biased when I talk about him. I have tried to look at it objectively and compare him with the recognised top drivers and I sincerely believe – given the car – he would be up there with the quickest. His attitude is right and that is important. It's the one thing you can go by. His knowledge of the car, his mechanical expertise and his confidence are the same as mine. He's also fairly similar in style to me. I'm sure some of that comes from dad. You're bound to pick up his characteristics watching him and being with him for so long, as we were.

Whether Alister and I will ever end up together in the same team, I don't know. We did try to pull it off at Ford but I think they were very nervous about having two drivers of the same nationality, let alone the same family, in the team. Maybe if he manages to prove himself in another team, by winning the World Championship or at least demonstrating his potential to be a champion, we'll get the chance to be team-mates. Otherwise, I can't really see it happening. More's the pity because we really would make a good partnership. We are the best of mates as well as brothers, we trust each other totally and we would genuinely do everything possible to help each other.

Alister still has time to get the break he needs but you do wonder whether he might have been luckier in bikes, if only he could have stuck at it. He's probably got the ideal build and strength to be a motocross competitor and there's absolutely no doubt he's got the ability to be a top biker. But because of his damaged knees he had to rule out that option, so rallying it is. One thing is for sure, he will keep trying and give it his all. He has the self-belief as well as the talent and, as Marcus Gronholm has shown, perseverance can pay off in the end.

Of the younger guys in the World Championship I think there's no doubt Norway's Petter Solberg has the talent to be a star of the future. He was given his break at Ford and Malcolm was very unhappy when he left us to join Subaru. He had nurtured Petter and had great hopes of him. There's no question Petter has the speed and the enthusiasm. When Malcolm sent for him at the last minute to drive on the Safari Rally, he slept the night on a bench in Oslo airport so he wouldn't miss the flight the next morning.

He's a very relaxed young guy, not the sort to get all hyped up. He has perhaps tried a little too hard at times and he has made mistakes, but I know one or two young drivers who have done that! The important thing is that he has the speed and the potential, so he needs the support and understanding of those around him. Every driver needs that.

Team Game

The drivers are the people at the sharp end of rallying and they receive most of the praise when things go well. They will tell you they also come in for most of the flak when things don't go so well, although the teams would probably dispute that! But everyone is agreed that no driver can be successful in modern World Championship rallying without a car capable of winning and the massive back up to ensure he remains competitive. That may be stating the obvious but I suspect not everyone appreciates the scale of the operation in rallying today. It is a team game of scores and even hundreds a side.

On an event the Ford Martini team of engineers, mechanics, medics, press and marketing people, caterers and so on numbers up to about 70, yet that represents less than a half of the total workforce at M-Sport. Malcolm Wilson expects to be employing 180 people at his headquarters by the end of 2001. Teams are notoriously secretive about their budgets and Ford are no different, but you can be sure it costs them well over £20m a year to pursue their Championship objective.

Malcolm and his team are now established at Dovenby Hall Estate, a 115-acre site on the edge of the Lake District National Park. He scoured the country before finding the place he was looking for right in his own neighbourhood. It used to be a mental institution, so you won't be surprised to learn he has had a good deal of Mickey-taking from within the rallying community. But when it comes to rallying and business Malcolm has his head screwed on the right way, you can be sure of that. He spent £10.5m converting the buildings – the oldest of which dates back to the 12th century – into a rally technical centre second to none. It is state-of-the-art and some. He reckons the company's turnover for 2001 will be about £30m.

M-Sport build Focus rally cars and nothing else. The company produces them not only for Ford's World Championship campaign but also for private customers. There are no fewer than 26 car bays in the huge main building. Step inside the spotlessly clean workshop – which has under-floor heating – at any time and you will see a bunch of guys working on our three cars for the next rally, and another bunch of guys working on our three cars for the rally after that. The preparation is as thorough as it is carefully planned. They strip the cars down, check everything and then rebuild them. Nothing is left to chance.

Malcolm will probably tell you I give them plenty of work because I trash the gearbox or whatever, but it is my job to get the maximum out of the car and that, ultimately, is what he and the team want. Everybody has to be pushed to the limit to get the best possible results. The guys in the team are just as eager for success as I am. They work incredibly hard. Some of them go to all the tests as well as the rallies, which is just a mind-blowing schedule. It's not a job for anyone who wants a cushy nine-to-five existence. It takes a certain kind of person to do it. But you need talent as well as commitment and enthusiasm in the team, and we have that in abundance.

The focus of the operation – literally in our case – is the car and the main responsibility for creating a winner rests on the shoulders of the designers and engineers. The driver can help in the development of the car with his input. I think I'm reasonably good at communicating with the engineers and mechanics, and with Malcolm and Martin. You have to be if you are to get the car to the competitive level required to win rallies. I have a good general relationship with everyone in the team and that's important as well. You need to have a good feeling about your work and what you are trying to achieve together. That enables you to build mutual trust and respect. I have to trust the guys who give me the car and keep it on the road in the rally. They have to trust me to drive it as well as I can. I believe we have achieved that situation at Ford.

Malcolm, as team director, is in constant touch with Martin and Ford. Around Malcolm are experienced and knowledgeable lieutenants. Gunther Steiner, who hails from Northern Italy, is project leader; John Millington is co-ordination manager; and Martin Wilkinson is the head mechanic on my car. The management set-up has been further reinforced by the arrival of Phil Short, a wily strategist who knows all the tricks of the trade.

But above all I think the strength of the team is the bond we have. You have to be dedicated and single-minded to survive in this business, let alone excel. Team spirit is vital to carry you through the tough times and in rallying you can be sure you'll get your share of those. The good times make it worthwhile for everyone, and the good times come with winning. The driver is the front man but all 180 people play their part in that victory and are entitled to take pleasure and satisfaction from it. Everyone at Dovenby Hall is given a huge boost when Nicky and I drive onto that ramp as winners.

The chassis and engine we all depend upon have been improved gradually, step by step, over the three years I have been with the team. By the middle of the 2001 season it was clear we had moulded a very good car. It was both competitive and resilient. A hat-trick of wins, in Argentina, Cyprus and the Acropolis, provided fairly conclusive proof of that. But those victories were achieved on rough gravel rallies. We were conscious we had to raise our game on asphalt, so a lot of test and development work went into making improvements specifically for the tarmac events due later in the year.

It is a constant process of tackling your weaknesses and enhancing your strengths. The worst sin you can commit is to assume you've cracked it. To a certain extent we had been guilty of that in '99. Those two early wins came too early, as Malcolm and everybody in the team will now concede. There is an old saying in motor sport: 'If you stand still you go backwards.' It applies more today than ever it did. But we were in no mood to become complacent when we made that breakthrough in 2001 and Malcolm pressed hard to ensure we maintained that forward momentum.

The Ford Focus RS World Rally Car has the basic shape and dimensions of a Focus road car but there the likeness pretty well ends. It is built to compete at the very highest level of the sport, driven to the edge in very varied, often hostile conditions, which is why each car costs around £350,000. It has to be as strong as the proverbial tank yet at the same time incorporate lightweight materials and highly sophisticated equipment. It has four-wheel drive, a two-litre, turbo-charged engine and a six-speed, semi-automatic gearbox. The gearbox is not operated by a pedal, as in a Grand Prix car. We still have a gear lever, which is positioned at a convenient height, close to the wheel, but we shouldn't have to crunch the gears. The lever operates an electric switch, which changes the gear.

I am often asked if the left-hand drive is a problem, and the simple and honest answer is 'No'. This is standard in our cars and I have long been used to it. I suppose cars used to be built with left-hand drive because most of the factory drivers were foreigners and preferred them that way. Some teams would change their cars to right-hand drive for British drivers but others wouldn't because all the parts were produced for left-hand drive. When my dad and Russell Brookes were around they had right-hand drive cars built for them, but if they wanted a full factory car it would have to be left-hand drive. Any right-hand drive cars around today are driven by amateurs.

I like to tell people I sit higher in the car than Nicky because I'm quite a bit taller than he is, but in fact my seat is positioned higher than his. The driver obviously needs the best possible vision, whereas it is not so important for the navigator to see as much. So he can be positioned lower in the car, and the lower the weight the more effectively the car will work. And no, we don't have back seats!

The Focus has a top speed of about 220 kph, and on most rallies we reach over 200 kph on a number of stages. The Safari is the rally where we have the longest stretches of top speed driving. There are sections in Kenya where the car is flat out for perhaps three or four minutes. The engine is set up to run at its maximum for each individual event. Safari would probably be the toughest because it's an event covering 1,500 competitive kilometres rather than 400, so the engine has three times as much work to do.

We drivers are protected by a cage built into our car and also by our clothing. Normally I wear a Nomex suit, gloves, balaclava, socks and shoes – all fireproof – and an open-face crash helmet. But on hot rallies it's nice to push up your sleeves. The heat has to get out somehow and if your body completely covered it can't dissipate. There is a belief that if you are fully covered inside a hot car you are subjected to more pressure and strain. You are more likely to feel the effects of the heat, which could result in your making a mistake and having an accident. On the Safari the local guys drive in T-shirts and shorts. I think the clothing of the driver should be left to the discretion of the crew.

A rally team's work schedule is like a never-ending conveyor belt. Within days, hours even, of one season finishing, the team head for the first of the winter tests. The testing and development programme goes on through December and into January, right up to the first event of the new season. Through the season there are regular tests before each rally, when teams prepare their cars and their strategies – set-ups, ratios, tyre choice and the like – for the specific demands of that event.

At some of the rougher rallies, such as the Acropolis, the team will reinforce the car's under-body protection. Stronger guards are fitted to the fuel tank and sump. It means adding perhaps 10kg to the weight, but that is a price worth paying if you get through the rally. Suspensions take a particularly heavy battering, so they are regularly changed at every service on the tougher events.

But also during any given season the team will be looking ahead to the following year, producing and testing parts they believe will further improve the car. Aerodynamic refinements will be designed and tried out. Sometimes a team will make a significant breakthrough with a certain section or component of the car they are testing and decide to introduce it ahead of schedule. And in some cases, of course, a team will be designing and building a completely new car, which really does pile on the workload and the pressure. Remember they will still be working on their current car, trying to squeeze as much performance out of it as they can.

Every rally now follows a fairly standard routine. As a working exercise it takes a week from start to finish. The whole trend in rallying is towards compactness and that is preferable for all concerned in a season of 14 events, possibly to become 16. Drivers fly out to the venue on a Sunday, start the recce on the Monday and fly home on the following Sunday evening if they wish. Members of the team will arrive at the start of the week because the rally cars have to be ready for the shakedown, on the Wednesday, and all the equipment has to be set up.

The drivers have two-and-a-half to three days to do the recce. This is a reconnaissance trip, an opportunity for the drivers to familiarise themselves with the rally route. Drivers and co-drivers make their pace notes or, if they already have experience of the stages, revise and amend them where necessary. It is only relatively recently that pace notes were allowed on the RAC Rally. A lot of traditionalists were up in arms about the change of rules but the fact is, if you want to see cars really attacking a stage, drivers have got to have pace notes. It is also distinctly safer when you know where you are going! Pace notes are now acknowledged as a standard feature of rallying. The one exception I would make is Safari, which is in dangers of becoming too like the others. It was traditionally an adventure event and should be restored to its original character. It should be larger and Pace notes should not be permitted. That would actually make it safer because cars would be running at a slower pace.

We are allowed two runs through each of the stages during the recce, but we don't use our rally cars. Through the 2001 season we have still been using Ford Escort Cosworths, which really are antiques. Francois Delecour, who returned to Ford at the beginning of 2001, reckons he's been driving the same recce car he drove when he was with the team in 1990. But Ford no longer produce a turbo-charged, four-wheel-drive road car, and these days teams are tending to opt for more standard-type cars, anyway. Depending on the rally, we have to stick to a maximum speed of 90 or 100 kph on the recce, which makes a monotonous job even more boring.

The recce takes us through to Wednesday lunchtime and in the afternoon we have a shakedown. This is, in effect, a final practice in the rally car before the event. It takes place at a location designated by the organisers. It is supposed to simulate, as near as possible, a representative stage of the rally. The shakedown stage is quite short, normally between three and six kilometres in length. But it is important. We drive it flat out because it is a last chance to check everything and make sure we are happy with the settings and so on. We still have time to make a few tweaks and if you feel you can gain something, no matter how minor, by making a slight adjustment you will want to do so.

After a day's recce, when the sun has gone down and it's a bit cooler, we'll take the opportunity to go out cycling for a couple of hours. Bernie Shrosbree sets the agenda and generally organises our fitness and training programme. He also works with the Benetton Formula One team as human performance manager and has all the latest facilities at their Cotswolds HQ. Once or twice a year he puts us through an assessment session, to make sure we are meeting his targets. If he identifies any weaknesses he'll work on them – and make sure we do.

Bernie has had a significant impact on our training and overall state of health. He is a guy to be respected because of what he has done. He is not like some doctors, standing on the sidelines, telling you what you should and shouldn't be doing. He's been there and done it. He served in the Marines and then reached the triathlon world rankings. He was second in a global 'Survival of the Fittest' TV programme. He's into extreme sports, Nordic skiing and all that stuff. We are talking one hell of a fit guy.

He has impressed upon me that I can extend my capability for top level performance in a rally car if I maintain and even improve my fitness, and clearly that awareness becomes more important with every passing year. It can be difficult fitting in training sessions with the hectic round of rallies and testing we have, so discipline helps and so does a trainer like Bernie. Some mornings the last thing you want is to get out of bed and go training, but if you have someone driving you out and leading the cycling you have no choice. Once you're out there, with company, you enjoy it. Well, usually, anyway.

We can be very competitive, even in training. Nicky and I really pushed each other when we cycled one of the toughest Tour de France stages, a 30 kilometre climb up in the French Alps. It was absolute torture of the puking-over-the-handle-bars variety. The last two kilometres were just impossible and Nicky couldn't believe it when I got to the top. But then I had to admit I'd cheated. Alison was driving alongside us and I grabbed on to the wing mirror, anything I could get my fingers onto to get me up the last couple of Ks. There was no way I could have done it otherwise. Poor old Nicky was dead.

Training, of course, is on my agenda between rallies, although, as I have already pointed out, we have to keep a sense of perspective here. We are not Olympic athletes. We are drivers and I believe I have a natural ability to drive a car. The driving we do is training in itself. The best training of all. I'm lucky in that I can eat virtually anything and not put any weight on, although the older I get the more conscious I become that I won't always be able to take that for granted. I'm six feet tall and my normal fighting weight is twelve and a half stones. The accident in Corsica restricted my training through the following winter and the early part of 2001 and I did move up a notch on the belt, so I was determined to tackle that and come back down a notch before Argentina. Chips were out, replaced by cycling for two hours a day.

It was good to be able to get back on motor-bikes again, as well. I enjoy skiing and jet-skiing, activities that also serve as training exercise and give me a lot of pleasure. At home I spend quite a bit of time on quads, which are great fun as well as hard, physical work. A lot of my friends, and Alister of course, enjoy the outdoor stuff and it's always easier to get out and get active when you have company. Sometimes though, you just have to get down to the training on your own and I have a gym at home where I work out.

On the Thursday of a rally week we usually have Press and PR commitments. We might also have a press or sponsors' dinner on the Wednesday evening. It is often said that I am not comfortable at these functions but I honestly don't have a problem with them. As long as they are organised properly, and start and finish when they are supposed to, then that's fine by me. Some sponsors' parties are pretty good but I'm there as a driver and, especially if they are held just before a rally, I'm not going to be throwing back the wine and having a good old carry-on. Drivers can't be totally relaxed in that kind of atmosphere. I can handle the tittle-tattle with strangers and in any case it's part of my job. I'm contracted to do this sort of thing, but I'm not going to pretend it's the same as going down to the pub to meet your mates and have a few beers. Of course it's not.

Totally separate from my commitments at events, Ford are entitled to my services for 10 days of the year for promotional purposes. I managed to negotiate that down from 20. The day after we won the 2001 Cyprus Rally I went to the

company's Boreham base and drove Hannu
Mikkola's London to Mexico 1970 World Cup
Rally-winning Escort to compare it with my Focus.
My thoughts and observations provided the
material for a feature to mark 100 years of Ford
motor sport. It was good fun and easy to drive,
but didn't ride the bumps too well. I wouldn't
have fancied driving all the way from London to
Mexico in it!

Some of the rallies start on the Thursday
evening with a superspecial stage. Occasionally
we have a ceremonial start. In Argentina we
began the 2001 event with two runs on the
superspecial stage. Australia set the standard for
these openers, which are not authentic rally stages
but provide the opportunity to cram the spectators
in to see something from start to finish. It is the
ideal corporate hospitality show. Companies have
their suites and entertain their sponsors with a
nice spread and a good view of the world's best
rally cars and drivers in action, head to head. It's
not representative of the rally proper, which starts
on the Friday morning, but again, if it is organised
properly I think it's okay. It's more of a social
event and as long as the driver doesn't do
anything stupid he can have a bit of fun, too.
Cardiff's debut as a host of the World Rally
Championship in 2000 wasn't much fun but then
they were very unlucky with the weather. It was
more of a mudbath than a special stage and the
organisers will have learned from the experience.

Whatever happens on the Thursday evening at
a rally, we get down to the real business on the
Friday morning. The rally lasts three days, with

Sunday the shortest day. That third leg usually finishes early in the afternoon. I never have a problem sleeping the night before a rally. I can sleep anywhere, any time. I normally have a breakfast of cereal and fruit and we eat three or four times during the day, at each service. It's a case of little and often, just topping up. Nothing too heavy. The diet is governed by Bernie, the physio, Paul Thawley, and the doctor, Simon Morris.

We have excellent caterers at our motorhome, which is run by Di and Stuart Spires, who worked for many years in Formula One. They became such established and respected figures in the Grand Prix paddock they were known as Mum and Dad. They have looked after the likes of Nigel Mansell and Michael Schumacher and many teams of mechanics down the years. They have fed them, watered them and given them a shoulder to cry on. Di makes sure I have my fruit and salad, but then lets me have a chocolate bar for a treat. She hides them behind the bottles in the fridge, for me.

On the hot rallies it is especially important to keep pumping in the fluid. What we drink is basically water with a fruit flavour. By the end of the day you feel water-logged! But you have to keep drinking when you can because if it ever gets to the point where you are thirsty it's probably too late. I can finish a day in even the hottest climate without losing any weight, but then I tend not to sweat. Carlos, on the other hand, does sweat so he probably loses weight over the three days of a rally.

I'm naturally pretty relaxed at the start of a rally and even just before a crucial stage. I'm not one to get sweaty palms, just a wee bit of excitement. When that goes you know it's time to stop. Many sportsmen and women have superstitions and rituals they follow religiously as they prepare themselves for action. David Coulthard famously wore a pair of 'lucky' underpants until they fell to bits. Mind you, I think the truth was that he couldn't get them off! Michael Schumacher always climbs into his car from the left. Footballers, rugby players, tennis players and boxers have little routines they go through as they psyche themselves up. I have no superstitions, no mascots, no magic potions. I have nothing like that. I'm just not superstitious at all.

I was once offered a supposedly 'magical' stone – from Jamaica I think it was – which I was meant to touch for luck before the Catalunya Rally. It didn't make any difference whatsoever so I told them they could chuck their bloody stone. The only thing I might do every now and then is touch wood, but that's about it. I'm not aware that Nicky has any superstitions, either. Unless he has some he wants to keep quiet about! There are no last words, no chants, nothing of that sort.

Rallies are no longer run through the night as once they were. We now have what dad sneeringly refers to as 'office hours'. The mechanics and engineers don't complain they miss the night sessions and I don't blame them. But they still have early starts, setting up the service area. Once that's done it's their base. When the cars return to service they spring into action. It can be quite a spectacle watching them at work in a pressure situation, when they know their efforts can save or cost you time and position in the rally. They can change a gearbox and more besides, in the permitted 20 minutes.

I wouldn't say the teams of today are much more professional than they were when I started. Prodrive were always a very professional outfit. But the scale of rallying and everything about it has changed. In the early 90s we had perhaps 25 people in the team at events, but now that figure has trebled. Everywhere you look you see evidence of money coming into the sport. The standard of the equipment, the motorhomes and vehicles, has gone up at the same rate as the numbers in the teams.

My dad and the gravel crews are among the early birds, driving through the stages before the rally cars and making final checks. You need all the help you can get on an event and that can include keeping an eye open for police speed traps. Finland is very hot on speed limits. The year we had all those rolls we were particularly tight on time so we used the helicopter as a spotter for police cars. The trouble was we were flat out leaving the service area to get to the next stage and the helicopter couldn't keep up with us. Fortunately we managed to get to the stage without losing time – and without being stopped by the cops.

Teamwork is crucial at every step of the way. We keep in constant contact with the team and they relay the stage times of the other cars. If something goes wrong and it has to be fixed before we get to service, Nicky and I have to tackle it. We are not allowed outside assistance between services but the team may give us advice and instructions by phone or radio. Sometimes, though, there is no technical or scientific solution to a problem and we have to resort to cruder methods. Anything to keep the car in the rally.

Organisation is vital and we certainly have that, from the factory to the road. Everyone has a job to do and gets on with it. Malcolm oversees everything on an event, just as he does back at base. He is calm and methodical, has an amazing eye for detail and is meticulous in his preparation and presentation. But rallies rarely run like clockwork and sometimes, when we are frantically trying to get out of a service on time, everyone has to pitch in – and that includes Malcolm. No-one in the team is frightened of getting their hands dirty. That's when the work ethic and team spirit come to the fore.

When the work is over, and especially when we've won, it's nice to unwind with the team, have a few beers and a laugh. Nicky and I, along with the mechanics, have been known to wander in at dawn, after a night of celebration.

I've painted a picture of Derek Ringer as the quiet straight guy but he got roped into something he probably wished he hadn't, when we went to a transvestite cabaret bar in Corsica a few years ago. He became the star turn! I think the night out was organised by Luis Moya, Carlo Sainz's co-driver. Luis is a bit of a character and he even managed to get Carlos along. The mechanics were with us, as well.

It was more of a pantomime than some erotic

show and they asked for a volunteer participant from the audience. Luis had set it up for Derek to be picked out and they took him off behind the curtain. Ten minutes later he reappeared wearing nothing except an old towel wrapped around him like a nappy and a big safety pin through it. They'd painted him some rosy red cheeks and nice red lips. He made a lovely baby. We'd all been taking bets on how long they would be able to keep him behind the curtain before he came running out but he was a great sport and went through with the whole act. In fact, he was surprisingly happy to go through with it!

Luis is always a good running mate for a bit of fun. On the Acropolis Rally one year we had a day off from the recce so the night before we went out and ended up in some club. We'd taken one of the recce cars, which was pretty low on fuel, and were on the other side of the bay, a long way from our hotel. We thought we didn't have enough fuel to get us back but as we were driving we came up to a railway crossing and I recognised the area.

I turned to Luis and said I knew a short cut. He said there was no short cut and we'd just have to go round the coast road. I said: 'No, here's the short cut.' And as we reached the crossing we turned 90 degrees right onto the railway line. I remembered there was another crossing close to the hotel so I reckoned it had to be the same line. The car sat with its wheels either side of the track. It was perfect. We were able to drive along, flat out, hands off the wheel. We laughed at each other all the way home. It must have been a three

With Nicky, celebrating our win at the RAC Rally, 1997.

Arriving through the forests of Sagen, during the Swedish rally, 1997.

With Mum and Dad at home.

Keeping fit is part of my job. Luckily there are plenty of ways to do it...

© Colin McRae

Good clean fun! Quad racing with the boys; (left to right) my brother-in-law Jimmy Anderson, me, Dougie Hamilton, David Rowe and my brother Alister.

© Colin McRae

Our favourite mode of transport – the six-seater Cessna Citation. In front are Alison, Hollie, my mate Colin Morrison, Alistair my pilot and Charlie Mike.

© Bryn Williams

Me and Alister taking a gentle bike ride.

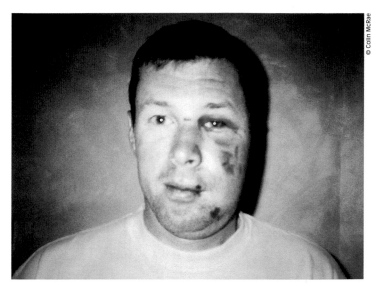

After the accident that could have killed me, Corsica 2000.
But I was still determined to be in the car for the next rally.

Let's Go

Alison, Hollie and I in Majorca, where we are renovating our holiday home.

or four kilometre drive. I did wonder about halfway down the line what would happen if a train came along as we were never going to be able to reverse back to the crossing in time. So we charged on and made it to the crossing near the hotel – and didn't run out of fuel. I figured we'd been highly responsible, not driving on the road after having a few beers. I'm not sure if you can be done for driving on a railway track, though!

We've had some fun pranks and parties down the years and there have always been girls throwing themselves around. But I've grown out of that. Honest! I'm old and sensible now. I leave it to the young guys. I'm still game for a laugh, though. I like to test the nerve of the Press and PR people by pulling the handbrake on when we are being driven from a function. Carlos went berserk when I almost put us into a wall, but Francois thought it was hilarious. I'm always up for a prank or a bit of fun.

There is a tendency in modern sport to be too stuffy about this sort of thing, but I believe that as long as you know when it's time to work and you don't allow your fun to affect the job, then it's good for everybody to enjoy their play. I'm not talking about binge drinking and I certainly don't know of any drug-taking – recreational or performance-enhancing. The authorities have introduced random drug tests for drivers so it wouldn't be too smart to get into either variety. What I'm talking about is acceptable recreation, normal social behaviour. We're human beings here, not robots. We all need to let go every now and again. If you allow people to have fun it builds team spirit and actually helps produce results.

I've been lucky in my World Championship career that I've worked with two outstanding teams. Both are excellent at their jobs, very professional, very committed. But both also create an environment and atmosphere you want around you. Without teams like these you cannot hope to be a successful driver.

Centre Stage

Rallying has undergone dramatic changes and made huge strides since I first competed regularly in the World Championship, yet I believe the most significant breakthrough is just around the corner. The reorganisation and packaging of the sport will, I am confident, turn world rallying into a far bigger, more popular television spectacle in the coming years. I am not saying it will challenge Formula One for prominence, but I am sure that as we tap the full potential of rallying it will become much more than a fringe show.

David Richards, my old boss at Subaru, has taken on the responsibility of exploiting and expanding the commercial possibilities of the Championship and, knowing DR as I do, I have little doubt he will be successful. He is chairman of International Sports-world Communicators, who own the television rights to world rallying, and is striving to raise the profile of our sport. To that end he has given Channel 4 a three-year contract, starting in 2002, to broadcast every round of the Championship in the UK.

Terrestrial TV coverage is vital to reach the whole population and ensure maximum exposure. We don't have Eurosport at home so Alison, for one, is delighted with the deal. Channel 4 are committed to producing comprehensive programmes after each leg of a rally and there are also plans for live transmission at the closing stages, on Sunday afternoons. Some of the camera shots we have already are outstanding and the intention is to extend and further improve the service. I feel that as more people tune in and watch the rallies regularly they will appreciate what we have to offer.

I think many sports fans still don't fully understand rallying. Hopefully we shall be able to reach a wider audience and viewers will get into the routine of following world rallying in the way they follow Formula One. That is why we had to standardise events and generally make our sport more compact, more media and television friendly. There's not much point in having this great show if the public don't know about it.

In my opinion rallying is much more exciting than Formula One. In fact, I find Formula One can be pretty boring. I watch it now and then but I wouldn't go out of my way to watch it. I definitely wouldn't get up in the middle of the night to tune in to a Grand Prix. That doesn't mean to say I don't appreciate the ability of the top drivers. You have got to admire a guy like Michael Schumacher. He does things the others can't. He is out on his own and what he has achieved in racing is staggering.

My feeling is that Formula One has its mass

appeal not because of what it is but because of what is made of it. It has developed this amazing profile and stature, and in turn its appeal, because of one man – Bernie Ecclestone. Bernie took hold of Grand Prix racing, packaged it and marketed it. He has made it the mega-business it is today. Rallying has had no-one to do that for it – until now. If DR can't do it then I don't think anyone can. I'm sure he's the man for the job and that this could be the start of something truly special.

As rallying gets bigger the commercial opportunities for all concerned will increase. Again, we have seen that in Formula One. Bernie has obviously done very well for himself but right through Formula One people are reaping the financial rewards of the sport's success. It's not just the leading drivers who have cashed in. The team managers and key personnel have also made fortunes. And why shouldn't they? Formula One generates enormous wealth and the people who deliver deserve their share.

In rallying I am referred to as something of a trail-blazer for the drivers in terms of salary, and if that is so then I am proud of the fact. I negotiated a new contract with Ford worth £5m for 2001. Is such a sum for a rally driver, a Grand Prix driver or any sportsman justified? I accept there are strong arguments against. But all sport at the highest level now is big business and Ford would not pay me as much as they do unless they were convinced my services were worth the price. Michael Schumacher has extended his contract with Ferrari until the end of 2004 and his salary is estimated at anything up to £25m a year. Is he

worth it? Ferrari clearly believe so. If my col-
leagues in rallying can negotiate for themselves
better deals on the back of my contract then good
luck to them.

The downside of making rallying more popular
and drivers more famous is the likelihood that our
privacy will be invaded far more than it is at
present. I prefer a quiet life away from the events.
I'm not one for the fuss and clamour of so-called
'stardom'. I honestly don't know how Schumacher
puts up with the attention he gets. Sure, he is paid
astronomical figures, but his life must be a
nightmare. I get recognised quite frequently but I
can at least go out and live more or less a normal
life. Schumacher has no chance. I couldn't cope
with that. By the time rallying really takes off I'll
probably be out of it, anyway.

Money brings pressures. The more money
manufacturers and sponsors put into the sport the
more they are going to want to take out, and
ultimately the responsibility for delivering rests
with the drivers. We are under ever increasing
pressure to get to the end of the rally and register
a result. Only when we have done that can we
relax and enjoy the achievement. It is definitely
harder from that point of view than it was 10 years
ago. The cars are just as much fun to drive and
when I am on a fast, flowing rally, such as in New
Zealand or Finland, I still get the buzz and
excitement that drew me to rallying in the first
place. It's the pressures from outside that are
difficult to bear.

The cars themselves have changed, of course,
and a lot of the frustration a driver has to endure

stems from the technology. As a driver I would prefer this technical trend to level off. The cars are still a challenge to drive and very responsive and I hope that is how they will remain.

One of the strengths of rallying is the depth of the competition. At the start of a season we have six or seven drivers with genuine prospects of winning the Championship. That number is inevitably whittled down during the year but any individual rally remains an open and unpredictable contest. In Formula One you can be almost certain at the start of the season that the Championship will be fought out by two or three drivers, and so it proved again in 2001.

But just as rallying can learn a lot from Formula One's commercial enterprise, so we can follow their example on safety.

The formation of the World Rally Championship Commission, under the chairmanship of Max Mosley, the president of the FIA, is a positive and welcome development. Perhaps we may now also confront the issue of safety as effectively as Formula One has. Max has concentrated a lot of his efforts to implement the best possible precautions for drivers and spectators in Grand Prix racing. He has introduced a policy of 'zero tolerance' in his campaign to eliminate fatal accidents and we must have the same level of commitment to that end in rallying. Max entrusts much of that work in Formula One to Professor Sid Watkins, president of the FIA's Research, Safety and Medical Commissions. We need a Sid Watkins in rallying.

It is imperative that we have a standard safety

team and medical back-up team on all the rallies. There have been a lot of discussions and good intentions expressed, but it is taking a long time to actually put things in place. The FIA have appointed a full-time medic, which is a step in the right direction. But we are still relying on each individual country to supply the safety and medical teams, and standards around the world vary greatly. For example, the emergency services and equipment – the helicopters, ambulances and so on – in Argentina are not up to the level of the safety measures and medical expertise in Britain. Australia were the first to introduce a proper emergency service and they set the standard. Unfortunately, not every country has responded satisfactorily.

The emergency button introduced in the cars following my accident in Corsica is another case in point. It's a great idea and, you would think, a very simple, straightforward mechanism. The trouble is that the teams can't decide how it should work and every organiser has slightly different technology. So we are still waiting for an effective emergency response system to be put in place. It is very annoying and frustrating for the drivers because these are the things that should be sorted out as a matter of priority. Costs should not come into it.

Max will be aware of these problems and the fact that they are not easy to unravel because we have so many manufacturers. There are people involved in the decision-making process who have no direct links or concerns with rallying and frankly don't understand it. If we are to get things done and moving smoothly we need a small working group of experts, people who do understand rallying and appreciate what is required.

To a certain extent we drivers don't help ourselves. We have never got together and formed an association, as Grand Prix drivers have, so we don't have a strong enough voice within the sport. This is something else that has been talked about over the years but nothing has come of all the hot air. The feeling of the drivers is that no-one among us has the time necessary to run an association. If we did decide to go down that road it would have to be run by a former driver, someone who did have the time to devote to the job and do it properly.

Even then, I'm not sure how much power and influence we would have. When you see how difficult it is to get things done through the recognised channels it makes you suspect we would have little affect. We have to rely on the manufacturers, the guys who have direct contact with us, and hope that if we pull in the same direction we will achieve the changes we seek.

The Rally Commission has also had to address matters such as the number of cars and events manufacturers should be required to enter. The sensible trend is towards standardising our sport so that the public can understand it and therefore feel more inclined to follow it. Yet again, they are going to compare our sport with Formula One, where every team has two cars for all 17 Grands Prix. It's simple and fair. We are thankfully heading in the same direction, except that in our World Championship the move is towards three-car teams, with manufacturers entering all the rallies.

In 2001 we had a situation where Citroën came in planning to compete in only four rallies. They were able to concentrate their resources – time, money and effort – on those events while the rest of us were committed to the full season. It is clearly not fair that a manufacturer can enter the sport at this level on those terms. No-one should have been amazed they were so quick in Catalunya. It wasn't surprising, either, that the other manufacturers declared they weren't prepared to sit back and let newcomers step in and beat them. Imagine how galling that scenario was for Malcolm when he was right on the limit of his budget, trying to give us the best possible chance of winning the Championship.

The only way it can be acceptable for a new team to come in with a limited programme is on the understanding that they cannot score points. In fairness to the likes of Citroën, they have to run the car in events to find out what it is like to compete at Championship level. You can do all the testing and planning you wish but it still doesn't prepare the driver or the team for the real thing.

Another contentious subject is the running order of cars on a rally. This was raked up again at the 2001 Cyprus Rally, where I deliberately slowed at the end of the second day to make sure I wasn't first on the road the following morning. That dubious distinction passed to Richard Burns, who knew he was going to act as road-sweeper on the loose gravel. Cars lower down the order would benefit because the roads would be cleaner, they would have more grip and consequently be able to go faster.

Richard's fears – and my expectations – were confirmed on the Sunday when I went into the lead and eventually won the rally. Richard was none too pleased and had a good old moan about it. In fact, he was a surprisingly sore loser. Richard had taken advantage of the rules previously and he admitted he would have done so again had he been in my position. Of course you shouldn't be penalised for being the quickest, but everybody knows the rules and there is a case for arguing that the opportunity to take advantage of those rules brings another intriguing element into the contest.

We are always coming up with possible solutions to the problem and various ways, such as reversing the top six, have been tried. So far, though, we have yet to come up with something that is acceptable to everybody. I think the only fair way is to run the manufacturers' cars in reverse order, but then if you are the last manufacturer you are going to suffer even more and you are not going to approve. Another proposal, to run the last 20 cars first, exposes you to the risk of having one of them break down in the stage and hold up the leaders. It's a real problem and there are no simple answers.

Casualties of the streamlining in World Championship rallying are the amateurs and privateers, the posse of drivers who bring their own cars and their chums along, and spend their own money and use up their holidays to live out their dreams by competing in the same event as the best. The guys – and women – at the back of the field have put the romance in the sport. But hard decisions have had to be made as the sport gears up for the new era and entry lists are due to be limited to 90.

In a sense it is a shame because the amateurs have certainly enhanced the atmosphere of rallies down the years. And for the young amateur hoping to make it in rallying this was always a great opportunity to aim for. But I'm afraid that the increasingly heavy Championship schedule meant this move was inevitable. On the positive side I think there may in future be more opportunities for ambitious young drivers in national championships. If these championships become stronger then, in the long term, rallying and aspiring rally drivers will benefit.

The FIA Super 1600 Championship which takes place over six World Championship rallies is a case in point, providing a showcase in front of the main manufacturers. Many of the drivers will tell you we already have too many rallies now, especially with testing between events. But there are moves to increase the number from 14 to 16. I would rather have 14 or even 16 rallies in their new, shorter, more compact format than seven of the old variety, travelling up and down the country. It may have been more fun and captured the spirit of adventure, but if I'd started a season in the good old days with four blanks, as I did 2001, I would have been screwed. That would have left me with only three or four rallies to catch up, which couldn't have been done.

The 14 rallies we have had for the last couple of years provide a mixed bag of conditions and challenges. The variety is an important ingredient. The broad division between gravel and tarmac events doesn't reflect the many different demands we face through the Championship year. Some gravel surfaces are little more than dust, others are car-wrecking rocks and boulders. We have to compete in searing heat and the deep freeze of Sweden. Some rallies I love, others I don't so much, others again I loathe. Well, one of them, anyway. Here, therefore are my opinions and ratings of the 14 rallies that made up the 2001 World Championship:-

Monte Carlo

This, you will have guessed, is the one that claims my 'loathe' ranking all to itself. It is the safety aspect of this rally that gets to me every time we go there. I appreciate that, just like the Monaco Grand Prix, it has a long history and a much-vaunted tradition; that manufacturers and sponsors value it as a shop window and wish to retain it. The Formula One drivers say Monaco would never be allowed in now, as a new Grand Prix, yet their race is a hell of a lot safer than our rally. Years ago the Monte Carlo Rally was a gentleman's jaunt, but now it is a professional event and we are expected to drive for victory. You aren't supposed to back off, no matter how dangerous it is.

That is what I cannot accept and do not agree with, no matter how much tradition it has. Tradition is no consolation if you have an accident. You are expected to drive in conditions that are not suitable for competition. Not with the specification of car and tyre we have. These are tarmac mountain roads, with a rock face on one side and a drop on the other, similar to the roads in Corsica. The difference on the Monte is that the dry surface gives way to snow and ice, and we come down that mountain road on a tarmac tyre. It's like asking Michael Schumacher and David Coulthard to race on a snow-covered race track. It just wouldn't happen.

Spectators like to make life even more difficult for drivers by throwing and shovelling snow onto the road. I know it's great fun for fans to have snowball fights up on the Col du Turini, the Italians on one side, the French on the other. The atmosphere is brilliant and, especially at night, with the floodlights on and fireworks going off, this has been one of the great theatres in sport, let alone one of THE stages in world rallying. But spectators will naturally congregate in places where there is likely to be some excitement – in other words where there is danger. And the conditions here are dangerous.

I've never gone off at Turini because I know what to expect and I respect it, but that doesn't make it easy or enjoyable. When I sit on the start line I do not look forward to it because I know I cannot be in control. I was happy we didn't have to go through Turini in darkness the last time. From a safety point of view Monte simply doesn't come up to standard. The scenery is stunning but these mountains are for skiers, not rally drivers.

My rating: 1 out of 10.

Sweden

Now when you go to Sweden you want snow. It is the one true winter rally, with temperatures falling below −20°C. A couple of times recently we haven't had so much snow, which has made tyre choice a bit of a lottery and taken some of the character from the event. But in 2001 there was plenty of the white stuff, making conditions perfect, and when conditions are perfect in Sweden, you are ensured some of the most enjoyable driving you can get in the Championship.

The event is fairly well supported, considering Scandinavia is hardly the most populous corner of the continent. The spectators are generally disciplined and respectful and they are also willing helpers when cars need digging out of the snow banks, as I discovered on the 2001 rally. That's part of the attraction for the punters. The trick, of course, is to use the snow banks to your benefit, but if too many cars lean on them they inevitably weaken and finally give way. They still act as a safety barrier because you tend to plough only halfway into the banks rather than career right off the road. I made my World Championship debut in the Swedish Rally as an 18-year-old so I have a special affinity with it and always enjoy going back there.

My rating: 8 out of 10.

Portugal

As a driving rally it is quite enjoyable because the gravel stages are varied and keep you alert all the way. But then there is another reason for being particularly attentive in Portugal – the spectators.

Crowd problems have long been a hazard on this event. It seems policing and controlling them is beyond the capability of the authorities. You want the fans to turn up and show their support and enthusiasm, but the Portuguese mentality is such that they too often step over the line into the danger zone. They don't only stand on the outside of tricky corners, they sometimes appear on the road itself.

I really don't think there is an answer to a lot of these problems. You certainly can't rely on the police to keep the spectators in check because they are sometimes just as irresponsible. That makes it a difficult one to sort out. You find yourself taking a deep breath and just hoping you don't hit anyone. In 2001 we had the added problem of waterlogged conditions, so it really was a testing weekend for the drivers. For all that, I do find it quite a fun event. The stages are drivers' stages, a lot of them fast and challenging.

My rating: 7 out of 10.

Catalunya

From the first genuine gravel rally, we go to the first dry tarmac rally. It is generally regarded as the best of the asphalt events. Conditions are usually good, although you can have slippery dust to contend with as cars cut the corners on some of the stages. Based at Lloret de Mar, it is a popular rally not only with the Spaniards but also with tourists from abroad, including a contingent of Brits. The Spanish fans, of course, are there to cheer on Carlos and they turn up in their thousands.

Unfortunately, Catalunya is a victim of its own success. The crowds have generally been better controlled in recent years and the event has been more enjoyable for the drivers. A lot of the stages are good and demanding, but it is another event where the spectators can give us grief.

My rating: 7 out of 10.

Argentina

I think Argentina is a great country and the rally is one of my favourites. We are back on gravel for this, the only Championship round in the Americas. The stages are varied, from soft sandy surfaces to unforgiving huge rocks. We climb the foothills of the Andes to a landscape you'd think was the moon. It's early winter when we compete in Argentina and the weather is unpredictable. It can be fine, but it can be foggy, wet and hostile.

You'll not hear many drivers say they don't like driving the Argentina Rally stages. There are fast stages and downright rugged stages. I've had my share of heartaches there over the years so I relished my victory in 2001. The crowds are usually reasonably well behaved, but some of the spectators got out of hand this time. We also had a nasty incident at a service area, where a water truck rushing to a fire hit and seriously injured Skoda's engineering director, and then turned over, smashing into the team's rally cars. The organisers did not handle that situation very well and it is to be hoped they learned from their mistakes.

My rating: 8 out of 10.

Cyprus

From the fast gravel of Argentina we switch to the slow gravel of Cyprus, which replaced China on the calendar a couple of years ago. In fact, it's the slowest rally of all. It is too slow and twisty for my liking with no real rhythm to it. You never feel as though you are really attacking it and because it is so hot, it can be very uncomfortable stuck inside the car for long periods. On other hot rallies you can at least be sure you will have reasonable air flow, but not Cyprus. It played havoc with the heat rash on my hands in 2001. It was too irritating to wear gloves on the final morning!

I had the consolation of winning that rally but I can't count Cyprus as one of the best. The stages are so rough you find yourself compromising to protect your tyres and retain adequate traction. When you can't drive flat out you can never feel totally satisfied. You have to be too cautious. At least we don't have problems with spectators here. They probably find it too hot to stand out on the stages. Most of the visitors are down on the beaches.

My rating: 6 out of 10.

Acropolis

Another rough 'gravel' event, but unlike Cyprus this is one of the classics. The stages can be very rocky and if you are not careful – or lucky – you can have your car broken beyond repair. Our cars are reinforced for the event with extra under-body protection but although it is rugged it is also fast enough to attack. Some of the stretches are very quick and a real test for the drivers.

Heat can also be a problem here so again you have to keep topping up with fluid. But at least the pace ensures you some air flow in the car and it is not as stifling as Cyprus. In every sense I feel much more natural and comfortable in Greece. Any driver is happier when he feels he can have a go at the stages. I've encountered no particular problems with the spectators, either, so all in all one of the better rallies.

My rating: 8 out of 10.

Safari

I really enjoy this middle sector of the season and Safari is, for me, one of the very best. As I have already explained, I'd like to be restored to an extended format without Pace notes, but it still stands on its own with its long, long stretches and, of course, its wildlife. Again it is rough, again it is a potential car-breaker, but the setting and atmosphere in Kenya make it unique. The speed helps counter the heat but you may need a snorkel to survive the water crossings, as we have discovered to our cost.

You have less control over birds and animals and we've had a few interesting close encounters, especially on recces. On one occasion we were nearly hit by an ostrich and on another, we had a zebra on the bonnet of the car. Thankfully there was no blood, though. The best near miss we had was when we ended up under a giraffe. We came around a corner, through a bush and the big fella was just standing there, straddling the road. We stopped right beneath its belly. That was probably the most dangerous situation we've had because if we'd caught one of his legs his body could have dropped on the car and flattened the roof. He just had a look at us and calmly walked off.

We have more problems with spectators than we used to since the event was concentrated around Nairobi. More people come out of town to watch and they can be a little undisciplined. But then different standards apply to different rallies and the authorities seem to turn a blind eye because it is the Safari Rally. It's still one of my favourites and one I firmly believe should keep its place on the calendar.

My rating: 9 out of 10.

Finland

I'm warming to it with every year. In fact, it is another of my favourites. I've always relished those super-fast roads and jumps, but because it is such a specialist event you need the experience and knowledge of the stages to feel comfortable here. That is why the local drivers have dominated the event while the rest of us have struggled to compete, but once you have had the opportunity to cover the stages, as I have in recent years, your confidence grows and you start to attack.

Then you sense you have a chance and begin to enjoy it. And this really is one to enjoy. You get a fantastic buzz when you are driving it well because it is so fast and the jumps are so spectacular. It must be almost as good for the spectators, as the cars launch themselves over the crests. Finns are mad keen on rallying and are as enthusiastic as they are knowledgeable. They don't cause any problems, they just enjoy the show.

My rating: 9 out of 10.

New Zealand

It is not quite as fast as Finland but still quick enough to be one of the great rallies, right up there in the top drawer. This rally has long had a special place in my affections because it was the scene of my first World Championship win. Any win I have to fight for is especially satisfying and that maiden success came after a great battle to the end with Francois, but it is still No. 1 for me because it was my breakthrough win. Returning to New Zealand is always a thrill. I think all the drivers agree this is the kind of event they want to take part in. These are genuine drivers' stages – nice and flowing, stages you can get your teeth into.

Rally people often compare New Zealand with Wales and certainly a lot of the scenery is similar. The weather can be as wet in the middle of the Southern hemisphere winter, as well. When it's dry the gravel tends to be quite loose, so running position can be important. The rally is usually well organised and the crowds well behaved. The folk down here are very sensible and create a good atmosphere.

My rating: 9 out of 10.

San Remo

We return to Europe and tarmac. This rally once gave us a long and spectacular tour of Northern Italy but in 2000 we are restricted to the craggy hills and mountains close to the resort. The organisers have to condense events under the current guidelines but I felt it was a mistake running stages in one direction and then in the opposite direction. It is easier for the organisers and safer for the drivers to re-run the stages in the same direction. We had to drive on dirty lines created by the earlier runs.

The stages can be quite tricky, with some nasty drops, but there are also quicker sections where you can open up and attack. Some of the stages are difficult for the spectators to reach but those who make the effort like to let you know they are there. We have had crowd problems. It is another rally with a long history but I can't pretend I'm wild about it.

My rating: 6 out of 10.

Corsica

We are still on tarmac, still on mountain roads, but here the roads are a lot tighter than they are in San Remo. It is all twists and turns and, as I found out the hard way in the 2000 rally, very hazardous. It is demanding on drivers and tyres, although you can at least push in Corsica. It's not like Cyprus, where your tyres can shred and when that happens you are helpless.

I was inevitably asked how I would feel about going back to Corsica after my accident and the honest answer was: 'No problem'. I genuinely wasn't concerned about that at all. I regarded it as just another event. What happened in 2000 was unfortunate, but these things happen in rallying. If you can't cope with them you should get out. In fact I was actually disappointed to learn that in 2001 we were not going to return to the stage where I went off. I hoped we would do so because I thought that by driving over it again I might remember what happened and why. I felt it might all come back to me.

My rating: 7 out of 10.

Australia

Another excellent event and another of my favourites. It is probably the one you would hold up as the model rally in terms of the organisation and professionalism. Based in Perth, the rally has a great feel about it. The country is great, the people are great and there is a sense of fun and freedom – yet in a safe environment. They are right up to speed on safety measures and you start the rally reassured that if you are involved in a bad accident you are going to get the best treatment and attention.

There are some fast and dangerous stages, and we have had a lucky escape here. Some of the stages aren't brilliant and it is one of the events where drivers have played cat and mouse over the running order. The gravel is like ball-bearings; very slippery and treacherous. If you have someone to clean the road for you, it makes the driving considerably easier. Despite the road surface, this is a hugely enjoyable rally.

My rating: 9 out of 10.

Great Britain

It may surprise some people to learn that my home rally has never been among my favourites.

Of course it's great to drive in front of your own fans and I've produced some of my most inspired performances in Britain. The emotional pull will always be strong and very special to me. The crowds really do lift me. But I believe it would be a far better event for drivers and spectators alike if it was moved to the summer from its current end of season slot in late November. The weather would be better (although you can never be sure in Britain!) and the stages would be quicker and more exciting.

The event became effectively a Welsh rally in 2000 and was confined to south Wales when the route was revised for 2001. Of course it was great fun when we used to go up to places like Kielder and Grizedale and we were all dashing about the country, but we have to face the fact that rallying has changed. The organisers have to follow the guidelines and have little room for manoeuvre. But at least we no longer have the Mickey Mouse stages and there are, make no mistake, some fast and testing stages down in south Wales.

My rating: 8 out of 10.

We keep hearing of countries wanting a place on the Championship calendar and I suspect there will be even greater demand when we move into the new television era. Germany hosted a non-Championship event in July, 2001, and clearly have ambitions. There has been a lot of talk about a rally in the United States and that would have to be widely welcomed. The problem is trying to accommodate more events. It is already a very demanding season with 14 events, not so much from a driver's point of view as the teams', but there is a growing commercial momentum for an increase to 16 rallies. The engineers and mechanics are flat out all the time, working at rallies and tests. Some of them can never be at home.

One or two of the present events have been under threat and I would be delighted to see the back of Monte Carlo, but I'm afraid that I am likely to be disappointed. All that tradition stuff. Portugal may not be safe and there is a suggestion Cyprus could go the way of its predecessor, China. I can understand the commercial lure of the Far East for manufacturers and sponsors, but China didn't really work. I'm not sure many of the locals had a clue what was happening.

Mind you, I was a bit confused the first time I went to China. I was on the Hong Kong to Beijing Rally and we stopped just across the border in China to re-fuel. It was a bit of a ram-shackle place, more like a bomb-site. I needed a pee and someone pointed me in the direction of a wee concrete shed. I walked in and saw about half a dozen Chinese men sitting on the floor reading newspapers. At first I thought this might be the queue for the toilet, but I looked around and realised this WAS the toilet. The Chinese men sitting on the floor reading newspapers had their trousers around their ankles. One guy stood up and there, underneath him, was a wee hole, so I stood over it and aimed. The five Chinese who were left watched my every move. I don't know what they found so interesting. I don't suppose it's often a white man uses their public toilets.

You can't expect luxuries out on the road and

rally drivers and teams don't. We're not pampered like those racing drivers. We're used to being left to our own devices. There is, however, a serious issue as far as organisation is concerned and the bigger rallying becomes the more important it will be for host countries to provide the structure, essential facilities and emergency services. They have to demonstrate they can cope with the modern requirements of our sport. The World Rally Championship is moving forward and standards at events have to keep pace.

Once you start winning rallies you like to win as many different ones as possible and I went into the 2001 season missing five from my CV. I knocked off two more in Argentina and Cyprus, leaving me needing victories at Monte Carlo, Finland and Sweden to complete the set. I have usually gone well in Sweden, I've got closer in Finland and as for the Monte, well, that would be my perfect revenge, wouldn't it?

Home Ground

I have travelled much of the world thanks to my work, which has also given me the means to buy just about everything I've ever wanted and more. I have a plane, a helicopter, a boat, and a number of cars and bikes. I am officially a resident of Monaco, where we have an apartment. We are in the process of converting a monastery into a holiday home in Majorca and we regularly ski in the Swiss resort of Verbier. But home for us is still Lanark and we plan to return officially in time for Hollie to start school in Scotland. That will definitely cost me in terms of tax, but it's a price worth paying.

With our second child due in December, 2001, we're keen to get settled again near our roots. Alison feels it's particularly important for children to be brought up with the family around them and Hollie's grandparents, aunts, uncles and cousins are all in and around Lanark. My parents, brothers and relatives are here as well.

I had thought we might stay in Majorca for

another two or three years so that Hollie could learn Spanish and make some friends over there, but then it's easy for me to come up with bright ideas like that – I'm not around most of the time. Alison would be stuck there on her own and although we do have friends there, it's not the same as having just about all your family within a 10 to 15 mile radius.

The only other option Alison would have considered was Canada. She's had a thing about the place ever since she went over there in 1994. She likes the big, wide-open spaces. It's the cowboy thing – and the farmer in her. I suppose she sees many similarities to Scotland but it has to be Scotland. We're proud of our country but it's not just that, it's our home and it is where we most want to be for the rest of our lives.

So now we're organising our house in Lanark for when it really is home and there will be four of us. Alison has already thrown me out of the room I used as my gym because she wants to turn it into a nursery. I'm having a new gym built in one of the outbuildings, which was the byre, and once that is finished all Hollie's stuff, which has been cluttering the house, will be moved into the nursery. No doubt there will soon be twice as much to cram in there.

We took over the house in Lanark in 1997. It used to be a dairy and we figured it had plenty of potential that we could develop. We've had the builders in ever since we've been there and needless to say the work is still not finished. We have plenty of land around us and yet we're only a mile from the town centre, so we feel it's the ideal location. Hollie's pony, Betsy, has a paddock that she normally shares with Alison's horse, Reilly, but he's been in livery since we discovered Alison was pregnant again and wouldn't be able to ride until after the birth. Hollie had been asking for some time whether we were going to have a baby and when we told her she would be having a wee brother or sister she was very excited.

I've turned another part of our land into a small track where Alister, one or two friends and I buzz around on quads. We've set up a few jumps to make it more interesting and challenging. A local farmer isn't so impressed and complains about the noise, but I've never complained about tractors disturbing our peace at the crack of dawn! Yeah, okay, I'm being a bit flippant. I appreciate it's his livelihood, but keeping fit is part of my job and in all seriousness that little track plays an important part in my training programme.

I keep my quads and a collection of bikes in the old byre. A recent addition is a copy of the first bike I ever had, a Honda 75. I got hold of it through a friend who has a bike dealership in New Zealand. Strangely, you tend to find older stuff in good condition in some of the far-flung countries so I asked him if he'd come across one. Sure enough, he had just renovated one, which a friend of his had taken for his son. So I bought another bike out of the shop and swapped it with him. I've also got a nice kart in there which I've had for some time now, but never used it. Ridiculous, I know, but I've just not got round to it.

A section of the byre will be home for my rally

cars. I've got an old Ford and a Talbot Sunbeam. I also had a Metro 6R4, simply because I'd always wanted one, but we had an accident during the renovations and unfortunately it was burnt out. The plan was to paint it up in the colours of my dad's car, but it wasn't to be. Pride of place so far goes to my Championship-winning Subaru. Although I'm not superstitious I hoped the No. 4 would be a lucky omen – that has also been the number of my 2001 Ford Focus. I like to get these old cars out every now and then because they are great to drive.

I'd like to get the Nova because of its significance in my career. I was offered one a few years ago but the guy wanted crazy money for it and it wasn't the original. It had the numberplate but it had been rebuilt. I'm not going to be held to ransom for it. The other one to have in the collection, of course, would be the Championship-winning Focus! I'd also like to get together all my results and photographs of my podium finishes, and any other bits of memorabilia from my career and stick them in there with the cars. Make a display of it. Just for my own satisfaction.

I've had one or two racy road cars but I'm not really into them. I had a Ferrari and got rid of it. I had a Porsche and got rid of that. The trouble is that these cars have to be doing 100 mph before they start working, and you can't do that now unless you take them to a track. But more recently I got a Cobra, and that *is* fun. It is as good as it looks and sounds. I don't have things for show though. It's the same with clothes. I'm not the fussy sort but I will do my own shopping. Alison doesn't buy my gear because, unlike most females, she hates shopping.

I'm not brash and I'm not on an ego trip. If I buy something it's because I genuinely do want it or need it. I have a plane because it makes my professional and private life easier. It is a Cessna Citation, a six–seater. I take it to all the European rallies. If I have to be in the UK for a business appointment or just personal reasons I can fly in early that morning and fly back out at night, without using up one of my 90 permitted nights in the country!

It costs me about £250,000 a year to run the plane, which is a lot of money. Because of where I come from and was brought up to appreciate the value of money it is still hard for me to shell out that sort of sum and at times it still seems so unreal. But I am in the fortunate position of being able to afford it and it is a cost I am prepared to write off. I'm sure there are those who earn £5m a year and quite happily write off £2m or £3m of it. I have to consider that I won't have this sort of income for ever so it is a case of striking a sensible balance between what I spend and what I save.

I certainly feel we should enjoy some of the benefits while we can. A good friend I'd known since I was 16 died of cancer not so long ago and it dealt me a big shock. That can happen to any of us. I had another jolt with the accident in Corsica which could have been the end of it for me. There's no point in having a healthy bank account when you're six feet under. There have been a couple of situations like that and I just thought:

'Sod it, let's do it. Let's get a plane.' I must admit it will be hard to give it up if and when we do have to go back to travelling on scheduled flights.

I haven't got a pilot's licence to fly a plane, though, because I don't have the time to build up the necessary flying hours. I do fly my helicopter, a five-seater Eurocopter 120, which I also have for the convenience. I can fly it to my door. That gives me an excuse to fly the Saltire outside my home instead of a windsock! I got my licence in Majorca after a friend spotted an article about helicopter flying instruction on the island. I rang up and explained to the instructor, Alistair Sutherland, that I had a very tight schedule. I had two weeks at the end of December, 1999, and another couple of weeks at the beginning of January 2000. He said we could manage it so I went over.

I thought I would pick up the actual flying quite quickly and was more worried about the theory. But in fact I found the flying just as hard. It was a real challenge, very different from anything I'd been used to. It's a bit like riding a bike, though, you struggle and struggle and just when you are thinking of giving up, it clicks into place. Suddenly you've got it. Alistair is now the pilot of my plane.

Flying around Majorca gave me the chance to see the island and appreciate how beautiful it is. The package tour boom left the place with a bad reputation. Tacky resorts were thrown up almost overnight, but the northern and western parts of the island are mountainous, spectacular and largely unspoiled. We had a look around at ground level and liked what we saw so decided to sell our place on the Spanish mainland and move over to the island. We have invested in what will be our holiday home. The climate and the atmosphere make it the perfect place to relax. It is also a haven for cyclists, which encourages me to keep on top of my training. We have a boat, which gives us the opportunity to enjoy yet another fantastic view of Majorca from the sea and really get away from it all.

Alison prefers any view from the one she gets from the air. She's not a good flier at the best of times. Hollie thinks mum's natural position on a flight is the crash position. Alison was near hysterical when our plane was hit by lightning. The bolt went straight through the plane and left scorch marks. Who says lightning doesn't strike twice? We were fine, though, and it wasn't a big drama. Planes are made to withstand bolts of lightning.

She was probably in even more of a panic on a helicopter trip we took in Majorca. I suggested we should go for a picnic up in the mountains, which she thought was a great idea. But when we got up there she was terrified. The ground was a bit rough and it was tricky to land the chopper. And then there was the small matter of the 1000 feet drop down the other side of the cliff. I tried to assure Alison it was perfectly safe but she wasn't convinced. She didn't appreciate my idea of a picnic with a difference at all. I think she expected to find the Sheraton up there.

I have to say, though, that she is more adventurous than I am when it comes to property. I had in mind a fully functioning, ready-to-move-in modern place when we were looking for something in Majorca. As Alison tells everyone, I like everything to be in place and in working order, automatic doors and all mod cons. She was keener on a place of character and she's happy to organise the renovation work. At least we won't have the builders working around us there. We'll let them finish the work before we move in.

Our apartment in Monaco is in the block next to David Coulthard's. I quite enjoy the odd week or weekend there but I've never really given myself a chance of settling in. David likes it there and that's fair enough, it obviously suits him. I'm more of a country person. I like space around me and there is none of that in Monaco. I find it very claustrophobic. If David and I are there at the same time we'll meet up for a drink or something but it isn't often that we are there at the same time.

The Stars and Bars, down by the harbour, tends to be the usual drinking hole. I've had one or two skirmishes with the police after having a few in there and playing around on a scooter. I've nearly ended up in the harbour with the police trying to catch me. Mind you, it's pretty easy to give them the slip because they're all on foot. I've got up to mischief and generally gone over the top like that, things that make you cringe the next morning, but it beats a boring life.

I'm beginning to grow up and mature now – but not too much, I hope. I suppose it comes to all of us. Age, experience, maturity – it's a natural process. I sense that change as a person and a driver. I think being a family man also makes a difference. You become more conscious of your responsibilities when you are a father.

I don't think I've ever been the 'rebel' that I was sometimes portrayed as. I am my own man and I'm prepared to stand up for myself. Okay, I've occasionally gone a bit too far messing about, but that's hardly unusual for any guy. Overall I think I've always been fairly level-headed. I am serious when I have to be. I am committed and professional in my work, but I also know when not to be serious. I know when to relax and enjoy myself. I consider myself a regular guy, a normal family man. My life and career have been anything but normal – from run-of-the-mill kid working in the plumbing and heating business to world champion with loads of money and being able to do what I want. I think that would go to the heads of a lot of young sportsmen and change them. But I believe I've managed to remain stable and sensible.

I'm sure it helps knowing who your real friends are. We have a close circle of friends and relations who would be as close to us no matter who I was, what I did or how much I earned. I don't really have a problem with hangers on. I'm pretty good at spotting them a mile away. Some people love being recognised. I don't. I'm quite a private person and prefer to be left in peace with my family and friends. When we're in Lanark I can go down to the pub with Alister and friends for a drink, or out with Alison for a meal and not be bothered. I don't want to talk about motor sport. Generally people respect the fact that you have a private life and even if they come up for an autograph they'll thank you and disappear. It can be more of a nuisance around rally time. You become aware that people are looking at you. Then they'll not only come up for an autograph but also start asking you about the rally. The odd one will cling on to you to the point where you have to be rude to them to get the message across. There's always a time and a place for everything.

I was sitting with the family one afternoon in Majorca and I could see this guy watching us. Sure enough, he came over, started chatting and asked for an autograph. He went away and sat down but a bit later he came back again. This happened four or five times and he kept repeating the same stuff. He'd obviously had a few glasses of wine at lunch and couldn't stop talking. But we just wanted to be left alone so eventually I had to tell him.

When I started to make a breakthrough in rallying there was a hint of envy in Lanark. It's a small community and people knew what I was doing. Everybody thinks that if they had the car they could do just as well and there was a local guy who gave me some hassle on Lanimer Day one year. That was the time I denied I was Colin McRae, and Alison noticed that when I lied my face twitched. But then as you move up another notch in rallying the same people realise there's more to it than having the car and you earn their respect. They don't have a dig at you any more.

I have to accept recognition comes with the territory but what does concern me a little is the effect my fame might have on our children. We want their lives and their environment to be as normal as possible. But we realise that when Hollie starts going to school there is a chance she will be picked on because of who her daddy is. She wouldn't be the first kid to find herself in that position and she will have to learn to cope with it. What we don't want to do is wrap her up in cotton wool.

Alison enjoys horse-riding and she'll be happy if Hollie sticks to four legs rather than wheels. But Hollie does love the bikes and cars. I wouldn't force her in any direction. I'll encourage her in whatever she wants to do. You see a lot of parents pushing their kids and I've seen youngsters being dragged up ski slopes with tears in their eyes. That's not right. If Hollie wanted to be a rally driver and she was truly committed to it then I would support her.

Hollie actually enjoyed her first taste of skiing so she may well take to it. Skiing has become a regular pursuit for the family and our friends, and Verbier has become our regular haunt. Alister and Stuart join us when they can. I first went there in 1993 with a Scot called Colin Morrison, who made his living as a ski instructor, stunt man and anything else he could think of. I spent four seasons with him, training and skiing between rallies.

Colin is also an excellent water-skier. We first met back home in Scotland, on Loch Earn. I was up there on holiday with friends. We were messing about water-skiing and he came over and gave us a few tips. He asked me if I'd ever tried bare-foot skiing. I told him I hadn't and that I didn't believe he could do it, either. So he said he would show us how it was done. He started on a mono-ski and, when the boat got up to speed, he put his bare foot on the water. Then he stepped out of the mono-ski and carried on with both feet on the water. He made it look so easy that he managed to talk me into having a go. I landed straight on my face and knocked myself out. I woke up in the water, floating around. But I stuck at it, despite a lot more spills and bruising, and eventually managed to do it.

Skiing apart, all my sporting interests are of the motorised variety. In the summer of 2001 I got the chance to ride John Crawford's Suzuki superbike around Brands Hatch. That was mind-blowing. It's got to be speed. I've never been into football, for example. In fact, I've never been to a football match in my life. Colin Smith, the guy who navigated for me in the first forest rally I did, the Galloway Hills, in 1985, is still a good friend and he's always on at me to go with him to a match at Motherwell, where he's got an executive box. I'm sure that if I went with Colin and his pals I'd end up getting smashed with the rest of them and not even see the football. That sounds okay by me, but I'd actually like to be in among the crowd and savour the atmosphere. I'll do it one day. Definitely.

As a Scotsman I suppose I ought to be a golfer but I play, at the most, once a year. I've never played it seriously and it's a game you can't expect to master unless you play it regularly. I'm not one for going to sporting events. I went to a Grand Prix at Silverstone when I was about 15 and haven't been to one since. When I have time off I prefer to chill out, doing the things I'm familiar with and enjoy doing, rather than looking for something new.

I would get very frustrated trying to do something and not being able to do it well. That's why I could never get into politics, even politics within the sport. I don't have the patience to tackle it. I'd need to understand all the angles and I know that's not likely, so it doesn't really interest me. While I am still competing I don't want to get involved in too many other things. The computer game is fine because it doesn't take up too much of my time and distract me from my driving.

A lot of people who have made a lot of money doing something they know and are good at, then get involved in things they don't understand and lose a lot of money. I don't want to get myself into that situation. By the time I finish driving, financial concerns shouldn't be an issue. I have money invested in the right places so I feel comfortable that we have the security we need. If I do get involved in anything it has to be something I enjoy. I am fortunate I am in a position to make that a condition.

When I've really got time on my hands, perhaps on a long flight or relaxing in Majorca, I quite like reading biographies. I'm not an avid reader but recently I read *Mr Nice*, the convicted drug-dealer Howard Marks' book, and I enjoyed that. It's quite funny and entertaining. I read magazines now and then. A bit of lifestyle, things like that, but *Motoring News* is about the only paper I read regularly.

We used to go to the movies quite often when

we were at home all the time, so hopefully we'll get round to seeing a few more films in the future. I don't watch much television and when I do it's usually *Teletubbies* or something like that. My taste in music is pretty varied. I tend to go in for the 'best of' compilations rather than specific tracks. I like blues, rock and roll, that sort of stuff. I'm definitely not a dancer. I'm terrible. No rhythm at all. I need to have had a few beers before I'd even consider stepping onto the dance floor. If it's not a night out with the guys I prefer a civilised evening: good restaurant, nice wine and perhaps a couple of gin and tonics.

My father still manages my financial and general business interests, but I also have a sponsorship manager, Jean-Eric Freudiger. He is Swiss and based near Geneva. I met him through Colin Morrison in Verbier a few years ago and he tried to convince me he could help me. At that stage I didn't think there was much scope for commercial enterprises but he came back to me and now he's working with me.

He negotiated a deal with Tunnock's, who are based in Uddingston, near Glasgow, and produce the best chocolate biscuits not only in Scotland but anywhere in the world! Who said I was a PR man's nightmare? Jean-Eric bumped into Mr Boyd Tunnock in Cyprus in 2000 and made the most of the opportunity. Some of the other things Jean-Eric is working on are long-term projects. One of them could be very significant and involve me personally after I retire from driving. Scott, another personal sponsor, supply me with mountain bikes, clothing and all the other bits and pieces. Ian Hughes, of Scott UK, gives me good advice on the equipment and cycling in general.

I'd like to be more active in charitable causes, although time will always be a limiting factor while I'm competing. However, we have set up a scholarship scheme, in conjunction with Ford and the Royal Scottish Automobile Club, to encourage young Scottish rally drivers. A Puma, supplied by Ford and built through the McRae Scholarship fund, is awarded to the driver, aged up to 25, who has shown most promise in the previous year. Mark Wheeler, from Hamilton, won the scholarship for the 2001 season. He's quick and began with a third place, but unfortunately the year was ruined by the restrictions imposed as a result of the foot-and-mouth outbreak, so we might look at ways of running him again in 2002. I also support Ford's 'Ladder of Opportunity', another initiative to encourage young drivers.

I know it can sound a bit trite when sports men and women say they want to put something back into their sport, but for what it's worth, I would genuinely like to do that. I intend to pursue the scholarship system and give young drivers the prospect of making headway in what can be an expensive sport for a normal family. I know from my own experience what it is like for a youngster trying prove himself and how much I appreciated any assistance I was able to get. If my name can generate the finances required to provide a few more young hopefuls with the equipment and opportunity to chase their dreams, then I will be delighted. That will give me enormous satisfaction. It's the same with the McRae Stages in the

Scottish Championship. We put something into the Coltness Car Club, who run the rally, which was the club I first joined when I set out. They helped me and I've never forgotten that. The 2001 event was another victim of the foot-and-mouth crisis, which probably spared the McRae clan a good deal of embarrassment. It was to have been the day after Alister's wedding so I'm not sure what state we would have been in. Well, I am, and we certainly wouldn't have been fit to drive.

I've always been convinced that Britain has the driving talent out there, but it has to be given a chance to develop. You look at the present World Rally Championship situation and it's terrific for Britain. We've got two drivers in the top bracket and I don't see why Richard Burns and I shouldn't be up there for some time to come. Given the right car, I've absolutely no doubts Alister would be rubbing shoulders with us. But we are not going to be around for ever. It is becoming a younger man's sport and there is the possibility of a vacuum when we have left the scene. So we have to do all we can to make sure we bring through the next generation of potential champions.

For years there hasn't been enough focus on this matter in the UK. I made it through the support I had from my own sponsors and the help of my father. Richard, too, has made it on his own and it is fantastic for the country when the two of us are competing for the World Championship. Until recent times we'd been used to seeing only the Finns up there in numbers. But we have to think about the future of British rallying and do something about it. The problem for me, and for Richard, is that while we are competing there is only so much we can do. What we need is for manufacturers to be more involved and committed.

Perhaps we could extend our scholarship scheme to a junior team, and a proper training school and rally centre. It would provide not only driving facilities and instruction but also cater for the wider aspects of preparation for competition, such as fitness, psychology and so on. That sort of expert coaching and guidance need not necessarily be confined to rallying or motor sport. It could be available to all sports people.

Primarily, though, I would like to put in place a structure that will ensure a flow of gifted young drivers. I'll give my advice and personal help whenever I can, but I don't think I would make the best instructor in the world. I couldn't tell anybody how to drive because for me it has always been instinctive. I can't analyse the way I drive so I can't explain it. I was lucky that I got the chance to express what came naturally.

I can't identify any 'secret' or 'magic formula'. The ability to drive a rally car at speed is something that was in me at a very early age and everything I have done since then has honed the basic skill. You obviously have to have the car control, the feel for the car. On a rally you must also have the alertness of mind and the concentration to take in the co-driver's calls, one, two and even three bends ahead, depending on the stage. You have to be able to react to the changing conditions and circumstances of a rally.

You will also hear people talk about rally drivers being brave, or courageous, or even fearless, and clearly this is no sport for the faint-hearted. You need the nerve to cope with the challenges of the stages and the opposition. But I prefer to call it 'belief' or 'confidence'. Everybody has a certain degree of talent and after that it is the psychological aspect that makes the difference between the winners and the also-rans.

When you have that total belief in your own ability, the confidence that you can pull off the victory, then you will push that bit deeper into a corner and you will brake that little bit later. It enables me to produce the time I need to make the difference in a close finish, or pull out a decisive lead on any given stage. There are certain stages where I know I can really go for it and I will even set out my stall at the start of the day to make, let's say, stage four my main target. If it is a long stage you can obviously take a huge chunk out of your time.

This confident approach is important in any sport. It is not arrogance or disrespect for your opponent, but merely the realisation that you have the ability to get that crucial edge over the next man. There's no better example of a sportsman who is totally positive and certain of his ability than Michael Schumacher. He has absolute belief in himself and that gives him the confidence to achieve what he has achieved.

If I can instil in our young drivers that sort of belief then they will have a far better chance of fulfilling their potential. Of course, they must have the basic talent to start with otherwise they'll get nowhere. But so much of sport at the highest level is in the mind and if I can get that message through to them then they might have a real chance of progressing and making names for themselves. To that extent management does quite appeal to me, but certainly not if it means being stuck in an office looking after bank accounts and the like. I'll be looking to work with manufacturers to establish and sustain a successful scheme for young drivers.

I'll certainly not be bored or a layabout when I retire. I'm looking forward to doing things I've never had time to do, such as little jobs around the house, sorting out this and that, things that have irritated me. The embarrassing part will probably be when Hollie's chums ask her what her daddy does for a living and she says 'nothing'. Mind you, I suspect she'd say that now, if asked. I'm very lucky and I am fully aware of the fact.

One ambition I have is to cycle along the coastline of Scotland and down through the islands of the west coast. It would probably take me about a month and I would love every minute of it. That's one thing I'm definitely going to do. I'm also going to compete in the Scottish six-day trial, a famous event in the motor cycle world, based in Fort William. I've always toyed with the idea of having a go at racing cars. Formula One is not a realistic aim but GT cars did cross my mind. One day I fancy it, the next I don't. I still can't be sure. I'm open to suggestions.

Alison and I have already talked about other things we want to do when I retire, such as buying a wee cottage and a fishing boat in Mull and living a reclusive life. That would be nice. We flew up there not so long ago and you forget just how magnificent the scenery is. I have travelled all over the world and although I haven't actually seen as much as I would have liked I do know nothing will ever beat Scotland for me.

I am asked constantly about when I plan to retire and the honest answer, at the time of writing, is that I don't know. Ideally I would like to quit at the top, as Champion. That would be the perfect way to sign off. But then that might also be the most difficult time to leave it all behind. When you have a car capable of winning the Championship and you are obviously still good enough it is hard to stop. There's nothing like the feeling that you are on top of the world. You want to stay there. Success pushes you on.

Right now I feel I am on top of my game. When you reach a certain level you can't expect to become any quicker, but you learn and fine-tune your driving all the time. Your overall performance can improve with experience and maturity. But what you must have to keep competing at the highest level is the desire and the motivation. I won't be interested in making up the numbers. I wouldn't enjoy it and couldn't take it. I'll be out of the sport before that ever happens. But as long as I have the ability, the hunger, the equipment that is necessary to do the job and the conviction that there is more to achieve, then I shall probably want to continue.

Renewed Challenge

Setbacks and disappointments are occupational hazards and I've learned to cope with them over the years, but making a full recovery from my accident in Corsica proved a less straightforward process than I hoped it would be. The winter testing programme leading up to the 2001 season followed a familiar pattern. The problem was my training schedule. The doctors told me that a full training programme was out of the question because the cheekbone was still fragile and I had to take care to keep my blood pressure under control.

The bad news was that I had to leave my motorbike shut away. Nothing works me harder than riding my motorbike but, for obvious reasons, I simply wasn't allowed to. The not so bad news was that I couldn't go out running either, because the constant jolting would have done my cheekbone no good at all. What a relief. I hate running. I was able to do some weight-training, though not as much as usual.

Fortunately I'm naturally fairly slim (I certainly don't remember being a Billy Bunter, mum!) so there was no real danger of my putting on weight. You would have to be pretty undisciplined – and stupid – to let yourself go. Gradually, through the year, I was able to build up the training routine again. I'd done quite a bit of cycling and some skiing, which was probably the best and most strenuous exercise I had during the early part of the year. The altitude also helps the conditioning. I was allowed back onto a motorbike by the spring, although the restrictions imposed because of the foot-and-mouth outbreak kept me grounded a little longer in Lanark.

I did manage to banish a few post-2000 Championship frustrations by winning the 'Race of Masters' rallysprint in Madrid, ahead of my Ford team-mate, Carlos. He didn't even bother asking me to let him win this time. For both of us the World Championship was the real objective and we had another experienced driver on board for 2001, Frenchman Francois Delecour. He was released by Peugeot and Ford stepped in to offer him a drive. Malcolm felt he could strengthen our line-up and give us some useful feedback from developments at his previous teams.

Testing was encouraging. The Focus had been further improved and refined in the on-going pursuit of better performance and reliability. Perhaps the most significant difference was in the engine. That was a definite step forward. We also had new tyres, switching to Pirelli. It tends to be a case of swings and roundabouts with tyres. On some rallies a certain tyre company will have the upper hand, on others their rivals have the advantage. Our early testing on Pirelli rubber gave us a clear direction and cause for optimism.

Tyre choice is absolutely vital at Monte Carlo, the event which again opened the new season. Despite my well-documented hatred of the Monte Carlo, it is a rally I have always dearly wanted to win – because it is Monte Carlo! The conditions that make it a spectacle for the public are the very conditions that make it a nightmare for drivers. Conditions on a stage can change dramatically from dry to wet to snow and ice. It can be very unnerving to have to negotiate snow and ice on a tyre better suited to dry tarmac but if you want to be competitive and have a chance of winning you must choose the quickest option, and the quickest option isn't always the safest.

Peugeot were wiped out by the end of the third stage and when we set fastest time on the next stage we found ourselves leading the rally. Carlos and Francois also recorded fastest stage times on the first leg, giving Ford three drivers in the top six at the end of that day. But my closest challenger was Tommi Makinen, in a supposedly out-dated Mitsubishi. He was due to have a new car in the autumn and a lot of people wrote off his chances for 2001. You do that at your peril. Tommi is such a resourceful driver and Mitsubishi had made a big effort to breathe new life into the old Lancer.

Carlos was his usual consistent self, running in third place, but it was clear that, given reliability, we were going to be fighting Tommi for victory. We were quite cautious on the second day, although we put in a fast stage time right at the end to give us a slender overnight lead. It was all set up for a classic last day battle.

I have to admit I wasn't particularly looking forward to it. We had been waiting for a straight fight to the finish, where neither of us had a problem, and it seemed this was to be THE one. But for me it was on THE worst rally possible. As I have already explained, Tommi is the opponent I most admire and respect. Had it been Carlos, or Francois, or even Richard in that situation I would have been confident of winning. But it was Tommi and I certainly wasn't super-confident I could beat him. Not at Monte Carlo.

It would have given me great satisfaction to beat Tommi, fair and square, on that final day of the Monte and that was my aim. At the same time I didn't want to push too hard and have an accident. Second place would still have been a good result there and given me some early season momentum.

The various scenarios were going through my head before we set out on the morning's first stage, the famous Col du Turini, but it soon became academic, anyway when about five kilometres into the stage, we spun on a slippery corner. But we kept going and lost only a few seconds, so I wasn't too concerned. Then we came into a hairpin – which was probably only half a kilometre up the road from where our engine blew the previous year – and the car spun again. There was no throttle response, which explained why it spun. I couldn't fire it up and get the throttle to work.

The motor which governs the fly-by-wire

throttle system had failed, so I followed the normal procedure in such circumstances. You put it on to a manual cable and re-set the ignition, put the failsafe on and it jams the throttle open. There's a switch in the bottom of the throttle pedal so you push the pedal right to the floor, hit the switch and the engine goes on, flat out. Eventually it started up and we could have driven through another stage like that. We would have been losing time, but there are occasions when you have to compromise and we could still have come away with third place.

Unfortunately, although the system had been checked on the rig, it hadn't been run for a prolonged period of time in the manual situation. With the switch on and the current that was going through the whole system, the electrical motor that runs the fly-by-wire just melted. It stopped altogether and that was it.

The TV cameras caught my frustration as I realised our rally was over. I tried to shut the car bonnet and resorted to kicking the thing. I wasn't exactly doing a Basil Fawlty on it but I couldn't get the bonnet over the pin so finesse wasn't going to be much use. I gave it a bit of boot to get it closed. I just couldn't believe what had happened. The performance was encouraging, no doubt about that, but it was the same old story. So many times we had been in the lead, or at least close to the lead, only for something to go wrong.

Carlos and Francois finished second and third respectively, giving Ford a good return from the first rally, but it might have been so much better for the team – and especially for me. Tommi was able to complete his third consecutive Monte victory without any pressure and put down his Championship marker. At least I had the consolation of knowing that Marcus and Richard had also left the event empty-handed, but it is difficult to look on the bright side when you suffer a hammer blow like that.

I felt better when we arrived in Sweden. The conditions were perfect for the first time in possibly 10 years. The snowbanks were really high, which is what you want on this rally. The trick is to use the banks to take the corners faster. As you exit a corner you bounce the back of the car off the snowbank, which lines you up for the straight. But because everything seemed so perfect, I was leaning on the snowbanks quite hard, which proved my undoing.

We were running down the order on the road and everybody ahead of us had been nibbling a bit out of the banks. That meant we were getting deeper into the ever thinning and weakening banks. On the third stage we went into a third gear right hander and hit the bank too hard. The back of the car broke through the bank and pulled the front in. The only thing you can do in that situation is keep it flat out and hope the car will plough through the snow. For a moment we thought we were heading back onto the road and Nicky and I had a sense of relief. But then we started slipping down again. The ditch seemed to get deeper and we were buried. My mistake had really dropped us in it and now we had to try and get out again.

You literally have to try and dig yourselves out

with your hands. There were quite a few willing spectators at that corner so we had plenty of help and eventually we managed to lift the car out. We'd lost five and a half minutes and knew the win was gone which was a severe disappointment as we had been in with a shout there. On the previous stage we'd passed Richard stuck in a snowbank and he lost far more time. I remembered almost feeling sorry for him because that is the worst thing that could happen to you. You've got a car that's absolutely perfect and there you are, stuck in a snowbank. And then on the very next stage it happened to us. Richard probably didn't feel quite so bad when he saw I'd done the same thing.

All we could do after that was try to make up as much ground as possible and hope others dropped out. It was a long shot to get among the points but we had nothing to lose. If nothing else, we were going to enjoy ourselves. We reeled off seven fastest stage times on the trot and reached the end of the second leg in 11th place. But even though we were going so well and beating everybody, we calculated that we were too far behind to finish in the top six and score our first point of the year. As it turned out, our final position was ninth, which at least earned Ford a couple of points in the manufacturers' standings.

Richard went on a similar charge on the last day but he had even less chance of making the points in the drivers' Championship. Marcus retired with engine trouble so three of the pre-season favourites still hadn't appeared on the scoreboard. We were all grateful that Tommi, launching a last-stage attack on Peugeot's Harri Rovanpera, pushed too hard and crashed out of the rally. Harri, another driver off Finland's production line, had his first WRC win, ahead of Thomas Radstrom and Carlos.

With Tommi, Carlos and Harri all on 10 points I didn't feel too uncomfortable about the Championship situation. No-one had got away and a win from the next rally could even have given me a share of the lead in the chase for the title. Since that next rally was Portugal, the first 'normal' event after the specialist tests of Monte Carlo and Sweden, it was generally regarded as the first true pointer to the season. We were confident about our prospects on gravel and I thought I was due a change of fortune.

No such luck – it was a nightmare right from the recce. We were told it had rained in the area for five months before we arrived and it never stopped while we were there. We managed to do the recce but the conditions on the stages were so severe because of the rain, that it was obvious to everyone that the rally was going to be horrendous. The stages are quite soft and sandy so they were just washed away by the rain.

Even on the start line of the first stage the sump guard was sitting on the ground and of course every car that goes through digs a rut of about two to three inches. I think they got to about car 15 before cars were getting stuck. They simply couldn't drive on the road. Our car felt more like a sledge on the mud. Four stages were cancelled but many drivers and team members reckoned the rally should have been abandoned. There were complaints that the stages were not only ridiculously difficult but actually dangerous. The rally was reduced to a farce because anyone running down the order had no chance of winning.

Nicky came up with a plan for a revised route after the recce. We knew which stages were going to be impossible to drive second time around so he suggested to the organisers that they should cancel certain stages and shorten others. It was a sensible solution and I'm sure it would have worked, but the organisers wanted to run the whole rally and were unwilling to make any changes. In the end they realised they had to drop stages, anyway. Had they made the kind of changes Nicky suggested in the first place I'm sure they would have salvaged more credibility with the FIA. Instead it wasn't a competition, it was a struggle for survival. That's the worst I've ever encountered. It was worse than Safari. The Safari Rally can be very bad but you know it's going to be very bad for everybody. Portugal 2001 got progressively worse for every car that drove onto the stage.

We knew we would lose time on the leader with every stage but just hoped we could climb up the order on the first day and give ourselves a chance of salvaging something from the rally. We drove tactically, taking no unnecessary risks and concentrating on keeping out of trouble. Late on the first day we were reasonably satisfied to be in seventh place and felt we would be able to improve our position on the second leg. Unfortunately, we didn't have the opportunity. A kilometre from the end of stage eight the engine stopped and our rally was over. We were only a couple of corners on from where we had retired the year before.

The team were very apologetic but it's not apologies you need in those circumstances. I couldn't help thinking: 'It always happens to me.' But considering all that had happened, I thought I was pretty easy on the team. Everybody was trying their best, nobody had slackened in any way. I just radioed them to tell them what had happened and asked them to send a car for us. Mind you, I suspect my body language left them in no doubt just how hacked off I was feeling.

Tommi had another win, Carlos second place, and Marcus and Richard picked up their first points of the season. I was still stranded. It had been a desperate start to the season.

Catalunya was next and having won there the previous year we were reasonably hopeful. It had to get better for us on this one. Wrong again. The only thing that was better was the weather. We were off the pace, largely because our tyres were not suited to the roads, and it was clear to us we had problems on tarmac. Everything seemed okay in testing but it's only when you get to the first event on a surface of that type that you face reality.

We were seventh by stage five, despite the sluggish response of the engine, and then on the road section it started misfiring badly. The car kept cutting out and we had to retire with a fuel pump failure. Four rallies into the 2001 Championship and I was on zero! The new

Citroëns, due to appear only four times in the year, showed ominous pace before dropping out. Didier Auriol took the victory, ahead of his Peugeot team-mate, Gilles Panizzi. Tommi's third place lifted him six points ahead of Carlos, who was fifth on the event.

I didn't need to be told my Championship chances were in danger of being washed down the drain, but I had no thoughts of throwing in the towel, even if I made no secret of my dismay. You can mutter things about 'giving up on the year' when you're down because you are only human. Some people interpreted that as meaning I'd had enough of Ford, but I had no intention of leaving. I'm not a quitter and I wasn't giving up on the Championship. There were still plenty of points to play for. We had work to do to improve our performances on tarmac, but coming up were rough gravel events where we expected to excel. I had to take advantage of them and start banking some results.

On the face of it Argentina is a rally where I ought to go well but the record books showed I had never won there. I had always been confident I could win the rally because I knew the speed was there, but we'd always run into problems. There was a build-up of frustration and anger inside me. I'd had enough of it, so I really went into the rally this time with a do or die approach.

I made my intentions clear with fastest times on the two superspecial runs and I kept my foot down through the first full day. We reached service on that Friday morning 39 seconds ahead of Carlos. I honestly couldn't believe how quick we were. We were fastest on six of the first leg's eight stages, setting record times on three of them, and reached the overnight halt with a 41.4 seconds lead over Richard. Carlos, who had a back problem, was third and Tommi fourth.

I would have been satisfied with a top three placing going into the second leg but our performance from the start had been fantastic. We had the cushion to be a bit more cautious, which is always handy when you are first on the stage. Those roads are very tricky in places and I had experienced too many mishaps over the previous months to feel we couldn't be caught out yet again.

There was no way I could have relaxed, though. Richard made sure of that. I just tried to keep the gap more or less constant and pushed when I felt I had to. Richard and I traded fastest times and no-one else was near us. I was quickest on two of the stages and second quickest on four of the other five. I ended the day still 37 seconds clear of Richard.

Our only real concern was when we encountered spectators on the road near the end of a stage, but that was nothing compared with the terrible ordeal of the Skoda camp. An out-of-control barbeque had apparently set alight a number of spectator cars and a volunteer fire engine was on its way to the scene, when it turned over at a service area. Skoda's chief engineer, Jens Pohlmann, was struck by the truck and seriously injured. The vehicle hit the team's two parked rally cars, but fortunately the drivers, Bruno Thiry and Armin Schwarz, and their co-drivers were unhurt.

The final leg of Rally Argentina was the shortest, with six stages, but the last two, Guilio Cesare and El Condor, were among the rockiest and most demanding in the Championship. So I was determined to make sure we retained a healthy lead and wouldn't have to drive too hard on those two stages to clinch the win.

We were a little too cautious on the first stage of that final morning and Richard, predictably, was intent on applying as much pressure as he could. He nibbled away at our lead and I sensed a little nervousness in our camp at the final service, but we were pretty much in control and set the fastest times on the last two stages to confirm our victory. We had been quickest on 10 of the 21 stages and won by 26.9 seconds. Richard had been there to the end, which made the win all the more satisfying.

Nicky and I shook hands as we crossed the line and, delighted though we were to have pulled off such a good and convincing victory, the feeling we shared above all was one of relief. After the wretched run we'd had, all the problems and heartaches of the previous 11 months, we desperately needed that. You could see the lift it gave the team, too. Everybody had suffered. All the team enjoyed their Sunday night celebration. We'd earned it.

The Championship table suddenly didn't make such depressing reading. Tommi, who was fourth in Argentina, still led the way, with 27 points, Carlos was second on 22 and I joined Harri and Didier in third spot with my 10. We hoped it was the start of our Championship challenge but clearly had to follow up that breakthrough with a few more good results to put us right back on track. Coming up next were three rough gravel rallies that reinforced our confidence: Cyprus, Acropolis and Safari. I figured that if we could win a couple of those and add a high finish in the other then we would definitely be on the title trail.

Ford were first and second in Cyprus in 2000, with Carlos taking the win ahead of me. I went looking for another Ford one-two – but in a different order! It is not one of my favourite rallies, though. It is slow and twisting. In fact, it is the slowest event on the calendar and it's difficult to get into a rhythm. The heat build-up in the car can be worse than in Greece or Safari because you are travelling so slowly.

I was content not to push too hard on the first day because it was obvious road position was going to be a factor. The roads were cleaner by the time we were on them and that suited us fine. If you strayed off line you lost valuable seconds – or worse. I'm sure Tommi was getting frustrated running at the front. When you are in that situation you can try too hard and run too wide and that's what happened to Tommi on that first day. He was caught out and went off. We ended the day fourth, behind Gronholm, Burns and Delecour.

Marcus had the worst of the conditions on day two and dropped to third place, but everything went to plan as far as we were concerned. I wanted to take back time from Richard yet not end the day in front and leave myself the job of road-sweeper for the final leg. So, on the last stage of the Saturday the team kept me informed of Richard's time and I knew how much to back off right at the end to make sure he was first overnight. I was well up on his time and did consider pushing to the end and pulling out what might have been a winning lead but I decided that on balance it was better to stick to our strategy and take second place.

I was happy with the way things had gone but on that Saturday night I wasn't as sure of victory as I had been in Argentina. Yes, I believed I could win, but I was ready for a tough fight from Richard and was aware that Carlos, in fourth place, would have even better road conditions. It certainly wasn't a straightforward situation for us and it is better to be prepared for a battle than to get complacent. That's asking for trouble.

On the second stage of the Sunday morning we took the lead and, although Richard kept pushing, we were able to stay in front without too much difficulty. The whole day was far more pleasant than I'd anticipated. I honestly thought Richard would make it tougher for us than he did and we had more than 16 seconds in hand at the end. Marcus dropped out and Carlos finished third to make it a great weekend all round for Ford.

Tommi still led the Championship on 27 points, Carlos was on 26, I was on 20 and Richard on 15. Ford led the manufacturers' table by three points from Mitsubishi.

Suddenly, from nowhere, back-to-back wins had put us in the thick of the title contest. We had been able to dominate Argentina from the front and now we had effectively controlled Cyprus from behind. The car had again proved its performance and reliability in tough conditions and the whole team operation had gone like clockwork.

Some of our opponents weren't so happy though. Richard complained that Ford had manipulated the rally to suit their needs and there's no doubt we took advantage of the regulations. We exploited them to the maximum, just as Richard had done at the Acropolis in '99 and I was surprised at his reaction. Okay, by all means have a bit of a dig and make the point about being first on the road, but he made such a big thing of our tactics and then admitted he would have done the same thing had he been in my position. He just came over as a sore loser and the team were clutching at straws, trying to knock us off the podium. I'd obviously wound them all up.

There were also moans from various quarters that I had driven that final morning without gloves and that a protest would be lodged. I found it all a bit petty and pathetic, frankly. It seemed some people were so desperate they were prepared to do anything to try and stop us. Despite what Richard said, we had won the rally fair and square. It didn't bother me that he was mouthing off like that. The fact that he was so upset he'd been beaten again, made it even more enjoyable. I was happy for him to continue whinging, as he did at the Acropolis. The more he got himself revved up the more he played into my hands.

We were on a roll and determined to maintain

the momentum in Greece, where I had won on three previous visits. The team reinforced the underneath of the car, even though it meant carrying extra weight. We felt our way into the rally, avoiding risks where possible on the opening morning before setting fastest times in stages four and six. But it was clear Subaru were intent on playing cat and mouse and reversing the roles of the Cyprus Rally. We ended the Friday schedule leading Carlos by 21 seconds, with Richard third. Marcus again retired and Tommi was struggling down the order, so it was all set up for another Ford v Subaru scrap.

The battle of wits continued on the second day and I had the job no-one else wanted, leading the way on the road. All we could do was press on and try to hold our advantage. We completed the second day with the gap to Carlos down to 9.8 seconds, while Richard was only five seconds further back. Richard was in the position he wanted and was ready to launch his attack on the final morning.

He did just that – and went off. He eventually got going again, thanks to the spectators, who pushed his car back onto the road, but he had lost three minutes and with it any chance of victory. In fact, he didn't even finish the rally as a broken propshaft forced him to pull out. That meant I was left with a head-to-head against my team-mate and I had genuinely felt Carlos was going to be a more serious threat than Richard on that last day.

Carlos edged closer and closer to me through the day and we reached the final, 38.69km stage separated by a mere 5.9 seconds. There were no team orders. Both of us had everything to play for: everything to win – and everything to lose. The slightest error by either of us would probably prove decisive. I wasn't massively confident I would do it, although we had been quicker on that stage in the morning. Carlos was on form. However, the showdown never materialised. Carlos' car stopped early in the stage with engine problems and we went on to win without any pressure. It was bad luck on Carlos but he had enjoyed a good run ever since he joined the team, while we had endured most of the setbacks.

He was unhappy and so was Richard. He had complained this time about the use of 'pit' boards, but then his team and others also started using them. There was a suggestion that he had been distracted by his own board. All I know is that he was going for it and went off the road. It happens. He tried to use the rules to his advantage and it hadn't paid off. If he still wanted to get himself wound up because of what I was doing that was fine by me. I thought it was great. As far as I was concerned Richard and I still had a good relationship. I didn't have a problem with him, but he kept on getting himself hot under the collar about me.

My season had turned around in the most dramatic way possible. I had won three rallies in a row, a record fourth at the Acropolis and 23 in all – equalling the all-time record shared by Carlos and Juha Kankkunen. It's difficult enough to win one rally these days, let alone three in succession. No-one had ever won four consecutive Championship rallies, I was presented with the prospect of achieving two records on the Safari.

But the main objective on my mind was the Championship. Satisfying though these other landmarks might be, what I really wanted to see was my name at the top of the drivers' table and there it was, alongside Tommi's, on 30 points. Officially I was actually leading the way, by virtue of my superior number of wins, three to two. Now we had to keep the ball rolling and with Safari coming up, we were optimistic we could sustain the winning sequence. There was a buzz in the team. Everyone was convinced this was no flash in the pan but there was still work to be done, a lot of work, to stay sharp and make sure we had the necessary reliability. When I am confident in the car I can concentrate on doing the job I am paid to do.

It had been a long time since my first Championship success, six years, and every season it seemed that second title had become more elusive. I had to dig deeper because winning had become harder. Some people may have wondered whether I had the resolve to do that after my accident in Corsica. I don't know how it would have affected other drivers but I knew it wouldn't break me. I have never felt lower than I did at that time so to come all the way back to the top again made it even more pleasurable. All the pain and commitment had been worthwhile.

But the job was only half done. The second half of the season lay ahead. Marcus admitted the Championship was over for him, but Richard was still clinging on. Carlos, as always, was there, and so, too, was Tommi. His new car was due in the autumn and that was going to be crucial to the Championship equation. No-one could predict how it would perform.

All we at Ford could do was concentrate on our own car and our own operation. We were looking good for the manufacturers' title but my vision of the perfect finale was the drivers' Championship. That was the aim when I signed for Ford and now the chance was looming for a Ford driver to take it. I was determined to make sure that Ford driver was me, but Carlos was driving well and we faced the possibility of another intense duel. I would be pretty hacked off to see Carlos receiving the award at the end of the season. I would be very happy, though, to see him finishing runner-up.

Safari turned out to be a big disappointment for both of us. My rally was over on the third stage, when the steering joint of the Focus broke. Nicky and I fixed it, but it popped out again and pitched us off the road. We tried to continue but the effort burnt out the clutch and we were forced to retire. It was a blow but we couldn't complain. We'd had three straight wins before going to Kenya and the Safari is always something of a lottery. This time our number didn't come up and we weren't the only ones to lose out. Carlos' engine failed him on the second morning. Richard had gone on the very first stage with a broken suspension. Tommi had no such bad luck and won comfortably. It was his 23rd career victory and, more importantly, put him 10 points ahead of me in the Championship, with his home event coming up next.

Finland's lakes and forests provide a picture postcard setting but have rarely proved welcoming for visiting rally drivers and I went to Jyvaskyla with a clear plan to ensure I took points from my trip. This, the fastest of all events, with its spectacular jumps and blind corners, had traditionally been dominated by the Finns and Scandinavians and I had no intention of drawing a blank through foolish bravado. Victory wasn't a realistic proposition but I thought that, with a disciplined drive, a podium finish was, and I set out with that objective in mind.

Tommi was, naturally, strongly fancied to win the rally yet to my great surprise – and relief – I passed his crippled car on the first stage. He had hit a tree stump, which apparently hadn't featured in his Pace notes, ripping away his front left wheel and suspension. His rally was over. It was a reminder of how easy it is to be caught out and we weren't about to tempt fate. At the end of the first day we were lying sixth, which gave us a more advantageous position on the road for the second leg.

We duly advanced to fourth on the Saturday, setting two fastest stage times in the process. Ahead of us were Peugeot's Finns, Marcus and Harri, and Richard. To be honest we would have been happy enough with the three points, but Harri broke a front left shock absorber just before the end of the penultimate stage and inevitably struggled on the final test. Even so, it was only when I had finished the stage that I learned from a television interviewer I had third place and that additional, potentially crucial point – by 1.6

seconds. Marcus had his first win since becoming champion and no one could have begrudged him that after suffering so much bad luck earlier in the season, while Richard's second place kept alive his interest in the Championship. Carlos managed a point with sixth place.

I felt our title prospects were good. We were six points behind Tommi with five rallies remaining, three of them gravel events where we could expect the Focus to be strong.

We had everything to play for, which is what any rally driver wants: the chance to compete, the hope of winning.

We made our longest trip of the year, to New Zealand, in a positive frame of mind. The Championship was definitely on the cards and I felt that if we could take good results from this rally, as well as Australia and Great Britain, we would be able to compensate for what were almost certain to be less productive events at San Remo and Corsica.

But when we got to New Zealand we realised we would have a problem. Dry weather had left a very loose gravel surface, which meant the running order was going to be crucial. We were second in the Championship and therefore second on the road on the first day, sweeping a firmer line for those coming up behind us. That wouldn't have been so bad if they had driven normally, but of course they were concerned about conditions and their positions for the following day, so they deliberately slowed. We finished that opening leg second, which meant we were going to be up against it, while Richard took full advantage and came in eighth.

We had managed to overcome difficult situations in the past and gave it our best shot. It was no surprise when Richard capitalised to go well clear on the second leg but we went all out and closed the gap on the third day until a spin finally put first place out of reach. Richard kept that and moved above Carlos into third place in the Championship. A couple of years earlier I might not have worried about a challenge from Richard but there was no question that he had to be regarded as a serious threat now. I was, though, joint leader with Tommi, who finished eighth and failed to add to his account, so we returned to Europe in a strong position. Richard was nine points behind us.

Next up was the tarmac of San Remo and we knew we were not going to be particularly competitive. Our strategy was to take what we could. It turned out to be even worse for us than we feared because we had a different problem that dogged us through the first day and into the second. Points for the Drivers' Championship were out of the question but at least Richard and Tommi weren't able to cash in. Richard went off on the first stage of the event and Tommi was never in the hunt.

As we had all anticipated, Peugeot and Citroen dominated the Italian roads. Our only hope was rain and it arrived on the final day, too late to make a significant difference. Our charge enabled us to take eighth place and add to Ford's tally in the manufacturers' standings, but I was still on 40 points, along with Tommi, in the drivers' table. Carlos' fourth place lifted him to 33, two ahead of Richard.

In the build-up to Corsica there was the inevitable media talk of my accident the previous year but going back to the island didn't bother me at all. The stage where we had gone off wasn't on the route this time anyway. During an earlier test I went to look at the road, just to see if it would trigger something in my memory, but it didn't. I half recognised the gorge and that was about it. My only concerns going into the rally were trying to salvage something from another tarmac event that wasn't going to suit us.

Citroen and Peugeot again set the pace, while a puncture put us up against it from the start. We got off lightly compared with some. Carlos had to retire after only two stages and Tommi was fortunate to walk away after a big shunt that left his car upside down, hanging over the edge of a cliff. His co-driver, Risto Mannisenmaki, injured his back and was airlifted to hospital. He had an operation a few days later and has thankfully made a full recovery. But it could have been so much worse. If the car had gone a foot further it would have fallen over the edge into the ravine and we would have had a tragedy. It is a real danger with tarmac rallies and a subject we took up with the FIA. We have to ensure there are proper barriers on sections like that.

We started the second leg in 11th place but rain helped our tyres and our cause, shooting us up to seventh. Then, on the day's penultimate stage, we hit a rock and lost the power steering. We had to struggle through the last stage and finished the leg back down in 12th spot. Our hopes of scoring points were gone and we ended the rally 11th. The only Championship contender to score points was Richard, who finished fifth but picked up an extra place and point when his Subaru team-mate, Petter Solberg, deliberately incurred a time penalty at the final service.

People argue this sort of thing is not in the spirit of the sport but it's an accepted practice and we have done it when the opportunity has been there. We have seen blatant use of team orders with Ferrari and Michael Schumacher in Formula One. The bottom line is that this is a team game and a huge business for the manufacturers, so I think it is fair enough. If manufacturers are spending millions of pounds to win a Championship they have the right to juggle their drivers as they wish.

Subaru's teamwork meant Richard was back above Carlos in third place, six points behind Tommi and me as we travelled Down Under. Despite the blanks of San Remo and Corsica we were in our best ever position for the climax of a season, and with only the gravel of Australia and Britain to come we were justifiably optimistic.

The top 15 drivers were allowed to choose their starting positions and running 14th ensured us relatively smooth roads on the first day in Australia. The car wasn't quite as quick as we would have liked but there was no pressure on us to win the rally and we were involved in a close four-way battle at the end of the first day. I was 5.3 seconds down on the leader, Marcus

Gronholm, with Burns and Auriol sandwiched between us. Tommi was sixth and Carlos 11th after hitting a tree stump.

That evening we were to select our positions on the road for the following day, the driver leading after the first leg choosing first and so on. I was obviously looking forward to running well down the order but didn't get the opportunity. I was told by Nicky to be at the service area at the Superspecial track at about 7.30pm. In fact, the selection process started at 7.25 and I arrived at 7.24, just as the drivers were being called up on to the stage. I heard my name read out. But Gary Connelly, the clerk of the course, pulled me back off, saying I should have been there at 7.20. He wouldn't budge and I was allocated first place on the road. It effectively meant I had no chance of fighting for a victory and that my prospects of winning the Championship had been seriously undermined.

Back at our team headquarters everybody was staggered and we lodged an appeal, but when it became clear we would have no joy it was withdrawn. Some people reckoned Gary Connelly was too officious and maybe he could have adopted a more sporting attitude and allowed me to make my choice. But the instructions were there in black and white and the other teams made sure their drivers turned up on time.

It is perhaps harsh to blame one person for what is really a team cock-up, but it's certainly not the driver who is responsible for keeping on top of the regulations and making sure we follow instructions such as these. I felt it should have been made clearer to me what time I had to be there and Nicky and I had a big row over it, the first like that we'd had. There are always going to be wee niggles and differences. You have to expect that when you're working together as we do. But we'd never fallen out like this. That mix-up, I am convinced, lost us the Championship and I shall always believe that. It will always rankle with me. There were a few stories going around afterwards that we were going to split but we never wanted it to come to that. Sure, there was a lot of friction between us for a while. You're not going to be able to sort out something like that straight away and we didn't. The bad feeling lingered for a while. But we both knew we had to get it sorted, otherwise it wouldn't have been possible to work together. We're both professionals and the next day we had a rally to get stuck into. There wasn't a lot of chit-chat between us, but we got on with our jobs.

Francois Delecour wasn't overjoyed, either, when he was instructed to check out of the service park 13 minutes early and run ahead of me on the road. He was to be released by Ford after this rally but he did what was required of him. I had the benefit of that assistance for only two stages. On the third, Francois had a big accident, smashing into a tree. He was unhurt but his navigator, Daniel Grataloup, was injured and taken to hospital. We were next car through and stopped to help. It was one thing on top of another. The whole episode was a nightmare. At least we had some rain to help us in the afternoon and managed to hold on to fifth place.

That was where we stayed to the end and, under the circumstances, two points were welcome. Marcus was untouchable that weekend and was never going to be caught by Richard. Tommi was having problems with his back as a result of the crash in Corsica, and managed only sixth place. So with only one rally, my home rally, left I led the Championship on 42 points, followed by Tommi on 41, Richard on 40 and Carlos on 33. Any of us could have become champion, although Carlos was very much the outsider. Victory for one of the top three guaranteed the title. I had never been better placed going into the final event, but we should have had at least another couple of points in the bag and not needed to win the Network Q.

Back in Britain the build-up to the decisive rally was incredible. Two Brits going for the Championship on home soil – it couldn't have been better for British motor sport. And of course the national Press lapped up the 'Battle of Britain' angle, making the most of our quotes to stir up the rivalry.

They picked up on the story that there was a feeling within the sport that Richard was becoming a bit precious. He'd checked into his hotel in Australia as Dick Keen, using his girlfriend's surname. Obviously the other guys gave him some ribbing over that. Richard let it be known, though, that he wasn't amused by a T-shirt we'd had done featuring a cartoon from Autosport, which showed him on his knees, polishing my shoes. That all went back to Cyprus, where he whinged about our tactics and the fact he had to sweep the roads for us. He then admitted he would have done the same thing and of course he has. So why whinge about it? The papers, TV and radio loved it. The rivalry was and still is keen enough, but there wasn't really any animosity. We had a healthy respect for one another.

By the time we got to Cardiff for the start of the rally Nicky and I had talked over our differences and sorted them out. We had a mission to accomplish and were concentrating our minds on that. The only way to approach it was to lead from the front, win the event and with it the Championship. We had a good start, outpacing Richard and everyone else in the Superspecial, and were fastest again on the first stage proper the following morning to extend our lead. Richard was fourth and Tommi was already out. On the next stage the rally was over for us as well.

It was a very fast section, a fifth gear right. I turned into it just a little earlier and tighter than I wanted to and realised I was going to cut right through the grass on the apex. I had time to correct it and take a wider angle but I was right on it, 100 per cent and feeling good. It was one of those split second decisions: you know, take a chance, it will be all right. Nine times out of ten the car would have driven through the grass and it wouldn't have been a problem. This was the one other time. It was a big, big mistake. I hadn't checked the cut through the grass and there was a hole. I hit the outside edge of that and we were gone. We rolled several times, although it wasn't as bad an accident as it looked. The energy is dispersed when a car rolls like that. It would have been a nasty one if we'd gone into trees.

The vision in my left eye was a little blurred and I went to hospital to have it checked but there was no real problem. Nicky had a bruised elbow. However, the real pain was the realisation that we had almost certainly lost the Championship. All Richard needed now was to collect three points and the title was his. Nicky took the disappointment better than I did. My pride was badly hurt. When it's clearly your fault, rather than mechanical failure, it's that much harder to take. And always at the back of my mind was what happened in Australia. If we hadn't had to win the Network Q, I would have taken a different approach. I would have done just as much as I had to. But to win the rally I was going to have to be right on the edge. I was thinking purely of the Championship.

All I could do was return to my lair, lick my wounds and hope something would happen to Richard's car. It's not the best way to win a Championship, sitting with your family miles away from the action. You want to be there at the finish, driving to the decisive result. But if Richard had gone out I would have taken it. A Championship is a Championship. DR and I had been talking before the event, agreeing it would be great if the three main contenders fought it out to the end, winner takes all. Yet here we were, on the first morning, and two of us were out. I'm sure Richard wasn't complaining and that's fair enough, but I think there was a general sense of anti-climax after all the hype.

Carlos was still in contention going into the second day, although he needed the four cars ahead of him to be spirited away. Instead he went off, injuring several people in what was not an official spectator area. Fortunately, no one was seriously hurt. The consequences could have been a lot worse. Those involved were marshals and their families. Marshals do a fantastic job in rallying and motor racing. We couldn't continue without them. They are volunteers who give up their time for the love of the sport and the British marshals are recognised as some of the best. They naturally want to bring their families and friends along, and safety hasn't been such an issue in Britain. But while rallies generally have improved I think standards have slipped a little on the Network Q and this was a wake-up call. The organisers have rightly called for tighter controls.

Ford responded to the incident by pulling out of the rally. It was a sensitive situation and they wanted to do the right thing, but there were no fatalities or serious casualties so I felt it was an over-reaction. It was a great shame for Mark Higgins, a British driver given his first chance in a Focus RS. He was having a great rally and had his sights on a top five finish. I could understand his disappointment.

There was to be no final twist in the rally and the Championship. Richard had a bit of a scare when his car wouldn't start on the Saturday, but he managed to stay out of trouble and finished third, behind Gronholm and Rovanpera. Alister's persistence was rewarded with fourth place. I called Richard that evening to congratulate him. I told him he'd deserved the Championship but that I wanted it back the following year. I didn't like losing the distinction of being Britain's only world champion. Worse still, I felt I should have been celebrating my second title.

Starting All Over Again

One of the good things about rallying is that you don't have time to sit around feeling sorry for yourself. You have to pick yourself up and make sure you're ready to start all over again. We were testing the week after the Rally of Great Britain, in preparation for the first event of the new season less than two months later. Our minds were switched to the next challenge and trying to make sure we could go one better in 2002.

There was still one more significant event for the McRae family in 2001, though – the birth of our second child on December 6. This time we had a boy, Johnny Gavin. My grandfather on the McRae side of the family was John, while Gavin is the name of Alison's dad and also my other grandfather. He was a tad jaundiced so he had to go under the sunlamp for a couple of days. He came home with quite a tan – didn't look like a Scottish baby at all. Family life always helps you put things back in perspective and I had a positive outlook for the New Year.

A few notable changes marked the arrival of another Championship campaign. At Ford we had Markko Martin, an Estonian, on board in place of Francois Delecour. Francois tends to be more consistent for manufacturers' points but he's one of those guys who runs on the wrong side of the luck barrier and it's a tough game. Having said that, Markko has had his share of bad luck already. I didn't really know him before he joined us but he's an easy guy to get on with, pretty laid back. He's put in some promising times and put together an outstanding rally in Greece. I was happy Carlos stayed with us because we understand one another, and work well together to keep pushing the team forward. We also had a new technical director in the Belgian, Christian Loriaux, who replaced Jaguar-bound Guenther Steiner. Christian, who joined us from Prodrive's Subaru operation, has made a big impression and backed up many of the development ideas Carlos and I had been putting forward.

Despite all the speculation about Nicky we were still in tandem and I was very comfortable with that. The relationship between a driver and his navigator is crucial and we make an excellent partnership. I certainly had no wish to break that up and was happy that we had put that unfortunate chapter behind us. There was, however, a change to our gravel crew. Dad went to join Alister, who switched from Hyundai to Mitsubishi. It was felt Alister might benefit from that bit of support and I didn't mind. Murray Grierson, a driver with a lot of experience, took over from dad alongside Campbell Roy. It seemed a good career move for Alister at the time, but after a few rallies with Mitsubishi I wasn't so sure. They needed to knock it up a couple of gears while Hyundai were going well. All too typical of Alister's luck!

Peugeot served notice towards the end of 2001 that they were going to be even stronger in 2002 and they had a new name in their driver line-up – Richard Burns. Subaru apparently had a clause in their contract with Richard stipulating they were entitled to keep him if he won the Championship and there was some legal sabre-rattling between the two teams. But once a driver decides he wants to leave you it's very difficult to hold him and inevitably the matter was settled. With Marcus Gronholm still in the team, Peugeot were under-standably confident. The other major transfer was Tommi Makinen's from Mitsubishi to Subaru.

Portugal had been dropped from the calendar to make way for Germany, which was bad news for us because it meant an extra tarmac event. It's not that I don't like tarmac, it's just that our car and tyres are better suited to gravel. We had a new ruling on the thorny issue of running order. Competitors were to start the first leg of a rally in Championship order, but for the second and third legs the top 15 would run in reverse order. We would have preferred a nomination system, as used in Australia, because it is not always an advantage to start in reverse order. You could, for instance, be caught out by rain. Having to choose your position would also bring another element into it. It's up to you to get it right – or pay the price. But overall I think this is a fair solution. You know where you stand and I'm quite happy with it.

It makes sense to limit the entry for each event to 90 cars, for reasons I have already explained, and further commitments by the authorities to ensure improved safety standards were also appreciated by the drivers. Crowd control, as we have seen time and time again, is so difficult to guarantee. Organisers have acted responsibly by cancelling stages, but how often can you do that? You would end up with no stages. Ultimately it's up to the spectators to regulate themselves if they want to see rallies. Of course we want to have fans out on the stages. We want the excitement and the atmosphere they generate. In Argentina 2002, for instance, it was amazing to see how many people lined the remote roads. There were thousands of them, with their four-wheel drives and barbeques, and most of them were 20 or 30 metres back off the road, which was fine.

Not so popular with the drivers was the decision to permit three rather than two recce runs on asphalt rallies. The thinking behind that is to give the younger drivers a better chance, but when I started in the World Rally Championship you accepted that you had to go through the learning period and I believe it should be like that for the guys coming in now. The WRC drivers suggested that the Super 1600 guys in the newly-named Junior World Championship could be allowed three or four passes, which would help them before they got into a WRC car, but it seems our advice was ignored.

Channel Four coverage of the WRC was

launched with the new season and that definitely represented a positive development for the sport. It's great to have a professional service at last, with regular programme schedules. I've had lots of calls from friends saying how much they enjoy the coverage and what a difference it makes knowing they can turn their TVs on at a certain time knowing they will actually see the rallying. Innovations such as virtual reality illustrations of the cars' relative performances have been terrific and so effective that the teams are using the technique for their own analyses. The endless interviews can be a bit of a pain for the drivers but I suppose we had to expect that! The next important step will be live coverage and that is a big challenge for the TV people. It will require a lot of cameras and a lot of careful planning to capture the best of the spectacle. We still don't get enough regular national newspaper interest, but hopefully that will come.

We at Ford had to make sure we were on top of our jobs. Peugeot were clearly going to be strong, both on tarmac and gravel. Subaru, like us, were expected to be especially quick on the loose. Mitsubishi were in a transitional period, while Citroen were stepping up their programme and Hyundai were improving their operation. It was going to be very competitive but I was looking forward to taking on the rest and having another shot at the Championship.

Monte Carlo may be a home event for me but, as everyone knows, we don't get on. I'm the first to admit that I hate the changing conditions, because they make it so dangerous. However, we do at least have a chance when competing in such circumstances, whereas dry tarmac simply doesn't suit our equipment. This year the weather was good – and the roads mainly dry. Despite that, we had a reasonable first leg. I understeered into a ditch on the penultimate stage, although we didn't lose much time and finished the day third. Sebastien Loeb led the way in his Citroen, followed by Tommi's Subaru. Peugeot were surprisingly off the pace but then this is one of those rallies that can throw up strange results.

A spin and a ten second penalty for a gearbox change that took longer than we anticipated dropped us behind Marcus on the second day, but we retaliated and climbed back to third only for the Turin jinx to strike again. We were within 500 metres of the spot where the throttle went the year before, and the engine blew the year before that, when we lost power. I couldn't believe it. I thought that it was because we were down to three cylinders. We had a coil failure but to our relief kept going. The team changed coils and plugs, and although it cost us two places we were still in business.

I had to make up 31 seconds if I was to catch Marcus on the last day and I managed it on the penultimate stage. Fourth was a satisfactory result for us. Far less satisfactory for the sport was the fiasco over first and second places. Loeb was penalised two minutes for illegally changing tyres at the end of the second day, but because Citroen lodged an appeal the penalty was not taken into account in the provisional standings. Tommi paced himself, believing Citroen had to be punished, and was understandably upset to be declared second. Citroen later dropped their appeal and came in for some stick from other teams, who claimed they had unfairly benefited from the media exposure. Tommi had a record 24th win.

I don't know all the ins and outs of the case but I do feel this sort of thing does the sport no good. There's nothing worse than sending people away from a rally not knowing who's won. If a team has broken the rules they should pay the price. End of story. Or it should be. The problem is that there are so many different interpretations of the rules. The rule-book for rallying was written many years ago and needs to be revised. Alternatively we should appoint one person, a lawyer who knows the rules like the back of his hand, to be present at every rally and adjudicate in matters such as this, and his word would be final.

Next up was Sweden, but not for poor Markko. He damaged his car so badly in the final pre-rally test that the team couldn't repair it in time for the event. We had a decent first day, enjoying the thawing conditions. We were fastest on the final stage and finished the leg third, behind the Peugeots of Gronholm and Rovanpera. The French team had obviously got their act together. We began the second day with another best time, but on the next stage struck a rock that caught out several drivers. It shattered the rear left wheel and we lost three minutes changing it. We were down to 11th place and points looked out of the question.

We had nothing to lose so we just gave it the

big charge on the last day and registered another stage victory as we climbed up to sixth. We chased Alister on the final stage but spun into a ditch and lost 20 seconds. We'd both slipped down a place behind a Finn called Janne Touhino, who happened to have been driving a Ford Focus. Malcolm Wilson asked him if he would do us a favour and he agreed to accept a 10-second penalty for leaving the final service a minute late. That relegated him to seventh, promoted me to sixth and Alister to fifth. I thanked Touhino because he wasn't obliged to help us, but then he no doubt felt it was in his interests to do so and he did a deal with Malcolm for some parts of the Cyprus Rally.

Peugeot followed up their success in Sweden by dominating Corsica, which had been brought forward to a spring date. I hoped that might mean a better chance of rain and we did get some to help us improve from ninth to seventh on the first day. We capitalised on further wet stages on leg two to reach fifth place and, although the skies cleared, we began the final day with a fastest stage time to move up another position. Then I was again airlifted from a Corsican shunt to hospital.

People go on about the curse of Corsica but if you started to think like that you'd stay at home. It was just an unfortunate coincidence that I had another accident on that island. Every passing car had dragged more mud onto the road and our car didn't turn in at a third gear right. We smashed helplessly and violently into a tree on my side of the car. The little finger of my left hand was stuck between the dashboard and the steering wheel but I soon managed to free it. The car seemed to have collapsed around my hips and my main concern was my leg, which was trapped with the roll cage stuck into it. I couldn't feel anything and looked down at it in horror, but there was no blood so it obviously hadn't pierced the skin. I thought I was going to dislocate my hip trying to force my way out of the seat, but eventually freed it. The leg, like my ribs, was bruised and my finger badly broken. At the hospital in Ajaccio doctors stitched up torn tendons and closed the wound. Nicky was fine.

I made another visit to Edinburgh to see another specialist, Chris Oliver. I told him I was driving again in Spain the following week and he looked at me as if I was out of my mind. He explained that the skin was right on the limit of healing and that if it didn't heal properly, or I broke the finger again I would lose it. They could try a skin graft but that rarely works and in any case that would have meant being out of commission for a lengthy spell and there was no way I'd agree to that. Amputation didn't sound particularly appealing but I told him it was a better option than missing three rallies. So I decided to do the rally against the specialist's advice, knowing it might cost me my finger.

Alison's reaction wasn't as bad as I'd feared. She was quite philosophical about it. As for Ford, they loved it. The publicity machinery played up the drama. I had the little finger strapped to the second finger and supported by a plastic moulded splint. The team did their bit, putting in a left-hand gear-shift. That meant I could keep my good hand on the wheel all the time. Occasionally when I set off from the start line I went to the right to change up to second and third, but then I quickly switched to the left and got used to it. The injury possibly cost me some time because I didn't want to push to the limit in case the car got away from me and I'd have to wrestle it back. That would have been awkward. But in the circumstances it wasn't really a problem. The team also lowered Nicky's seat to improve the balance of the car. He could hardly see where we were going, which he probably thought wasn't such a bad thing!

Carlos, making a record 155th WRC appearance in his home rally, had a big shunt in testing and Luis Moya, his co-driver, sustained injuries that ruled him out of the event. We were seventh and eighth at the end of a first day, which confirmed the superiority of Peugeot and Citroen on tarmac. The opening stage had been cancelled and two more were dropped from the schedule at the start of the second day because of crowd congestion. Spectator control had improved in Spain but such is the popularity of rallying in that part of the world that things got out of hand again. Carlos, ironically, was a victim of that enthusiasm. Spectators' cars were parked at the side of the roads and Carlos crashed out avoiding them.

I moved up to sixth place when Loeb went off and that point felt almost like a victory. My ribs were aching more than my finger and it certainly justified my decision to compete. Not that we were able to provide any competition for Peugeot. It was so easy for Gilles Panizzi that he could afford to treat the fans to a 'doughnut' spin on his way to victory.

We were thankful to reach a gravel sector of the season, starting with Cyprus, where we had won the previous year. I was able to return to a right-hand shift and although the roads were even rougher than usual we duly put ourselves back in business, leading after the first day. On the second day we also had a thunderstorm and torrential rain to contend with. Conditions were atrocious. The roads were like rivers and the second run on the long stage had to be cancelled. We weren't complaining, though, because we extended our lead over Marcus to 26.2 seconds.

On the last day it all went pear-shaped. The board indicating my split time on the first stage showed '+1' to Marcus, so I backed off a little, believing I could afford to drop another one or two seconds. But at the end of the stage I discovered I'd lost 12 seconds to Marcus. The board should have said '+9'. That put pressure on me to step up the pace on the next stage and I followed tracks cutting a corner, only to hit a concrete culvert which we hadn't seen on the recce because it was behind a bush. We rolled and although we came to a halt the right way up, the power-steering was broken and by the end of the following stage we were 50 seconds down on Marcus. Those tracks turned out to be Markko's and he, too, had rolled.

Worse was to come. The weather seemed to be improving so we opted for dry tyres, but the heavens opened again and we aquaplaned into a bank, flipping over again. I was disorientated and set off in the wrong direction. Nicky realised after we'd travelled about 700 metres. One of our wiper-blades had been ripped off so we had to stop again to wipe the mud-splattered windscreen. That little drama cost us another two minutes and pushed us down to seventh. We charged over the last two stages to make up a place and salvage a point.

I expected a productive rally in Argentina but had a disappointing first day – a spin, the dust and then fog conspiring to hinder my progress. We were ninth overnight. There were stories that Malcolm felt I was suffering the psychological effects of four big offs, going back to the Network Q, but that wasn't the case. I needed a result from this rally and couldn't afford another non-finish. We had a better second day, posting two fastest times, and advanced to sixth. We were fortunate a rock thrown by a spectator merely caught the edge of our windscreen. Markko's windscreen was hit by a better shot. Must have been some upset landowner.

I couldn't see us getting much more out of the last day. Then Tommi went off fighting Marcus for the lead, giving us fifth place. Marcus thought he had his third win of the season until he was excluded for receiving illegal assistance from his team. That appeared to hand victory to Richard, yet he was also disqualified because his engine had an underweight flywheel. Carlos inherited a record-equalling 24th win and I had the bonus of third place.

The break after Argentina gave me the chance to chill out with family and friends at home in Monaco, and also take in the Grand Prix. It was good to see our neighbour and fellow Scot David

Coulthard hold off Michael Schumacher to win the race.

We needed a result like that if we were to retain any hope of challenging for the Championship. We simply had to end the 12-month victory drought on the Acropolis. Our start scarcely inspired confidence as we struggled to find a rhythm, but we got it right in the afternoon and completed the first day third. Markko had a stormer, pulling 53 seconds clear of me at the front. Only a problem could have prevented him from winning, and on the second day a shredded tyre did just that.

We began the final leg leading Richard by 32 seconds and maintained our consistent form. We had another stroke of luck when we passed a Peugeot, parked on the stage. I couldn't tell whether it was Richard or Marcus and asked Nicky. He said he thought it was Richard but wasn't sure. The distraction broke my concentration and in the brief confusion I took a corner in sixth instead of third. We ran wide, clipped a tree and bent the rear left wheel arch. I took out the wheel jack to hammer the bodywork clear of the wheel and we got away with it. We pushed just hard enough to make sure Marcus didn't get too close to us and won by 24.5 seconds. Carlos was third and Markko, who shows signs of becoming a strong competitor, was sixth.

We have learned how to win this event, where to go for it and where to take extra care. That experience paid off. This was my third victory in a row and my fifth in all on the Acropolis. It also put me level again with Tommi and Carlos on 24 career wins. When you retire it's nice to be able to look back on records like that, but uppermost in my mind that evening in Greece was the Championship. Halfway through the season we were joint third, on 20 points. Marcus led, on 37 points, and Carlos was second, on 23. Marcus still had a healthy advantage but we had put ourselves back in contention and given all the team a lift. We looked ahead to the Safari and beyond with renewed confidence.

Sometime before the end of the year I had to make an important decision about my future. My contract with Ford was expiring and I had been made aware of interest from Subaru and Citroen. I intended carrying on and wanted, above all, a car capable of winning rallies and competing for Championships. I certainly wasn't in any rush to leave Ford and the team were striving for success just as I was. Malcolm was pushing hard with his development projects and would no doubt make good use of further support from Ford. Rallying is, after all, Ford's best chance of World Championship fulfilment.

That was definitely my goal and I was as hungry as ever to achieve it.

But I needed another good result on the Safari and I went there with a game plan to run at my own pace, determined not to take unnecessary risks on that most unforgiving of rallies. We stepped it up when we felt comfortable to do so and set fastest times on two of the opening day's four stages to reach the overnight halt just 16.1 seconds behind Tommi, which is nothing on this event. Marcus had already gone with an engine problem and we were confident we could take the lead on the second leg.

We did just that but only after running for ten miles in the dust and stones thrown up by Tommi's struggling Subaru. He had a damper problem and apparently wasn't aware I was on his bumper because he's lost communication with his helicopter. Luckily we came to a mud hole and as he went one way round it I went the other and got past him. I was annoyed because he was clearly in trouble and holding me up, but he later apologised. It's certainly not like Tommi to do something like that deliberately. He eventually retired and so did Richard, stuck in sand as he tried to reach his crew at the service park.

Harri pushed hard but we kept to our strategy and I had my third Safari win. It was my 25th in all, giving me the WRC record outright. It was great to have that distinction but more satisfying still to have put myself firmly in title contention. Our second consecutive victory and the non-finishes of the other contenders had lifted us from nowhere to second place in the Championship, seven points behind Marcus. We were on that glory trail again, and there's no better place to be.